Mañana es San Perón

Mañana es San Perón

A CULTURAL HISTORY
OF PERÓN'S
ARGENTINA

MARIANO BEN PLOTKIN

Translated by KEITH ZAHNISER

A Scholarly Resources Inc. Imprint
Wilmington, Delaware

Scholarly Resources Inc.
104 Greenhill Avenue
Wilmington, DE 19805-1897
www.scholarly.com

Library of Congress Cataloging-in-Publication Data

Plotkin, Mariano Ben, 1961–
    [Mañana es San Perón. English]
    Mañana es San Perón : a cultural history of Perón's Argentina /
Mariano Ben Plotkin; translated by Keith Zahniser
        p. cm. — (Latin American silhouettes)
    Includes bibliographical references and index.
    ISBN 0-8420-5028-0 (alk. paper) — ISBN 0-8420-5029-9 (pbk. : alk.
paper)
    1. Argentina—Politics and government—1943–1955.
2. Propaganda—Argentina. 3. Communication—Political aspects—
Argentina. 4. Education and state—Argentina. 5. Peronism. 6. Perón,
Juan Domingo, 1895–1974. I. Title. II. Series.

F2849 .P5813 2002
982.06'2—dc21   2002066865

∞ The paper used in this publication meets the minimum requirements of
the American National Standard for permanence of paper for printed library materials, Z39.48, 1984.

To Osi and García, the two Ps of my life,

and to the memory of Victoria Cerrudo

ABOUT THE AUTHOR

Mariano Plotkin received his Ph.D. in history from the University of California, Berkeley. He taught at Harvard University, Colby College, and Boston University. In 2000, after fifteen years of living in the United States, he moved back to Argentina with his family. Until it closed in 2002 he was the director of the New York University Center in Buenos Aires. Plotkin is the author of *Freud in the Pampas* (2001). He also edited *Argentines on the Couch* (forthcoming), and coedited, with Samuel Amaral, *Perón, del exilio al poder* (1993), and with Ricardo González Leandri, *Localismo y globalización* (2001). He is now a researcher at the Consejo Nacional de Investigaciones Científicas y Técnicas based at the Instituto de Desarrollo Económico y Social in Buenos Aires, and professor at the Universidad Nacional de Tres de Febrero, Buenos Aires. He is married to Piroska Csúri and has one son, Pascuel.

CONTENTS

INTRODUCTION

This book is a study of the mechanisms for the generation of political consent and mass mobilization created by the Argentine state during the Peronist regime. By political consent, in the context of this work, I mean both an open and active support for the regime (active consent) and a passive support that might be characterized as benevolent neutrality toward the government (passive consent). In the case of political regimes of an authoritarian nature such as Juan Domingo Perón's, the creation of political consent also implied the repression and exclusion of all those who refused to participate in it.

This work approaches the subject from three angles. First, it analyzes the process of the creation of myths, symbols, and rituals, which constituted what can be characterized as a Peronist political imagery. Although the generation of some kind of political imagery is necessary to assure the legitimacy of any political regime—legitimacy, after all, is based on beliefs[1]—Peronism, with its symbolic systems, attempted to occupy the totality of public symbolic space. This goal made it impossible for alternative systems to coexist with it and was aimed at generating what Perón called "spiritual unity." Peronist political imagery was not designed to reinforce the legitimacy of a political system defined in abstract terms but to assure the undisputed loyalty of different sectors of society to the Peronist regime and to Perón in particular. This imagery became a crucial component of Argentine political culture, and it would have a profound impact on the political life of the country for almost thirty years after Perón's fall. This book analyzes the substance, reach, and limitations of the messages conveyed by the Peronist regime in support of its political imagery.

Second, this work seeks to describe the evolution of the institutional framework that made the creation of the symbolic apparatus possible. In this sense, it analyzes the changes introduced by the regime in areas such as education, the provision of social services, and others.

Third, this study presents the mechanisms designed by the Peronist regime to broaden its social base through the incorporation and mobilization of sectors that had traditionally occupied a marginalized position within the political system. After obtaining the support of the unionized workers through his policies as secretary of labor and welfare, Perón sought to attract the support of other sectors that would serve to counterbalance the excessive influence trade unions had acquired during his governance. These new sectors included women, nonunionized workers, the poor, and others. Peronism, like other authoritarian regimes, attempted to blur the border between public and private space.

Finally, on a more general level, this work also treats broader themes such as the creation of charisma through the manipulation of political symbols and the generation of legitimacy in the context of a profoundly polarized society.[2]

As Peronism is one of the most studied topics of Argentine contemporary history, any new work requires some kind of justification.[3] Most of the initial studies on the period following Perón's fall were heavily influenced by the heated debate the Peronist experience had provoked. Peronism had divided Argentine society into two irreconcilable sectors. For the great majority of the working class and other previously marginalized groups, Perón's regime had brought concrete improvements in their living conditions and a redefinition of their place in society. Other sectors, in particular the middle class and the intelligentsia, interpreted the ten years of Peronist government as the result of a pathological development in the history of the country. For most of the anti-Peronists, the Peronist phenomenon and its survival after Perón's fall did not fit within the "normal" historical process of Argentina. Therefore, the first analyses of the Peronist experience tended to focus their attention on the problem of how and why it was even possible. Specifically, the main question the analysts tried to answer was why the working class (and which sectors within it) had supported Perón, making possible the creation of a powerful system of Peronist unions. Starting with the classic study by Gino Germani, *Política y sociedad en una época de transición*, working-class support of Perón was explained as an aberration, the product of manipulation and irrationality.[4]

Throughout the 1960s, however, it became clear that Peronism had become a permanent component of crucial importance in the Argentine political system. Interpretations of Peronism that tried to explain it as a pathology were no longer satisfactory. In this context, Miguel Murmis and Juan Carlos Portantiero published their pioneer work *Estudios sobre los orígenes del peronismo.*[5] Instead of characterizing the Peronist experience as a rupture with the past, Murmis and Portantiero explained its emergence as the result of certain structural characteristics in the developmental process of Argentine society during the 1930s. In this way, Peronism was no longer presented as an aberration, but as the almost natural result of a process that had begun in the decade before its appearance. This short but valuable work opened up an important debate over the origins of Peronism, which, although reaching its peak in the 1970s, continues today.[6]

Until recently, in part due to the impact of the debate begun by the Murmis and Portantiero work, the main focus of studies on Peronism was the relationship between Perón and the organized working class.[7] However, it soon became clear that Perón's era had left another important legacy beyond the powerful system of Peronist unions. It reformulated the relationship between the state and society and redefined the identity of various sectors of Argentine society—in particular, but not exclusively, that of the working class. The long-standing historiographical focus on the problem of Peronism's origins had left this important aspect of the phenomenon understudied for a long time.[8]

The survival and impact of Peronism could not be explained only in terms of the improvement of living conditions introduced during Perón's era, although this factor should, of course, not be ignored. If Peronism was successful in redefining the identity of important sectors of Argentine society and in creating what could be called a Peronist subculture,[9] this success was in part the result of the creation of a powerful political imagery and an efficient system for symbolic interchange between Perón and the masses. This system, while reformulated, continued to function even during the exile of the leader. The mechanisms used to create this symbolic system, a subject that has only recently captured the interest of scholars, constitute the central problematic of this book.[10]

This work is not, and does not pretend to be, a general history of Argentina during Perón's government. It is not even a chronological history of the Peronist movement. Some undoubtedly relevant topics, but ones already treated extensively by other authors, have been omitted or mentioned only marginally. Issues not discussed in depth include the relations between the Peronist state and the trade unions, as well as the conflict between the Catholic Church and the state that began toward the end of the period. Although the repression of opposition, especially after 1950, was an important component of Perón's policy, it is only briefly considered. Furthermore, this study centers its attention on the state and its policies and not primarily on the real impact that these policies had, which would have implied the use of sources and methodologies of a different kind.[11]

The first of four parts analyzes the crisis of the liberal consensus in Argentina during the 1930s and the birth of Peronism in the context of this crisis. It also focuses on the reach and limitations of Peronist ideology and on the failed attempts of some Peronist intellectuals to create an "alternative Peronist culture." Part II studies the creation of political rituals and their role in the generation of Perón's image as a charismatic leader. In particular, this section examines how the Peronist regime appropriated and redefined the meaning of the political celebrations of the Seventeenth of October and May Day. In Part III the Peronist regime's attempts to transform the school system into an enormous mechanism for the political indoctrination of youth are examined. Further discussion describes the institutional changes introduced in the educational system by the military authorities established in 1943 and by Perón's government after 1946. A discussion on the content of the textbooks introduced by Peronism concludes this section. Part IV explores the regime's politics, aimed at obtaining passive consent, and the incorporation of sectors previously marginalized or excluded from political life. It deals with the Fundación Eva Perón and its double role as counterweight to the powerful union apparatus and as generator of myths and symbols of the regime. The final chapter focuses on the mechanisms used to attract women and children through the Partido Peronista Femenino, which was closely linked to the Fundación, and through the children's sports tournaments organized by the Fundación and the publication of a Peronist children's magazine, *Mundo Infantil.* The government not only tried to gain the support of women as voters but also as potential "missionaries" who would spread the Peronist word in the privacy of their homes. In this sense, women and children would serve as a link between the Peronist state and the family.

In the preparation of this book, I have incurred so many debts that it would be impossible to list completely all those who helped me in one way or another. This work began as a doctoral thesis presented to the Department of History at the University of California, Berkeley. My first debt, therefore, is to my thesis adviser, Professor Tulio Halperín Donghi, for his support, patience, and inspiration, and to the other members of my thesis committee: Professors Linda Lewin and Francine Masiello. Later the thesis was published in Spanish as *Mañana es San Perón: Propaganda, rituales políticos y educación en el régimen peronista (1946-1955)* (Buenos Aires, 1993). This book is an updated translation of that work.

Many people in Argentina facilitated access to sources in private or nonpublic archives, without which this work could not have been written. Here, I am especially thankful to Dr. Ramón Cereijo for granting me access to previously unused documents of the Fundación Eva Perón. Dr. Manuel Molinari gave me access to the almost complete collection of *Hombre de campo*, as well as other documents, besides having submitted himself to innumerable questions. Susana Bianchi and Norma Sanchís did what almost nobody else in the field would have done: they allowed me to use the originals of their interviews with women members of the Partido Peronista Femenino, some of which were used in their 1986 book *El Partido Peronista Femenino*. Clara Brafman granted me access to her unpublished work on the magazine *Billiken*. Professor Laureano García Elorrio and the personnel of the Dirección de Estadística y Documentación of the Ministerio de Educación not only gave me carte blanche to dig into its archives and photocopy what I needed but also provided me with a desk. The same warm hospitality was shown me by the authorities of the Distrito Escolar 5 and the Instituto Bernasconi, who also worked hard to make me feel at home.

Claudia Perel, head of the Film, Audio, and Video Document Department of the Archivo General de la Nación, besides being an excellent friend, eased my search for film material. Finally, I wish to thank the authorities of the Biblioteca del Maestro, of the *La Nación* newspaper archive, and of the Estrada and Kapelusz publishing houses.

Lila Caimari and Joel Horowitz read and criticized drafts of the original thesis. Their suggestions were essential in transforming a shapeless mass of data into something that made sense. Later, they made valuable comments on the Spanish edition. Raanan and Monica Rein have been great interlocutors during the production process for this new version. Marcela García, Nora Charlín, and Ana Gutman efficiently collaborated with the collection of sources during the different stages of the creation of this work. Victoria Cerrudo amicably helped with the correction of the original manuscript. Naturally—and it goes without saying—with them I share only the credit for the possible merits of this work but not the responsibility for any mistakes.

My friends in Buenos Aires, particularly Adrián Lerner, Telma Liberman, Moira Fradinger, Jorge Myers, Anahí Ballent, Claudia Frana, Patricia Chomnalez, Susana Bianchi, and Raúl Mandrini, each helped me in his or her own way, and all of them more than they can imagine. I also want to express my gratitude to Keith Zahniser for successfully translating the Spanish edition into English.

The research for this book was made possible by a grant from the Social Science Research Council of New York; two travel grants provided by the Centro de Estudios Latinoamericanos of the University of California, Berkeley; and a Humanities Research Grant from the Graduate Division of the same university.

Finally, but most important, I wish to thank my wife, Piroska Csúri ("Osi"), and my son, Pascuel ("García"). Without them, this book would not be what it is, and I would not be what I am.

1

CONSENSUS IN ARGENTINE SOCIETY AND THE RISE OF PERÓN

During the 1930s, Argentine society suffered a profound polarization. The long period during which liberalism had provided economic and social elites with the bases of a unifying myth, one used by these elites to lay the foundations of ideological consensus, had come to an end.[1] Although the economic crisis accelerated the breakdown of the liberal consensus, the first symptoms of the process could be perceived in the decades preceding 1930.

The first part of this book explores the characteristics of the crisis of the liberal consensus in Argentine society. Chapter 1 analyzes the origins of the process during the 1920s and 1930s. Chapter 2 examines Perón's response to the breakup of the liberal consensus and his attempts to create a new one based on different fundamentals. This chapter also explores Perón's ideology, its scope and limitations, and the role played by the Peronist intellectuals in attempts to define an "alternative Peronist culture."

1

THE CRISIS OF
THE LIBERAL CONSENSUS

Since its entry into the international market in the second half of the nineteenth century, Argentina had experienced a long period of unprecedented economic expansion based on the exportation of agricultural products. This undoubtedly successful growth was made possible by a combination of domestic resources: abundant and fertile land; and foreign resources: the influx of foreign capital and manual labor provided by massive immigration.

From the 1860s to 1930 the country enjoyed relative institutional stability under a formally democratic system. However, until 1916 the country had been governed by a landed elite whose interests were closely tied to the export market. The vast majority of the population was excluded from participation in the political system by means of electoral fraud and coercion. The exclusion of the masses from politics, moreover, was facilitated by the high proportion of immigrants in the population, the majority of whom lacked the incentives to acquire Argentine citizenship. They were thus unable to participate in the national electoral system.[2]

The characteristics of this social and political order were consistent with the existing consensus among the dominant sectors regarding the proper social and political conditions for continued economic growth. This consensus, based on the ideological premises of nineteenth-century liberalism as understood in Latin America,[3] stressed the need of maintaining a society without conflicts and democratic in form, although, in fact, the country was governed by an enlightened elite. It would be the responsibility of this elite to administer the seemingly unlimited wealth generated by international trade and the work of the "invisible hand" that, according to liberals, would handle the economy with minimum interference from the state. The democratic institutions provided, at least in theory, an adequate legal framework for this development. The strength of this consensus among the elites who controlled the state was one of the most important characteristics of the Argentine political culture until the second decade of the last century. As Cristián Buchrucker has pointed out, until the First World War none of the relevant Argentine institutions had developed political conceptions incompatible with the liberal consensus.[4]

In such a context, party ideologies played a secondary role within the Argentine political system. If political parties wished to present a viable alternative, they were forced to do so within the dominant consensus. Even the Socialist Party, in spite of its theoretical attachment to Marxism, continued to express its confidence in the liberal institutions and in the market economy.[5] The same can be said about the Unión Cívica Radical (UCR), a party that was born as a result of a severe political crisis that took place in 1890 and which would become the first modern mass party in Argentina.

By the second decade of the twentieth century, however, the problems associated with this model became clear. The process of development begun a half-century earlier had so profoundly transformed Argentine society that important adjustments were necessary to assure its continued success. Mass immigration had had a strong impact on society, and some of the newcomers—the most fortunate, or their direct descendants—began to climb the social pyramid with such success that they threatened the monopoly of economic privileges traditionally enjoyed by the landed elites. The expansion and increased visibility of an organized working class, whose demands were sometimes violently expressed, was also perceived as a potential threat by the dominant sectors. Consequently, it became clear for some within the ruling elite that a deeper intervention on the part of the state in social matters (not yet in economic ones) was needed. "The absolute liberality, as it has been understood by us until recently, is now a serious threat," wrote Joaquín V. González in the first decade of the last century.[6] The result of this awareness was a combination of repressive and reformist social policies. Thus, for example, in 1902 the Residence Law was passed that authorized the government to summarily expel from the country any foreigner considered dangerous to the social order. In 1910 a new Law of Social Safety was passed by Congress that granted the government even more repressive powers. Congress also debated and passed some of the first social laws; and in 1904, Minister González proposed (without success) that a new labor code regulating the relations between labor and capital be enacted.

At the same time, during the 1910s, the Consejo Nacional de Educación, presided over by José María Ramos Mejía, set up a program to provide "patriotic education" in the schools, aimed at inculcating nationalist feelings in the children of immigrants. Such nationalist sentiments would also serve as a barrier against "dissolvent ideologies" (in particular, anarchism, which was influential at that moment within the workers' movement).[7] Paradoxically, the ideological consensus was so strong that among the teachers who dutifully complied with their obligation of patriotic indoctrination, it was possible to find sympathizers with anarchism and, later, even a few Communists.[8] In fact, the educational bureaucracy included people from the most diverse ideological orientations, from nationalists such as Leopoldo Lugones and Manuel Gálvez to anarchist sympathizers such as Julio Barcos. As state agents, however, they fulfilled their mission regardless of their personal ideology.

During the 1910s the need for significant reform of the political system also became evident. The closed political system, which prevented the active participation of the masses, no longer provided adequate responses to the problems of an increasingly complex society. The UCR was a political party that, under the leadership of Hipólito Yrigoyen, was on its way to becoming a party of the masses. This party's refusal to participate in an electoral system that, as it existed, gave them no chance to win also contributed to the delegitimization of the traditional political system.[9] The most progressive members of the dominant classes, among them President Roque Sáenz Peña, realized that in order to ensure the survival of the system, drastic changes were needed. Such a transformation did not entail a rejection of liberalism, but rather a broader and more accurate application of its principles. This would imply the incorporation of the masses into the political system. An important result of these changes was the so-called Sáenz Peña Law passed in 1912, which established the secret ballot and mandatory universal suffrage (for all males over eighteen years of age). As the immediate consequence of the application of the law, Hipólito Yrigoyen won the elections in 1916 and became the first president elected by popular vote. This marked the beginning of a new era of massive political participation.

During the first Yrigoyen administration (1916–1922), the state took a more active role in political and social issues, acting in many cases as the arbiter in social conflicts. However, in spite of the expanded role assigned to the state in certain areas, the Radical Party did not abandon, at least in theory, the principles of liberalism. After all, Yrigoyen claimed, as another Radical president would do almost seventy years later, that the program of the UCR was the Constitution of 1853, the backbone of the liberal economic and political system.

Despite the fact that the Sáenz Peña Law was fundamentally a more rigorous application of the principles on which the liberal consensus of the dominant classes was based, the results of the incorporation of the masses into politics led some less progressive members of these classes to question the validity of those principles. As historian José Luis Romero has pointed out, the governing classes, who had proudly proclaimed their liberalism and progressivism, became the vocal advocates of conservatism when forced to face what they perceived as a threat "from below."[10] For those groups, the Sáenz Peña Law resulted in what Buchrucker calls "the period of democratic danger."[11] Confronted with the evidence that they could not hold on to power through the application (although perverted) of the principles of liberal democracy, the now conservative sectors began to question the validity of these very principles.[12]

Yrigoyen contributed to the breakup of the consensus. Although he lacked a concrete program of government, he believed that his legitimacy was derived from the fact—which seemed to be confirmed by the electoral victories of his party—that his government and party were "the fatherland itself": the incarnation of a civic unity that represented the aspirations of the Argentine people. While Yrigoyen and his official propaganda referred to the governments that had preceded him and to his opponents as "the regime," his own government was characterized as "the cause."[13] To be fair we must recognize that freedom of speech was not suppressed during Yrigoyen's government (particularly during his first term), and the truth is that the official discourse tried to deprive the opposition of its status as a legitimate contender in the political arena.[14] Therefore, a process that can be characterized as "double delegitimization" took place. Yrigoyen's followers refused to recognize their opposition as legitimate political actors, while the conservative opposition questioned the legitimacy not only of the radical government but also of the ideological and institutional framework that had made it possible.

The Emergence of Nationalism

The real threat to the system based on the principles of democratic liberalism came from those segments of the elite who perceived their own situation as threatened by the newly enfranchised sectors, and from the radical right-wing nationalist groups that emerged in the 1920s.[15] The Soviet Revolution of 1917, the social upheavals of post–World War I Europe, and the events of the Tragic Week in 1919 (a series of strikes that were harshly repressed by the government) only served to confirm the fears of the elite. Yrigoyen's government was portrayed by the conservative opposition as the prelude to a Soviet-like revolution in which Yrigoyen would perform a role in Argentina similar to that played by Alexander Kerensky in Russia. Numerous right-wing nationalist groups sprang up during the 1920s, such as the Liga Patriótica Argentina. They fought for the recovery of a "true nationality" and for the establishment of some sort of authoritarian control over public order so as to prevent the rule of the masses and the dangers of communism.[16]

Nationalism was not a new phenomenon in Argentina. In the 1910s there had been an emergence of nationalist thought. The aim of the nationalist thinkers of that decade had been to keep alive a system whose flaws were already obvious by infusing the state with new vitality and by fostering nationalistic sentiments in the children of immigrants. The new nationalists, however, proposed the destruction precisely of this system.[17] In 1924, poet Leopoldo Lugones had already predicted with enthusiasm the coming of "the hour of the sword." For him, as for other militant nationalists, the army was the only repository of national feeling. From the 1934 book *La Argentina y el imperialismo británico* by brothers Julio and Rodolfo Irazusta to the "Manifiesto de la Liga Republicana" of May 1933, all the nationalist groups and authors coincided in their celebration of the death of liberalism. However, the nationalists were never able to form a viable political party and remained deeply divided. Their inspiration came mostly from the works of French nationalist intellectual Charles Maurras, but some of them admired Italian dictator Benito Mussolini, Portugal's Antonio de Oliveira Salazar, and Spanish general Miguel Primo de Rivera. The nationalists were essentially antiliberal, profoundly anti-Communist, generally staunch Catholics, and deeply distrustful of democracy.

Nationalist thought became influential in the Army.[18] The nationalist newspaper *La Voz Nacional*, founded by Juan Carrulla in 1925, had among its subscribers General José Félix Uriburu, a Facist sympathizer. One of the junior officers involved in the 1930 coup that removed Yrigoyen from power, Captain Juan Perón, would later recall that the group of officers who organized the conspiracy distributed among themselves issues of the nationalist paper *La Nueva República*.[19]

The challenge to the liberal consensus became a real threat in the 1930s when a combination of factors, including the effects of the economic and concomitant ideological crisis, made it evident that the line of historical evolution based on the principles of liberalism had come to an end.[20] The result was a coup led by General José Uriburu that ended the second Yrigoyen administration (1928–1930) and almost seventy years of continued political stability in the country. As became clear after the 1930 coup, the political elite, which now included some members of the army, was divided. Some, led by General Agustín Justo, who became president through fraudulent elections in 1932, believed that the restoration of the pre-1916 political order was desirable and viable, while others (including General Uriburu) wished for a complete transformation of that order to be based on the principles supported by the authoritarian regimes emerging in Europe. Although this latter group, made up of nationalists who completely rejected the liberal tradition, was marginal and remained divided, some of their ideas succeeded in permeating the period's "climate of ideas." In any case, there was a shared feeling that the era of liberalism was coming to an end.

The breakup of the liberal consensus was evident not only in the differing evaluation that various groups made of the current situation, but also in their interpretations of the past. During the 1930s, a new school of historical analysis was born: the so-called Historical Revisionism, closely linked to nationalism. This historiographical movement attempted to challenge the version of the past presented by the liberal historiography in order to justify the nonliberal political alternatives that were supported by its followers. The revisionists worked to recover the Hispanic–Catholic tradition of the country as an alternative to the cosmopolitan liberal one. According to these revisionists, Argentine history was in reality the history of the penetration and exploitation of the country by British imperialism. The "founding fathers" of Argentine liberalism were mere agents of this imperialism. The antiliberal caudillos of the nineteenth century who had been portrayed by the liberal historiography as representatives of barbarism—in particular, Juan Manuel de Rosas, who had ruled the country for more than twenty years—replaced the liberal heroes in the nationalist revisionist pantheon. Although Rosas's image was already under reevaluation in the 1920s, it was only during the following decade that remaking it would acquire an open political connotation.[21]

Throughout the 1930s, the debate surrounding these competing interpretations of national history became an important component of the political debate. Different political groups used history as an instrument to legitimize their own political aspirations. As clearly explicated in a 1937 political pamphlet of the Fuerza de Orientación Radical de la Joven Argentina (FORJA) group: "History is a political weapon."[22] The political use of the past was not only the patrimony of the nationalists. Political groups from diverse ideological orientations saw themselves as the last link in a chain of historical events that represented, according to each of them, the true and legitimate history of the nation. In 1928, for example, the Comité de Jóvenes Intelectuales Yrigoyenistas was created by some members of the group that published the avant-garde *Martín Fierro* literary magazine and that included writers such as Jorge Luis Borges, Leopoldo Marechal, and Raúl González Tuñon, among others. This group approved a resolution acknowledging three periods in the national history: revolution (1810–1816), organization (1853–1860), and national awareness (1916–1922).[23]

In addition to ultraright authoritarian nationalism, a populist tendency within nationalism arose during the 1930s. In 1935 a group of dissatisfied young members of the UCR created FORJA under the intellectual leadership of Raúl Scalabrini Ortiz.[24] The young men of FORJA were particularly angry at the "participatory" policies that Marcelo T. de Alvear had adopted for the party. Alvear, who had been president between 1922 and 1928, led the anti-Yrigoyen faction of the UCR that continued participating in elections during the thirties. FORJA members claimed to be the heirs of the true *yrigoyenismo*, and they declared that their objectives were to recover its true ideology and carry on the fight of the former president. Like the "other" nationalists, the *forjistas* also became attracted to the revisionist version of national history, and they concurred in the perception that British imperialist penetration was the main, if not the only, problem facing Argentina.

However, despite the similarities between FORJA and the right-wing nationalists, and the existence of personal ties between some members of both groups, there were important differences. FORJA's discourse, which made constant appeals to "the people" and to its trust in the popular will, could not have been further from the hierarchical and reactionary conception of society upheld by the right-wing nationalists. The *forjistas* denounced the members of the oligarchy as agents of imperialism, and clamored for the economic emancipation of the country as well as for the "true exercise of the popular will."[25] But the commitment of the *forjistas* to liberal democratic institutions was ambiguous, resting on a distinction between "formal democracy" and "real democracy." In 1942, Arturo Jauretche, an influential member of FORJA who would later hold official positions in Perón's government, wrote: "The thing is simple: they want us to believe that democracy is simply having a parliament, a judicial system, the institutions—in a word, the formal aspects that the regime manipulates. To us, democracy is the government of the people, with or without a parliament, with or without judges."[26] As Ernesto Laclau points out in his now classic study, "The decade of the 1940s thus challenged Radicalism with the disarticulation of its traditional political discourse: it now had to opt for liberalism or democracy. The perfect synthesis between the two which had characterized *yrigoyenismo* was dissolved."[27]

The model of society that the *forjistas* had in mind was one in which there was no place for social conflicts; these would be replaced by social harmony. "National liberation could only come about as a result of the union of classes and not from their opposition."[28] Like Yrigoyen two decades before, FORJA wanted the "true" UCR to have a status superior to that of a mere political party. The UCR had to provide the basis of a new consensus that would cement the unity of society. In 1942, Jauretche said in a tone similar to the one habitually used by Yrigoyen: "Now, there are radicals who do not dare say that the UCR is not a political party, but rather the civil union of Argentines, in order to place the Nation beyond the factions of the regime found in the political parties. This is said to be totalitarian. . . . The definition was perfect, and I find that there was never a revolutionary force that was not totalitarian, that is to say, which totally does not negate all factions in order to constitute itself as the Nation."[29] Even as late as 1945, Jauretche wrote in the newspaper *La Víspera*: "For those who see in Radicalism a political party, this may sound like an easy way to avoid a concrete definition. But the UCR is not a political party. . . . In repeated documents [Yrigoyen] had established and developed the concept that [the UCR] was the civil union of all Argentines in order to achieve nationhood 'radically,' and not a mere political party contesting for power . . . that is why [Yrigoyen] could say that radicalism was the Nation itself."[30]

Many of the members of FORJA, including Jauretche, would see in Peronism the fulfillment of the old radical dream. After October 17, 1945, FORJA was dissolved because its members considered that in view of that day's events the existence of the group was now unnecessary. Although some of the ideas of the *forjistas* would acquire great influence later, the group was never able to claim more than 2,500 members in the entire country.[31]

The *Década Infame* and the Redefinition of the Role of the State

Those sectors that regained power as a consequence of the 1930 coup worked hard to make sure they would keep it. Their aim was to recreate the conditions existing before 1916, when the masses had been excluded from the political system. To achieve this, the neoconservative governments that ruled the country during the 1930s made wide use of electoral fraud and political corruption. This corruption helped to generate a crisis of legitimacy in the political system. Moreover, the traditional parties underwent internal crises, leaving no real alternatives in sight.[32] After 1935 the UCR, following a five-year absence from the political arena, returned to take its old place. This move was interpreted by many members of the party as a sell-out of their principles. The deaths of former presidents Marcelo T. de Alvear, Agustín Justo, and Roberto Ortiz within months of each other in 1942 and 1943 also contributed to the feeling of political instability. The loss of President Alvear had left radicalism with no relevant leader. The long illness and subsequent death of President Ortiz frustrated his plans for revitalizing and cleaning up the political system. The presence of General Justo, who had his own political ambitions and prestige within the army, had served to guarantee the democratic commitment of the military. His death left the democratic sectors of the army without a leader.

The situation in the 1930s, however, was very different from the one prior to 1916. The economic crisis of the 1930s had two important consequences that contributed to the definite breakup of the consensus on which the pre-1916 system was based. First, as a result of the new economic conditions, the role of the state was reformulated and expanded, particularly in the area of the economy. In 1933, President Justo (1932–1938) implemented economic policies resembling Franklin Roosevelt's New Deal.[33] The state took an active role in the regulation of market forces, mostly to the benefit of the upper classes, whose fate could not be left to the mercy of the "invisible hand" any longer. The heated discussion generated around defining the functions of the state can be followed in congressional debates from this period and in the pages of such publications as *Revista de Economía Argentina*.[34] And second, the increased visibility of the working class could no longer be ignored. During the 1930s the economic crisis limited Argentina's ability to maintain its traditional levels of importation of manufactured goods, thereby bringing about a wave of import-substitution industrialization. Between 1935 and 1946 the number of industrial plants grew from 38,456 to 86,400, while the number of industrial workers increased from 435,816 to 1,056,673 in the same period.[35] This rapid industrial growth, however, was not matched by an improved distribution of income. Rather, as Juan Carlos Torre points out, during the 1930s the state functioned as an instrument for the benefit of the economically dominant bloc, which now included the industrialists.[36]

Nevertheless, partly as a result of fear that the social conflict that followed World War I would be repeated after World War II, the topic of "social justice" became an important part of political discourse. This was true of groups ranging from the ultraright to the reformist-Catholic industrialists grouped around the *Revista de Economía Argentina*, led by Alejandro Bunge. All these groups saw a possible solution to the economic and social problems in a more vigorous intervention of the state. Luis Colombo, for many years president of the Unión Industrial Argentina, expressed his worries in this way in 1943: "Among them [the problems that the countries would have to confront in the postwar era], one of the most important is the one linked to the provision of social welfare, because poverty and misery are the sources of all rebellions. . . . It is on this point that the big powers are worried. . . . We want to protect the worker 'from the cradle to the grave.' And we will."[37] Similarly, in 1942, businessman Torcuato Di Tella had presented a bill for the creation of a system of a universal social security similar to (although much less generous than) the one proposed by Sir William Beveridge in Great Britain.[38]

The question of "social justice" also worried many within the body of officers in the army. Many saw the existing poverty in various regions of the country as a threat to national security. In 1936, for example, 45 percent of the potential conscripts from the province of Santiago del Estero were found unfit for military service during their medical examinations due to problems of malnutrition and other factors associated with poverty.[39] Various publications and speeches within military circles cited the need to improve living conditions of the working class through state policies.[40]

It may be concluded that during the 1930s Argentina, like many other countries, was characterized by a crisis of the liberal democratic institutions and of the ideology sustaining them. The functions of the state were being redefined, and the viability of the system itself was being questioned. As Ernesto Laclau notes, "[In the 1930s] liberalism and democracy ceased to be articulated."[41] This crisis of the liberal consensus was candidly acknowledged in 1934 by President Justo, who, speaking to a group of schoolteachers, said that "we are witnessing the most varied experiments of social organization, and we see that principles and beliefs that only yesterday were accepted as unquestionable truths are today rejected. We sense the return of old procedures that were formerly repudiated. Perhaps tomorrow we will see the repudiation of all that today is claimed as the absolute truth and the panacea of the peoples."[42]

Liberal democracy was no longer perceived as the only legitimate political system, and diverse political groups agreed that some form of corporative system might be appropriate. In 1934, for example, Carlos Ibarguren, in a piece that, with minor variations, could have been pronounced by Perón fifteen years later, said:

> The moment has come for us to push toward a spirit of unified national-
> istic ideals as the firm basis of the New Argentina. In these times of turbu-
> lent confusion, it is necessary to transform the state so that in the
> Nation—without factions which weaken it, and without class struggles

which divide it—the concerted effort of organized interest groups representing the collective interest (unions, professionals, corporative, economic,
and social associations), prevail over selfish individualism. Thus, by bringing about social justice and solidarity, we will reinforce national unity, as
well as encourage the work and productivity that will bring us economic
independence. We will make sure that all those who work in this country
enjoy an acceptable standard of living, provided by an egalitarian distribution of income.[43]

Yet it was not only admirers of the authoritarian solutions in vogue in
Europe at the time who were enthusiastic about solutions of a corporate
slant but also corporatism was part of the "climate of ideas." Socialist leader
Alfredo Palacios, who could hardly be considered an admirer of Mussolini,
accepted the possibility of establishing some sort of corporative representation system. In a speech delivered in Córdoba on September 6, 1930, he
recognized that "professional representation, not to suppress a political Congress but to complement it, has been studied by publicists of authority," and
it was therefore an alternative to be seriously considered.[44]

The State and the Catholic Church: Redefinition of an Old and Conflicted Relationship

Another symptom of the change in the ideological and political climate
was the close relationship that developed between the Catholic Church and
the state during the 1930s. During the government of General Justo, this
relationship was probably the strongest it had been in the twentieth century.
The state and Church would come to be even closer at the beginning of
Perón's government.

Traditionally, the relationship between the state and the Catholic Church
in Argentina had been complex. During the final decades of the nineteenth
century, when the liberal governments passed most of the laws establishing
some moderate form of separation of Church and state (for example, civil
marriage, lay education), this relationship had been particularly tense.[45] In
the following decades the emergence of a common enemy—militant anarchism among the working classes—contributed to the softening of these
tensions. In 1910, Father (and later Bishop) Miguel de Andrea, who had
always shown a strong interest in the "social question," still found it necessary to warn the liberals (that is, the state) that their real enemies were not
the Catholics but the anarchists disseminating "dissolvent ideas."[46] Nine

years later, after the Tragic Week, the identity of the "real enemy" had been made very clear. After the events of 1919, some sectors of the ecclesiastical hierarchy organized the Gran Colecta Nacional, with the aim of improving the living conditions of the working class. The idea behind the Gran Colecta was that a better standard of living would prevent the workers from being attracted to anarchism or communism. The public manifesto of the Gran Colecta, published by the group's organizers, ended with: "Tell me: if you found yourself surrounded by a pack of hungry beasts, wouldn't you at least throw them morsels of meat in order to placate their fury and shut their mouths? The barbarians are already at the gates of Rome."[47]

The ideological divisions permeating society in general were also present within the Catholic sectors.[48] But in the 1930s the ideological current known as *integrismo* was gaining ground among important figures within the Catholic hierarchy. According to Msgr. Gustavo Franceschi, director of the influential Catholic magazine *Criterio*, democracy was unacceptable as a system of government because it was based on liberalism; and "a Catholic," said Franceschi, "cannot be a liberal."[49] The more right-wing Catholics developed strong ties with the nationalists of the same ideological persuasion. Gradually the Church (or at least some sectors of the hierarchy) began to participate actively in the political struggle. In 1930 the nationalist priest Julio Meinvielle said in *Criterio* that the Church, in order to fulfill its mission, could and must encourage and direct the participation of Catholics in politics.[50] After 1931, the ecclesiastical hierarchy began to publish pastoral letters before each presidential election, advising Catholics on how to vote.[51]

During the administration of Justo the relationship between the Church and the state became closer. The International Eucharistic Conference celebrated in Buenos Aires in 1934 provided President Justo with an opportunity to show off his Catholic devotion and piety. The conference was attended by Cardinal Eugenio Pacelli, who at the time was Secretary of State of the Vatican and was later elected Pope as Pius XII. Justo attended every event at the Eucharistic Conference, going far beyond the requirements of protocol. Conference officials duly noted Justo's devotion and felt it deserved the recognition of the ecclesiastical hierarchy. Cardinal Pacelli apparently agreed, commenting in a piece published by *L'Osservatore Romano*, and reprinted in *Criterio*, that he had never seen a head of a nation pronounce in such a solemn manner the consecration of his people to the King of Kings.[52]

Justo's attitude toward the Church, which Halperín Donghi attributed to his need to use "forces that were not strictly partisan as instruments of extortion against the organized political forces,"[53] was also reinforced by an awakening of popular religiosity. This rise was in part the result of the Church's policy of "going to the people"—particularly the lower classes—implemented during the decades of the 1920s and 1930s. On "men's night" during the Eucharistic Conference, 175,000 men received Communion from the hands of Cardinal Pacelli, who could not hide his emotion at the apparent outpouring of faith.[54] Although it might be true, as has been suggested, that among the faithful there were many members of Catholic Action and other Catholic groups, these never numbered more than 11,000 people. Even if all of them received Communion that night, there was a considerable number of people who could not be characterized as militants who did attend "men's night."[55] As Msgr. Gustavo Franceschi would say in 1936, religion was becoming fashionable.[56] Catholicism, traditionally confined to the upper sectors, was now also penetrating the popular sectors.[57]

The new kind of relationship between the Church and the state was also evident in the crucial area of primary education. In June 1937 a group of Catholic teachers organized a meeting outside the Consejo Nacional de Educación to thank its president for "the spirit which, by law, has been infused in public schools through moral education and the worship of national traditions."[58] He responded to the homage by pointing out that Law 1420 of 1884 that had established mandatory secular primary education in territories under federal control in no way required "Godless" education. After 1938 the celebration of Christmas was authorized in public schools, and it was attended by the president of the Consejo Nacional de Educación and other civil and ecclesiastical authorities.[59]

However, education was, in the end, one of the last arenas in which the crisis of consensus became evident. In spite of the ideology of government-appointed officials at the top of the educational hierarchy, a strong undercurrent of the liberal tradition remained deeply rooted in the lower levels of the educational bureaucracy. Moreover, as in the 1910s, when some within the educational bureaucracy publicly supported anarchism but nevertheless faithfully fulfilled their task of strengthening the weakened consensus through patriotic education (along with right-wing functionaries who also performed the same tasks), it was also possible to find people with widely divergent ideologies in the educational system during the 1930s and 1940s. Thus, for example, in 1946, Perón would have no problem finding people of Catholic nationalist ideology among the career education officials to occupy positions of importance, as we shall see. But at the same time, in 1945, the Communist newspaper *Orientación* featured an article criticizing the anti-liberal educational policies of the military government, in particular the adoption of historical revisionism. The author of the article was Juan Nissen, presented by the newspaper as a distinguished reader of *Orientación* and, therefore, we might assume, a Communist sympathizer. His ideology, however, had not prevented him from having an admirable career within the educational system. His appointments included professor at the prestigious Escuela Normal de Paraná, secretary of the school board in Mercedes, inspector of primary schools in Entre Ríos, principal of many schools, and secretary for Technical Inspection of the Consejo Nacional de Educación, among others.[60]

The Crisis of Consensus, the Polarization of Society, and the Intellectuals

The crisis of liberal consensus, combined with the emergence of nationalism in all its varieties, divided society, and the elite in particular. This division, nevertheless, became unbridgeable only when international events such as the Spanish Civil War and World War II forced the dominant classes, and in a certain sense all of society, to take more militant and rigid positions.[61] In his memoirs, the revisionist historian Julio Irazusta recalls the climate of peaceful coexistence among intellectuals of various ideologies that was still possible at the beginning of the 1930s. Referring to a meeting in the home of liberal writer Victoria Ocampo:

> Eduardo Mallea, Pedro Enríquez Ureña, María de Maetzu, Cármen Gándara . . . and many others I cannot remember now, frequently met with us in a spirit of civilized coexistence . . . if such an experiment ended, it was partly because the European War confused people's minds and divided them along the lines of international factions. But I think that it was also because nationalism degenerated into an international ideology, and, already manipulated by the regime, it collaborated with successive governments and subsequently failed in practice.[62]

Such "civilized coexistence" would become unthinkable by the end of the thirties.

The crisis of confidence in the consensus that had held society (or at least the elite) together also became evident in the repressive measures taken by the neoconservative governments against intellectuals of leftist tendencies. In the previous decades, while the state had reacted with violence against material threats to the social order, the free dissemination of ideas had never been seen as a serious threat to the official ideology. The consensus was strong and was able to absorb alternative ideologies. In the new climate of the 1930s, however, ideas began to be seen as dangerous, and the intellectuals who generated them were harassed by repressive measures. Thus, although at the end of the nineteenth century the famous Italian anarchist Pietro Gori had been invited to deliver some lectures in the Law School of the University of Buenos Aires, in the 1930s the Marxist thinker Aníbal Ponce was dismissed from his chair in Psychology at the Instituto Nacional del Profesorado and forced into exile. The poet Raúl González Tuñón was prosecuted for the content of some of his poems.[63] As Jesús Méndez points out in his doctoral thesis, in the 1930s Communist leader Héctor Agosti was jailed for repeating the same things as José Ingenieros but with no consequences decades earlier.[64]

The "death of liberalism," as lamented by Eduardo Mallea from the pages of *Sur*, was accompanied by a deep pessimism among the intelligentsia.[65] In 1933, for example, Ezequiel Martínez Estrada published his *Radiografía de la pampa*, a work which won him the National Literature Prize of that year. *Radiografía* is an exhaustive catalogue of the problems and maladies of Argentina. Naturally, the perception that things were not going well in the country was nothing new. Previous writers, such as José María Ramos Mejía or Ricardo Rojas, in the 1910s had diagnosed the problems of the country and had blamed them on the unassimilated immigrants, or on an imperfect, but perfectible, political system. Martínez Estrada, instead, traced the causes of the national problems to the very origins of the country's history. According to this vision, Argentina was now paying the price for its flawed geography and the economic and social configuration of the pampas.

This critical version of Argentina was shared by authors such as Mallea, who, in *Historia de una pasión argentina*, distinguished between a "visible Argentina"—materialistic, pretentious, soulless, and urban—and an "invisible Argentina"—spiritually rooted and rural. Mallea's book, which was extremely popular, was written as a response to his "need to cry out my anguish caused by my land, our land." Unlike Martínez Estrada, Mallea did not blame Argentina's problems on its geographical configuration. Rather, Mallea found the cause in the "visible Argentina," and particularly in the behavior of politicians and intellectuals during the existing crisis. Mallea's vision was, in this sense, less pessimistic than Martínez Estrada's because it admitted the possibility of redemption. One of the chapters of *Historia de una pasión argentina* was entitled "The Country as Lazarus." Although the current situation as analyzed by the book was characterized in the darkest terms, eventually, as in the story of Lazarus, there would be a resurrection.

Some politicians and intellectuals, overwhelmed by the crisis, saw suicide as the only solution. The 1930s was the decade of the "great suicides," including those of Leopoldo Lugones and Lisandro de la Torre, among others.

In many aspects the 1930s marked the end of a period that had begun more than fifty years before. In part a result of the economic crisis that broke up the bases of the successful Argentine experience (which themselves were weaker than anyone expected), and in part the result of the natural evolution of a society that had become more complex and conflict-ridden, the consensus holding the elites together fell apart. As Beatriz Sarlo points out, Argentina, which in the nineteenth century had been "a cause and a program," was in the 1930s "a problem that admitted few optimistic solutions."[66] The climate of discord generated a "structure of feelings" that permeated Argentine literature and culture in general.[67]

By the end of the 1930s, Argentine society was profoundly polarized. The illusion of unanimity and social harmony became difficult to maintain. In addition, the political system, corrupted and fraudulent, had lost its legitimacy. Political parties were in crisis, and the army had become an important factor in political power. It was in this context that the Revolution of 1943 took place, out of which Perón emerged. However, the liberal tradition was still strong among some sectors of society, and it would reemerge as the ideological glue that would bind together the anti-Peronist bloc.

2

PERÓN AND THE PROBLEM OF CONSENSUS

J uan Perón emerged in public life as one of the main leaders and ideo-
logues of the secret military lodge made up of midrank officers, the Grupo
de Oficiales Unidos (GOU), which organized the coup that on June 4, 1943,
brought down President Ramón Castillo. Soon afterward, he took the rather
obscure position of director of the National Labor Office, which he transformed into the powerful secretary of labor and welfare. From that office,
Perón undertook a policy of attracting loyal union leaders while repressing
those who would not toe the line (particularly Communists). Gradually
Perón increased his power within the government, and by early 1945 he
was simultaneously secretary of labor and welfare, war minister, and vice
president.

In general terms, the ideological principles supported by the lodge were
nationalism, anticommunism, and ultra-Catholicism tainted with anti-
Semitism.[1] Just as other right-wing nationalist groups, the members of the
lodge were afraid of the possible social consequences of the postwar situation. Also like the similar groups discussed in Chapter 1, the officers of the
GOU believed that it was imperative to improve the standard of living of
the workers in order to avoid social conflict. In a secret document circulated
among the members of the lodge in May 1943, the situation of the moment
was described in the following terms: "The important employees and 'friends'
of the bureaucracy enjoy their high salaries and think of nothing but making sure this situation lasts and that the government remains ignorant of the
situation. The poor can afford neither food nor clothing."[2]

According to the document, the politicians in power were servants of
the usurers, foreign businesses, and the Jewish merchants. The solution within
the document for these problems was "the suppression of the political, social, and economic intermediary." "To do so," it continued, "it is necessary

that the state transform itself into a body that regulates wealth, directs politics, and harmonizes society. All this requires the disappearance of the professional politician, the annulment of the dishonest merchant, and the extirpation of the social agitator."[3]

On June 5, one day after taking power, the new government issued a proclamation, probably written by Perón, making public its objectives. According to this proclamation, the principal problems of the country, whose resolution the new authorities took it upon themselves to solve, were: immorality in public administration, the absence of God in public schools, the excessive power of "usurious capital" to the detriment of national interests, the lack of moral authority of the judicial system, and the Communist threat.[4] The military authorities also stressed the importance of industrial development as a prerequisite for attaining "economic independence."

Perón's Ideology and the Problem of "Spiritual Unity"

It is very difficult to establish a genealogy of Perón's ideology, and in any case it is not clear that it is relevant to do so.[5] Perón, as he himself never tired of saying, was not an ideologue but a pragmatic politician. There are, however, some points worth noting. Many of the social, political, and economic ideas supported by Perón—the role the state should play, the need to establish some kind of corporative system of representation, the importance of achieving "economic independence" for the country through the protection of some industries—were part of the climate of ideas of the time. Many of these ideas, and even some that he would adopt as slogans of his own, can be found in publications such as the *Revista de Economía Argentina* or the *Boletín del Museo Social Argentino*, among others, during the 1930s. The ideas of the Catholic right also clearly influenced Perón's ideology. There were two experiences in his life, however, which proved to be crucial for the formation of his personality and his mental universe: his military life; and his trip to Europe, in particular, to Italy and Spain at the beginning of World War II.[6]

It was during his military career that Perón developed the basic structure of the ideas he would later apply to politics. León Rozitchner has pointed out the continuities between the textbook *Apuntes de historia militar*, written by Perón in 1934 for his classes in the War College, and Perón's 1952 book *Conducción política*, a work based on the classes that Perón had given the year before in the Escuela Superior Peronista, an institution for the formation of political leaders.[7] Moreover, as an army officer, Perón had the opportunity of traveling throughout the country, journeys which opened his eyes to the problems caused by poverty in the provinces of the interior. In 1919, Perón was among the forces that repressed the workers during the Tragic Week. The events triggering the repression were recorded in his mind as an ever-present danger.[8]

The other experience that proved to have a crucial influence in the development of Perón's mental universe was his trip to Europe between 1939 and 1941. There he not only came to appreciate firsthand the achievements and organization of the Fascist regime, but he also personally witnessed the horrors of immediate post–Civil War Spain. Perón never hid his admiration for Mussolini, nor even for Hitler.[9] However, as Halperín Donghi points out, Perón did not believe it was necessary to familiarize himself with the content of the theoretical works of fascism.[10]

One of the most important conclusions Perón drew from both experiences was the need to control the masses. It was uncontrolled masses that provoked the events leading up to the Tragic Week. From Fascist Italy, Perón learned some practical ways in which the masses could be organized and controlled. As he himself would say in *Conducción política*, "The value of the people . . . does not reside in the number of men who are organized. Its value resides in the rulers who lead the people, because *action is never generated by the mass or by the people, but by the rulers who lead them.* The mass goes wherever its rulers take it; otherwise, it overflows, and God forbid!"[11]

Perón sought the controlled mobilization of the masses through political rituals during his governance for two ends. First, he wished to recreate the image of direct contact with the people, one of the main sources of his legitimacy; and second, he used the organized masses as a way to warn the "oligarchy." The regular flooding of human masses into the streets of the city, whom Perón constantly reminded that he had rescued from the oppression to which the oligarchy had subjected them, served as a valuable restraint on the opposition. It was warned not to forget the consequences of what might happen if Perón eventually loosened the strict control he held over those masses. From his first days as secretary of labor and welfare, one of Perón's favorite slogans was "From Home to Work, and From Work to Home," a clear illustration of the passive role he attributed to the working masses.

Another important idea that Perón took from military doctrine and that would later be applied to politics was the importance of "spiritual unity." In his *Apuntes de historia militar*, first published in the 1930s before Perón showed any political ambition, he wrote, "The leader will say: *This is my idea. It turns itself into action.* From that moment the main task of the command will be to assure *that one single thought dominates the whole army. That thought will be the commander in chief's.*"[12]

The idea of obtaining a "single thought," that of the commander in chief, in order to limit the level of disagreement, was developed by Perón (or, more accurately, taken by him from other classic authors) as a necessary doctrine for armies at war. Later, Perón extended this doctrine in order to make it applicable to society in general. The need to establish a single doctrine, one generated by the state that fixed the objectives of the whole nation, would become one of the crucial components of the Peronist discourse. The state needed to inculcate this doctrine to the degree that it became a kind of "collective mental framework" through which all reality had to be interpreted. This doctrine had to unify all readings of reality and, at the same time, clearly fix the acceptable limits of dissent. But let us follow the evolution of this conception step by step. In his *Apuntes*, Perón had written: "The doctrine will be extended to all the high command during war by developing the faculties for a similar mode of seeing, thinking, and acting. . . . The war doctrine is aimed at providing the necessary moral and intellectual cohesion to the commanders, establishing shared criteria, wills, feelings."[13]

This is Perón the military teacher writing in 1934. Ten years later, in June 1944, already a high-ranking official of the military government with known political ambitions, Perón was invited to give the inaugural lecture to the faculty of national defense at the National University of La Plata. Perón used the opportunity to expand his 1934 ideas. "In matters concerning forms of government," he said, "and matters of economic, social, financial, and industrial problems, along with problems concerning production, work, etc., all sorts of opinions and interests are admissible within the state. In the political objective derived from the people's feeling of nationality, because it is single and indivisible, no divergent opinions are acceptable. On the contrary, this shared myth serves as one more glue with which to cement the national unity of a given people."[14]

Differing from its original formulation, in 1944 the uniformity of doctrine was no longer solely a need for armies at war but extended to the whole nation. During his presidency, Perón never tired of stressing the importance of the uniformity of doctrine. In his speech presenting the First Five-Year Plan to Congress in 1947, for example, Perón gave a more specific meaning to his words of 1944: "The doctrine is the collective sense and feeling which must be inculcated in the people, and through which it is possible to arrive at unity of action in achievements and solutions."

It is therefore not surprising that during Perón's governance the "Peronist doctrine" had been declared "national doctrine" by congressional law in 1952, and defined as such in the Second Five-Year Plan. This doctrine had to be inculcated in the minds of the population and "preached": "one has to go out and preach this Doctrine; not teach it, but preach it."[15]

One way in which the Peronist regime expected to inculcate the doctrine was through the publication of books such as the *Peronist Manual*. There were at least two editions of the *Manual*: one in 1948 and another in 1954. If we compare the two editions, it is possible to follow the evolution of the concept of "spiritual unity" in Peronist discourse. In its 1948 edition, the *Manual* stressed the importance of the "unity of action" and of the "unity of conception" in holding together the Peronist Party: "From a single way of seeing, there will result a single way of understanding, and from a single way of understanding there will result a single way of resolving problems."[16]

In the 1954 edition, however, the "Peronist doctrine" is presented as the frame on which the orientation of a whole people had to be fixed: "The doctrine is a total conception of life; it fixes the orientations of the people toward the great common obligations of nationality. It is the set of postulates that respond to national—and by extension popular—aspirations, needs, and convenience. . . . The Peronist doctrine, which is the national doctrine, is exclusively Argentine and is based on what we call Peronism, the principle of our present political organization, which will be applied in each country in a different way."[17]

The actual content of this doctrine that would become so important in the organization of the country, however, was defined only in the vaguest terms. To begin with, the doctrine was never coherently systematized. The books published under the title *Doctrina peronista*, of which there are several versions, are only fragmentary compilations of Perón's speeches on the most diverse topics and contain contradictory messages. In general, all that can be said about the doctrine is that it was oriented toward the happiness of the people through the attainment of the three basic principles of social justice, economic independence, and political sovereignty. It also alluded to a humane and Christian "third position," which located itself between individual capitalism and its opposite and necessary consequence, collectivist communism.[18] In what was perhaps the most sophisticated presentation of the doctrine, Perón delivered a speech (probably written by the priest Hernán Benítez) to the Congress of Philosophy in 1949, in which he declared that for Peronism, "society will have to be in harmony and there will be no room for any dissonance, nor a predominance of the material, nor a state of fantasy. In a harmony presided over by the norm we can talk about collectivism achieved through improvement, through culture, through equilibrium. In such a regime, freedom is not an empty word, because its condition is determined by the sum of freedoms and by the ethical and moral state."[19]

At first, Perón used elements taken directly from Catholicism in order to legitimize his discourse. His programs were presented as the application of the principles delineated by papal encyclicals. Catholicism served as the starting point from which it would be possible to generate a new consensus.[20] This association of his message with Catholic doctrine won Perón the sympathy (at least at first) of the ecclesiastical hierarchy and of the right-wing nationalist groups. Gradually, however, during Perón's government, the state monopolized the public symbolic space, and the Peronist doctrine replaced the Catholic one as a kind of official religion. Peronism was becoming a political religion, and this made the relations between the Church and the state quite tense. Toward the end of the regime, this tension produced a violent rupture between the two.[21]

The basic ideas behind Perón's discourse and policies were, as we have seen, not new. His model of social organization was a society organized through a corporative system, held together by "spiritual unity," in which the state would arbitrate social conflict while working to eliminate all future possibility of such conflict. "We want capital and labor, in a tight embrace, to forge the greatness of the fatherland, while the state watches over the good of both, assuring justice for the rich and the poor. . . . We envision the disappearance of all causes of anarchy, in order to provide harmony, based on social justice, and to assure the impossibility of the alteration of good relations among capital, labor, and the state."[22] However, Perón and his group, born in part as the result of the 1930s crisis of the liberal consensus, "updated" this idea by redefining the role of the state and adding some elements taken from recent European experiences and right-wing Catholicism.[23] Later, Perón also borrowed some ideas from his collaborators, some of whom, such as Angel Borlenghi, had Socialist backgrounds.

Spiritual Unity and Consensus: A Failed Attempt

From the beginning of his ascending career in 1943, Perón tried to gain the support of all possible sectors of society. His policies concerning the working class were based on the redefinition of the relationship between the state and the trade unions. After the 1943 coup, the state began to grant benefits to the loyal unions while repressing those whose loyalty was questionable. This policy was complemented by a controlled mobilization of the working class.[24] Trade unions had always attempted to establish friendly links with the state.[25] Now, for the first time since the beginning of Yrigoyen's government, unions found a state that, through the secretary of labor and welfare, was receptive to their demands.

However, Perón's plan was essentially conservative, and, at the beginning, the support it most required was that of the elite, in particular of the financial and industrial sectors.[26] Before he was elected president, Perón tried to win the sympathy of the conservative sectors by reviving fears of a seemingly inevitable postwar social revolution, which only Perón, through his policies of controlled delivery of social justice to the working class, would be able to prevent. This line was evident in his famous and often-quoted speech delivered at the Bolsa de Comercio de Buenos Aires in 1944, when he urged employers to "give something so as not to lose everything."[27] This message would be repeated ad nauseam during the Peronist government. In 1947, for example, Perón reprimanded the "conservative classes" for opposing the Peronists, who "in the end had come to save them from a tragedy which they had brought upon themselves with their attitude."[28]

The problem was that by the time Peron began his rise to power, obtaining consensus along the lines he proposed was no longer possible. Society was already profoundly polarized even before the 1943 coup. Although Perón was undoubtedly successful in obtaining the support of the unions, the same cannot be said about his efforts to secure the support of the conservative sectors. The opposition of the industrial sectors to Perón did not derive only from the possible economic losses his new social policies might inflict on them. These sectors were also concerned—and this may be the most relevant point—that these policies, rather than serving as a barrier against social agitation, as Perón never tired of proclaiming, would, in fact, work to increase the lack of discipline among the working class. In 1944, for example, the Unión Industrial Argentina (UIA) complained of "the lack of discipline in the industrial plants generated by an ever-increasing use of a language which presents the employers as being in a position of dominance [and which presents] each agreement not as an act of justice but as a 'conquest.' "[29] As Juan Carlos Torre pointed out, "In fact, the policies of the secretary of labor looked like a self-fulfilling prophecy: his social policy, instead of pacifying [the working class], caused further mobilization of labor, [and] invited the proprietary classes to act in response."[30]

As we have seen, there had been agreement among the industrial sectors in the 1930s that more extensive participation of the state in social issues was necessary as a barrier against social disorder. The UIA stressed that it

supported improvement of the living and working conditions of the working class. Some industrialists had already established paternalist policies in
their companies. As mentioned before, Torcuato Di Tella had presented a
bill in Congress (with the institutional support of the UIA) to establish a
system of universal social security. Perón's policies, however, went far beyond what the industrial sectors were willing to tolerate. As Joel Horowitz
points out, the industrialists could not countenance the idea of delegating
the control of their plants to workers and unions.[31] One businessman recalled years later, "After two years of Perón's protection, workers wanted to
obtain more, while working less. The means used by the workers to achieve
their demands created moments of anxiety [among the industrialists]. Workers accused the foremen of being against Perón's policies, and this affected
the role of the foremen to such an extent that few people wished to be in
that position."[32] The perception of the empowerment of the workers brought
about by the Perón regime is evident in testimonies collected from working-
class activists.[33] Perón was right when he told a group of union representatives in August 1945 that "the Republic is divided into two groups which
are clearly recognizable. This division had its origin in the work of this house
[the Secretariat of Labor and Welfare]."[34]

However, Perón was able to convince two important groups of the im-
minent danger of a social revolution and of the need to rely on him as the
only leader able to stop it; these were his colleagues in the army (or at least
some groups within it) and certain sectors of the Catholic right, including
members of the ecclesiastical hierarchy. The army was always ready to believe in the immediacy of the Red threat, and the Catholic group was being
treated by the state with a deference they had not enjoyed since colonial
times. Some sectors of the ecclesiastical hierarchy also envisioned the benefits they might be able to obtain for the Church in a country governed by
Perón. But his arguments did not persuade the industrialists, who found the
evidence of the dangers Perón prophesied unconvincing, and therefore saw
no reason to accept him as their self-proclaimed savior.

The Reemergence of Liberalism as
the Basis of an Anti-Peronist "Unifying Myth"

Paradoxically, the polarization of Argentine society discussed in the previous chapter served, on the one hand, to consolidate the support the working class gave Perón and, on the other, to unify against him and the military

the government groups that traditionally had been separated or even opposed to each other. Liberalism, in crisis during the 1930s, emerged again,
particularly after the triumph of the United Nations in World War II, as the
basis of a unifying myth for those groups opposed to Perón. The military
government and Perón were characterized as Nazis by their opposition. In
the University of Buenos Aires, for example, where the repressive methods
of the military regime had had painful consequences, Halperín Donghi notes,
"in their now unchained rage, those who used to march separately in university life unified; from conservative liberalism . . . to the reform positions
of the reformist student sectors, the common aggravations created a unity, a
solidarity earlier ignored."[35] It should come as no surprise that when those
who had been hurt by the military government saw the possibility of obtaining their revenge, they used the same methods that they had cried out
against when these methods had been used to victimize them. A resolution
of the University of Buenos Aires dated July 1945, after the anti-Peronist
opposition had gained control of the institution for a short time, ordered an
investigation of all the professors who "in their behavior as citizens had
shown an orientation against the democratic principles which are the essence of our constitutional organization."[36] Once again, although this time
from the opposite side, professors were being judged for their political ideas
and not for their academic performance. Members of the UIA who opposed
Peron (including its president, Luis Colombo), who during the previous
decade had not hidden their sympathy for Mussolini, now presented themselves as the champions of liberal democracy.[37]

The degree of the polarization in Argentine society became clear in the
last months of the military regime when, cornered by internal and external
pressures, the regime was forced to liberalize its policies. In September 1945
the opposition—which now included a political spectrum extending from
the Communist Party to the conservatives—organized a march suggestively
called the "March of the Constitution and Freedom," in order to demand
that the regime immediately surrender power to the Supreme Court. The
march was a notable success and attracted the participation of between 65,000
and 250,000 people (according to which source is consulted), including
politicians ranging from the conservative doctor Antonio Santamarina to
the Communist Rodolfo Ghioldi.[38] The march showed that the opposition
was not only questioning the military's right to govern but also the legitimacy of its place in the historic development of the country. The participants carried maps of the Republic, flags, and placards that read: "This is
Argentina: May Revolution, Assembly of 1813, July 9th, Caseros, Civil Code,

Penal Code, and individual guarantees. This is not Argentina: anarchy, barbarism, Rosas's tyranny, decree-laws, stage of siege."[39] There was a "true Argentina" represented by the liberal tradition, whose history was a line of continuity from the May Revolution of 1810 against Spain to this very demonstration, although many of the participants came from ideological positions antithetical to liberalism.[40] Everything that was not included in this line of historical development was characterized simply as "not Argentina." The participants in the march were not only appropriating a place in the streets of the city, but also establishing their place as the heirs of the country's "true tradition." Again, the appropriation of the national past was becoming a political weapon.

The events of October 17, 1945, discussed in the following chapters, would serve as the mirror image of the march. In the demonstration of October 17, the Peronist masses challenged this symbolic appropriation of the urban space and the national past. What is interesting is that in both cases, the dispute was over the same symbols.[41] According to *La Epoca*, Perón had accomplished nothing less than the completion of the conquests of the 1813 Assembly, which was the corollary of the Revolution started in 1810.[42] The meaning of the Seventeenth of October was the same as that of May 25, 1810, and Perón was the heir of San Martín and Sarmiento.[43] Both groups, Peronists and anti-Peronists, saw themselves as the representatives of the true nationality, which they defined in similar terms.[44] However, the very weight of the liberal tradition in Argentine culture had a paradoxical effect. By linking this tradition directly with anti-Peronism in order to deprive Peronism of legitimacy, the anti-Peronist opposition forced the Peronists to look for an alternative source of legitimacy. Another tradition, recovered by the supporters of "historical revisionism," was available. In 1949, in addition to the unquestioned heroes of the national past, the members of the group now called *descamisados* (the shirtless, meaning the poor) were also brought forward as the heirs of the "popular uprisings and revolutionary crowds of our elders."[45]

Perón, however, made it clear from the beginning that he had no interest in associating himself with an alternative vision of the national past. Although Perón was certainly not a liberal, he had no intention (at least at the beginning) of dissociating himself from the liberal tradition that, after the Allied triumph in the war, could claim once again its role as the "true" tradition of the country. In any case, Perón tried to appropriate—and integrate—the two versions of the past (liberal and revisionist) by shifting the terms of the debate. As he himself stated in 1946, "The real truth is this: in our fatherland there is not a debate between 'freedom' and 'tyranny,' between Rosas and Urquiza, between 'democracy' and 'totalitarianism.' What deep down is being debated here is, simply, a championship match between 'social justice' and 'social injustice.' "[46]

Official Peronist history presented Peronism as a rupture with the past, negating the relevance of all the history of the country between the declaration of independence and the rise of Peronism. The *Political Plan for 1951* ordered Peronists to refrain from participating in the discussions between "revisionists" and "antirevisionists."[47] When some prominent revisionists asked Perón why he refused to support their version of history (something he would do for very specific motives after his fall in 1955), he simply answered that the past was dead and that therefore he saw no need to add a new and unnecessary element of discord to an already divided Argentine society.[48]

In view of his failure to attract business groups to his heterogeneous coalition, and aware that in such circumstances the working-class sector's support was crucial, Perón radicalized his speech.[49] He began to characterize his base of support as "the people," while referring to the opposition as "the oligarchy." With the approach of the February elections, it became obvious that Perón was succeeding in displacing the terms of the debate from the political to the social sphere. As Daniel James points out, "By constantly emphasizing the social dimension of citizenship Perón explicitly challenged the legitimacy of a notion of democracy which limited itself to participation in formal political rights, and he extended it to include participation in the social and economic life of the nation."[50]

Besides, as is well known, Perón received the unexpected help of an official of the U.S. State Department, the former ambassador to Argentina, Spruille Braden. His open support of the Unión Democrática, the political coalition that opposed Perón, and the publication of the "Blue Book" in which Perón was characterized as a Nazi agent, implicitly supported Perón's argument that the opposition was not only oligarchical but also in collusion with foreign imperialism.[51] The Peronist campaign received another important forward push when it became public that the UIA had financially supported the Unión Democrática. Peronist propaganda referred to the opposition as "anti-fatherland." There developed, therefore, a process of double delegitimation similar to the one occurring in the Yrigoyen period. The opposition characterized Perón as a Nazi, and he, in turn, characterized the members of the opposition as oligarchs who were selling out the country. This time, however, polarization reached new extremes.

The Invention of Consensus

Once in power, after wining the elections of February 1946, Perón faced two important tasks. First, he had to discipline his own party's forces, which were made up of dissimilar groups from diverse ideological extractions. Second, unable to create a true consensus, he was compelled to create the illusion of one. By 1947, Perón had achieved his first objective.[52] The second was extremely important, given the peculiarities of the Peronist regime.

The legality of Perón's government was unimpeachable. He had been elected by a clear majority in clean and honest elections.[53] Even during his governance, Perón scrupulously followed the form (if not the spirit) of the law. Therefore, he could declare proudly that he was the first president in the history of Argentina who always inaugurated the sessions of Congress on the day required by the Constitution, May 1. However, as Jürgen Habermas points out, formal legality does not guarantee legitimacy: "The organs which are responsible for making and applying the laws are in no way legitimated by the legality of their modes of procedure, but likewise by a general interpretation which supports the system of authority as a whole."[54] By depriving the opposition of its role as a legitimate political contender, Perón also undermined his own source of legitimacy. By displacing his discourse from the political to the social sphere, Perón created the image that his legitimacy was derived not only from his legal election but also from his direct and unique contact with "the people." The elections were only incidental evidence of such contact. The opposition, of course, characterized by the official discourse as the "anti-people," found this source of legitimacy unacceptable.

The Peronist regime tried to generate the image of a "spiritual unity" (which they could not create in reality) by excluding the opposition from the realm of legitimate political discourse and by creating a system of myths and symbols that served as the base for a true Peronist political imagery. This political imagery would function as the glue that would reinforce the cohesion of the heterogeneous Peronist "constituency" characterized as "the people." The exclusion of the opposition was achieved through the strict control of the media, open repression, and the control of all the institutional mechanisms of the government. The creation of the political imagery was achieved through the organization of a machinery whose purpose was to indoctrinate and organize the masses as well as to create Perón's own charisma. This machinery included, among other elements, the use and manipulation of the educational system and the creation of political rituals. Although Perón had indeed emerged as a charismatic leader on October 17,

1945, it became necessary to keep that charisma alive through an impressive propaganda effort orchestrated from the Subsecretaría de Prensa y Difusión. Under the direction of journalist Raúl Alejandro Apold, during Perón's regime this agency published more than 2.5 million pamphlets of various types and more than 3 million posters, in addition to producing movies and other propaganda materials.[55] The *Organic Political Plan, 1952–1958*, a secret government document, clearly stipulated that the Subsecretaría de Prensa y Difusión was supposed to mount an enormous propaganda effort in order to counteract the campaign of the opposition. The document also established that one of the objectives of the government in this period was to "openly orient the teaching of *justicialismo* among students, and to eliminate those teachers who put up any barriers against it." The document specified that "this direction should begin in primary school."

The structuring of the Peronist political imagery was not, of course, the work of Perón alone. People working in the Subsecretaría de Prensa and in other official broadcast media created different and sometimes contradictory images of Perón and his role in the various events linked to the birth of Peronism, in order to make the message relevant to the different sectors within Peronism. In Part II this topic is analyzed in connection with the "mythological creation" of the Seventeenth of October.

Failed Attempts at Creating a Peronist Culture

The attempts on the part of the Peronist government to generate a "new unifying myth," one which would fill the role played by liberalism in the previous decades, failed. Beyond Perón's own inconsistencies and ideological limitations, one of the reasons for the failure is linked to the inability of the regime to attract intellectuals who would be capable of creating this message. The anti-intellectual rhetoric in some sectors within Peronism contributed to the alienation of the "intelligentsia."

For important segments of the middle and upper classes, the birth of Peronism was very difficult to swallow.[56] The new phenomenon of Peronism was seen as an aberration that did not fit in the "natural" history of the country. This perception became even more evident in different aspects of cultural life, including literature. Ezequiel Martínez Estrada, in a short novel published in 1944, *Sábado de Gloria*, made clear and direct allusions to the current political and social situation. Although the action occurred in the present, he had woven into the narrative images of the "invasion" of the city of Buenos Aires by the caudillos in 1820, a clear allusion to the current "invasion" of political and social life by new social groups. These images were combined with allusions to the current political situation. The "invasion" of 1820 had traditionally been presented by liberal texts as examples of the inundation of "civilization" by "barbarism": the rural world taking over the urban world. It is therefore not a coincidence that Martínez Estrada took the historical references to these events from the works of nineteenth-century liberal historians.[57] The idea of the "invasion," with or without direct references to the current situation, was already present in the works of other famous authors who, as Andrés Avellaneda points out, had produced an ideological replica that existed in literary texts even before Perón formally took power in 1946.[58]

Jorge Luis Borges made even more direct references to the birth of the Peronist regime and its development in some short stories he wrote with Adolfo Bioy Casares under the collective pen name of Honorio Bustos Domecq.[59] A case in point was, for instance, the short story titled "La fiesta del monstruo," published in Montevideo when Perón was still in power. The story is about a group of people who go to celebrate "the feast of the monster" (an obvious reference to one of the political rituals described in the following two chapters) and end up committing all kinds of crimes, including the senseless torture and murder of a Jew (a reference to Peronists' alleged anti-Semitism). Not only are the protagonists of the story criminals, but they are also aesthetically disgusting. Borges and Bioy Casares do not spare their readers from detailed descriptions of the odors emanating from those people as well as their gross physical attributes.

These authors presented Peronism as the "other absolute." To them, the rising movement was a monstrous and incomprehensible phenomenon (in any case, one they had no intention of trying to understand). Even after Perón's fall, Borges evaluated the fallen regime in the following terms:

> During the years of opprobrium and foolishness, the methods of commercial propaganda and of the *littérature pour concierges* were applied by the government of the Republic. Thus, there were two histories: one of a criminal nature, made up of jails, torture, prostitution, robberies, deaths, and fire; another one pertaining to the stage, made up of nonsense and fables for the consumption of the churlish. The dictatorship hated (pretended to hate) capitalism but copied its methods, just like in Russia. . . . Even more curious was the political use of the procedures of drama, or of melodrama.[60]

The intellectual establishment remained, by and large, in the opposition.[61] Only some well-known intellectuals, such as the popular anti-Semitic writer Gustavo Martínez Zuviría, and others such as Elías Castelnuovo, Manuel Gálvez, and Leopoldo Marechal, and popular artists such as Enrique Santos Discépolo, Homero Manzi, Cátulo Castillo, and Tita Merello, sided with Peronism.[62]

The problem was that Perón not only lacked a consistent cultural policy, but that the role he pretended to assign intellectuals within the regime also conspired against the development of alternative cultural patterns. In his attempts to "organize everything," Perón tried to organize the intellectuals. In 1947, for example, he set up a series of meetings with artists, writers, and teachers led by Gustavo Martínez Zuviría, who, as noted, had been responsible in 1943 for the introduction of Catholic education in the schools during his tenure as minister of education. In the first of such meetings, Perón introduced his ideas on the role intellectuals and culture had to play in the New Argentina: "I hope that you [the intellectuals] organize yourselves as a society; I hope that you unify, no matter what you think, what you feel, and what you want; but that you fulfill your role within the orientation that the state will no doubt fix."[63]

According to Perón, it was necessary to create a Subsecretaría de Cultura—which, in fact, would soon be created within the Ministry of Education—to assure that the arts and literature also "belonged to the state": "It is necessary that the state also provide in this realm its own orientation, that it set the goals and control the execution to see whether or not it is fulfilled."[64]

As a result of these meetings, in 1948 the Junta Nacional de Intelectuales was created. Its objective was to promote the country's artistic and scientific creation. The Junta, whose members were appointed by the President of the Republic, was made up of right-wing Catholic intellectuals, such as Martínez Zuviría, Carlos Ibarguren, and Delfina Bunge de Gálvez. Bunge de Gálvez had been excluded from liberal intellectual circles after she wrote an article on the events of October 17 in which she had compared them to Christ's passion.[65]

The attempts by Perón to organize the intellectuals failed in part because the Junta was not representative. Other attempts to create a body of intellectuals loyal to the regime also failed. The Asociación Argentina de Escritores (AADE), created in the 1930s by a group of nationalist writers in order to oppose the Sociedad Argentina de Escritores (SADE), and which after Perón's rise attracted many Peronist writers, also had limited success. AADE was never as prestigious as SADE, and after 1951 its activities declined sharply. Manuel Gálvez, who had been nominated by AADE for the Nobel Prize in Literature, recalled in his memoirs that in AADE "there was an abundance of school-text writers and a shortage of men of real prestige, most of whom were in SADE."[66]

The lack of a consistent project to create an alternative culture was also evident in what was probably the only serious attempt to create a "Peronist cultural magazine": *Sexto Continente*. Edited by Alicia Eguren and Armando Cascella, *Sexto Continente* proposed a Latin American and Argentine approach to culture against the cosmopolitan approach of magazines such as *Sur*.[67] *Sexto Continente* prided itself on having correspondents in six different Latin American countries, including some famous intellectuals such as the Mexican José Vasconcelos. However, this project was also doomed to failure. The final product was a combination of thinly disguised official propaganda[68] and articles on political and economic topics. What *Sexto Continente* understood by artistic and cultural production was well summarized in an article by Jorge Beryastain entitled "Argentine Reality in Art," in which he wrote: "The body which presides over artistic education must provide uniform directives in order to encourage those aesthetic activities that glorify the fatherland, our founding fathers and heroes, and the outstanding events of history. They should eternalize on canvas or in stone our physiognomy as a nation, without pretexts, because this is how it is written in the principal pages which guided our formation."[69]

Notwithstanding the contributions of some well-known intellectuals, including philosopher Carlos Astrada, most of what *Sexto Continente* presented was an incoherent mixture of nationalism, nativism, right-wing Catholicism, and praise for the regime. Its inability to create a forum of alternative culture was implicitly recognized by the editors, who complained that the first issue of *Sexto Continente* had been coldly received by the press and traditional intellectual circles, most of whom were anti-Peronists.[70] The editors of *Sexto Continente* were aware that they were fighting for a legitimate place in what Pierre Bourdieu called the "intellectual field," which was controlled by anti-Peronist circles.[71] Given the evident impossibility of changing the rules of the intellectual field, *Sexto Continente* had to content itself with having a secondary place in it.

Other Peronist intellectual groups, such as the Agrupación de Intelectuales del Partido Peronista, presided over by Pedro Baldasarre, or the Centro Universitario Argentino, organized during the electoral campaign of 1946, opted instead to anchor themselves in a totally different intellectual tradition. Highlighting the complete rupture that the Peronist revolution implied in the history of the country, the Centro Universitario Argentino took it upon itself to explain the profound meaning of this revolution. For the

Centro, the Peronist revolution represented no less than a return to the fundamental principles of the nation. Resulting from this attempt to find the deeper meaning of the revolution was a collective volume in which we once again find the usual combination of mythical nationalism, anti-imperialism, and the search for national roots that Carlos Astrada had located in the myth of the gaucho Martín Fierro.[72] Astrada repeated his argument in another collective volume edited by the Comisión Nacional de Cooperación Intelectual, entitled *Argentina en marcha* (Buenos Aires, 1947).

These failed attempts to create a new cultural consensus based on the never clearly explicated principles of the "National Revolution" were not restricted to the sphere of "high culture" or, as will be discussed later, to the creation of myths and political rituals for the masses. Efforts were made to create a "popular Peronist culture of everyday life." One such attempt was through the magazine *Argentina* published by Minister of Education Oscar Ivanissevich (1949–50). It was a relatively expensive magazine (the cover price was one peso) printed on high-quality paper. Among its collaborators were the above-mentioned Gustavo Martínez Zuviría, Manuel Gálvez, Carlos Ibarguren, and Delfina Bunge de Gálvez. The nature of the ideological message that the magazine tried to transmit can be summarized in the opinion of Gálvez on Peronism: "Perón has solved the social problem in the manner that I have always wished: advanced, orderly, from above, and rapidly."[73]

Although the editors of the magazine never tired of stressing the fact that most of its readers were workers, it seems clear that the intended audience for *Argentina* was not limited to that social sector. Apart from its high price, which probably placed it outside the reach of the working class, the material included in the magazine suggests another target audience. *Argentina* had fixed sections on how to set an elegant table, written by the expert on these topics, Count Chikoff, and a fashion section by his wife, Eugenia. In addition, the magazine stressed petit bourgeois values such as the importance of the family, religion, and patriotism.

Argentina also treated a variety of topics ranging from the place of the writer in society (in articles written by Gálvez or Martínez Zuviría) to aspects of popular culture. In fact, *Argentina* emphasized the importance of creating a popular culture that was *truly Argentine* and would replace cultural aspects that had been imposed from outside. One of the examples of the "foreign culture" that so worried the editors of *Argentina* was the custom of setting up Christmas trees, which, according to the magazine, was totally alien to the national traditions.[74]

The fashion section also attempted to replace "foreign fashions" with some of a more domestic character, which, of course, could not totally deviate from the dictates of Paris. Countess Chikoff suggested that instead of wearing gowns of the Directoire style then in vogue in Europe, Argentine women should wear dresses from her own clothing line, which had a more national character but were modeled more or less on the same historical period that had inspired the current French fashion.[75] *Argentina* disappeared in 1950 when Ivanissevich was dismissed from the Ministry of Education.

These somewhat grotesque attempts at creating a "national culture" were not isolated instances. It is possible to find second-rate intellectuals eager to show their loyalty to the regime who became active in other areas as well. In 1953, for example, Ramón Asís, a civil engineer who had been vice governor of the province of Córdoba and a university professor, published "Hacia una arquitectura simbólica justicialista" (Toward a Symbolic Peronist Architecture). In this pamphlet we learn that "architecture must be useful for unifying the people, not for the goals of the individual, and when we talk about collective property, we do so from a psycho-social perspective, and not from an economic and legal one."[76] Asís proposed the construction of buildings shaped as enormous statues of the Peróns. These buildings would have not only an aesthetic function but also an ethical and educational one, since they would symbolize the purest values of the fatherland, embodied in Perón and Eva. Of course, Asís also had in mind the functional aspect of the architecture, and he tells us that the sculptures would not be merely ornamental, but that practical use would be made of all the various anatomical parts of the building. No serious attempt, to my knowledge, was ever made to follow the program proposed by Asís. In this sense, in architecture as in other areas of culture, Peronism had little to offer in the way of alternatives to accepted styles.

From the beginning, Peronism presented itself as a complete rupture with the past. This mythical image was in some way reinforced by the opposition, which in its efforts to deprive Perón and his government of legitimacy, symbolically associated both with portions of the national history seen as pathological in the traditional view of the past and unrelated to the line of legitimate historical development. Some intellectuals close to the regime took the image of rupture seriously and attempted to create new cultural patterns to replace the old ones, still based in large part on the liberal tradition. These new cultural patterns would create a new consensus around the regime on the cultural level. Similar attempts were made within the realm of public education (see Part III). Although Peronism was successful in creating what could be called a "political subculture," which survived the fall of the regime, the attempts made at generating a new consensus clearly failed. In fact, what Peronism did achieve was the deepening of the polarization already existing in society to the point where it could be said that the entire Argentine political system, at least until the 1970s, defined itself in terms of the dichotomy "Peronism/anti-Peronism." The attempts at creating a new consensus were necessarily doomed to failure for various reasons.

First, Peronism never had a coherent ideology that could provide the basis of a new consensus. Second, the same dynamic of self-glorification in which the regime enveloped itself, turning itself into a "political religion," contributed to the generation of an "anti-Peronist consensus" among the opposition, which included most of the country's well-known intellectuals. This new consensus brought together people of diverse and sometimes antithetical ideologies under the umbrella of liberalism. Partly as a result of the end of World War II, liberalism once again became a unifying myth, this time working against Peronism. Near the end of Perón's governance, even the Catholic Church participated in the consensus.[77] As Oscar Terán points out, this liberal anti-Peronist consensus would disappear after Perón's fall in 1955.[78]

Moreover, the anti-intellectual discourse of some Peronists contributed to the alienation of intellectuals from the regime. Semiofficial publications such as *Mundo Peronista*, for example, printed numerous articles against the cultural manifestations of the avant-garde. The artists and intellectuals who followed the new trends were characterized with contempt as dirty, crazy, and anti-Argentine. According to *Mundo Peronista*, the only legitimate function of the intellectual within the new order was to preach the Peronist doctrine.

Many historical revisionists, such as Carlos Ibarguren or Arturo Jauretche, supported Perón from the beginning. Perón accepted them and appointed some to official public positions. The regime also tolerated the publication of revisionist articles in some of its newspapers. *La Epoca*, for example, in 1949 published a long series of articles on history with a clearly revisionist slant in which all liberal national heroes were expelled mercilessly from the national pantheon.[79] But even *La Epoca* had an ambiguous attitude with respect to this vision of the past. In the same issue of the newspaper in which we read an article urging the government to eliminate Sarmiento's *Facundo* from the school syllabi since it "disowns our Hispanic origins and our 'barbarism,' " the very masthead of the newspaper contained Sarmiento's phrase (with signature) "I bring my fists full of truths," likely a remnant of the paper's *yrigoyenista* period.[80]

As we have seen above, Perón discouraged a full revision of the national past, and, as will be discussed later, revisionism never fully permeated the school textbooks of the Peronist period. The official version of the past simply ignored the period between the declaration of independence and the birth of Peronism. Officially, however, the regime endorsed the traditional liberal version of the national past. The newly nationalized railroads were named Urquiza, Roca, Mitre, and Belgrano. It is therefore not surprising that in a series of conferences organized by the undersecretary of culture, one of the participants clearly said that the historical revisionism was still in its "pamphlet stage," and referred to Rosas's government as "the dictatorship."[81] In other areas not related to the vision of the past, however, Peronism did present antiliberal visions of society.

The failure of Peronism to create an alternative "Peronist culture" was implicitly recognized by the regime when it was forced to incorporate some publicly anti-Peronist writers (some of whom, at the time, were being persecuted by the regime) in a list of the top Argentine writers. An official publication of the Subsecretaría de Prensa y Difusión in 1952, *Síntesis de las letras argentinas*, included the names of some of the best writers, including Jorge Luis Borges, who had been forced out of his position as head of the Municipal Library by the regime. And Victoria Ocampo was briefly jailed by the government without its ever revealing the criminal charges against her.

Peronists never obtained recognition within the area of culture as legitimate contenders in the struggle over the control of the "intellectual field." Although some Peronists tried to negate the validity of the rules of the game in the contest over symbolic capital, they were, in fact, unable to formulate their own alternative rules and therefore were forced to accept the existing ones. However, Peronism was to be successful in generating a symbolic interchange with the masses based on the creation of a Peronist mythology.

Peronism's attempt to generate unanimity while simultaneously excluding the opposition (which represented the preferences of a firm 30 percent of the electorate even at the peak of Perón's popularity) ended by alienating not only the middle and upper classes but also such sectors as the Catholic Church, which had originally supported Perón.

II

MAY DAY AND THE SEVENTEENTH OF OCTOBER: POLITICAL RITUALS AND PERÓN'S CHARISMA

For decades after the fall of the Perón government there were two dates closely associated with Peronism: May Day and the Seventeenth of October. During the Perón regime those were the days when the organized Peronist working class would march to the Plaza de Mayo, where the governmental palace is located, to renew its loyalty pact with the "leader." After Perón was gone, on these two days the masses remembered their fallen ruler and promised to keep fighting for his return. The importance of the Seventeenth of October was such that the anti-Peronist military that overthrew Perón (the so-called Liberating Revolution) criminalized the mere celebration of the date.

Nevertheless, the process of "Peronizing" both dates was not simple. Although October 17, 1945, was closely linked to the origins of Peronism—on that day workers mobilized to rescue Perón from his arrest—originally the date meant different things to different people. It took a few years until the Peronist state could impose a single meaning on it. In the process, the date lost its commemorative nature and became one of the political rituals in which the communion between Perón and his people was recreated. The case of May Day was even more complicated since it was a celebration that predated the emergence of Peronism by more than a half-century. Originally, it was a Socialist celebration. Therefore, it took a tremendous effort from the Perón regime to appropriate the date and redefine its meaning into a Peronist celebration. The next two chapters analyze the process of Peronization of the Seventeenth of October and May Day.

3

THE ORIGIN OF TWO RITUALS

In an interview given some twenty years after the events it narrates, General José Sosa Molina recalled the impression that the May Day celebration of 1943 had made on him: "I remember that many chiefs and officers were commissioned to appraise *de visu* the parade [of workers]. It was really striking. [There was] a huge multitude with red flags in front . . . with their fists upraised, and singing 'The International,' foreshadowing truly tragic hours for the Republic."[1] In 1949, Juan Perazzolo, a Peronist who was a member of the National Constitutional Convention, delivered a speech before that body in which he referred to May Day in these terms: "Years ago, the May Day parades had the character of acts of protest against the execution of the Chicago workers [Martyrs of Chicago]. They were therefore an expression of hatred, rebellion, and struggle against capitalism. But now that General Perón is in charge of the fatherland's destiny, we no longer harbor hate or resentment: we gather around the May Day tribune to bless God and celebrate the happiness of Argentine workers."[2]

These two quotes are consistent. As Sosa Molina points out, before the revolution of June 4, 1943, the celebrations of May Day were occasions on which the working class threatened the social order, displaying all kinds of revolutionary symbols: red flags, fists up, and the like. After Perón took power, as Perazzolo claims, a new era began in which the Día del Trabajo (Workers' Day, on May Day) became a Fiesta del Trabajo (Celebration of Work), an eminently patriotic and peaceful holiday. This version of the evolution undergone by May Day celebrations would be one leitmotiv of Peronist propaganda.

The facts, however, were not that simple, and General Sosa Molina's recollections are inaccurate. The Socialist parade organized to celebrate May Day in 1943, the only parade of any real significance, was saturated with patriotic symbols, as the Socialists were celebrating that year not only

Workers' Day but also the ninetieth anniversary of the enactment of the National Constitution. The red flags were not present in 1943, as they had not been since President Justo prohibited them in the 1930s. Instead, as reported by the local press, workers carried placards with the colors of the national flag.[3] As was customary during the celebration of May Day since the 1930s, the national anthem was sung before "The International."[4] The placards carried by the protesters, according to the "bourgeois" press, contained positive references to the Constitution and to democracy, along with criticisms of the high prices of certain basic products.[5] The parades organized by the Socialist Party to celebrate Workers' Day, in fact, had always had a festive and peaceful character.[6]

In truth, General Sosa Molina's comments were self-serving. At the end of his statement, he claimed that given the revolutionary threat he had witnessed, the army had been forced to act, seizing power on June 4. Peronist propaganda also successfully created a myth around May Day that became a part of the Peronist political imagery. This myth held that Perón's rise to power ushered in a period of happiness for the working class. Therefore, the peaceful character that had since marked all May Day celebrations demonstrated the distance that separated the "New Argentina" from the old one. Moreover, Peronists believed that workers supposedly had all their needs met by the Perón government's policy of social justice. The working class thus continued to observe May Day, which became an official holiday, only to thank the government for all the benefits they had received. May Day, then, became one of the two highly ritualized events (the other was the Seventeenth of October), in which year after year the organized working class renewed its vote of confidence for, and loyalty to, the leader. The Peronist regime transformed the celebrations of May Day and the Seventeenth of October into two important political rituals.

A wide array of political regimes, not all of them authoritarian, has used the power of political rituals and festivals as mechanisms for the generation of consensus (or the illusion of its existence). Similar to the function of ritual in religion, political rituals seek to create a sense of belonging among the participants of a certain community through religious belief or concepts such as "the nation," ethnicity, or "the party," in the case of political rituals. But while religious rituals reinforce the sacred image of certain values and justify the sanctity of certain ideas, political rituals symbolically recreate the conditions that legitimate a given political regime. As Mona Ozouf points out, while the legislator makes the law for the people, festivals and political rituals make the people for the law.[7]

Anthropologist Clifford Geertz has shown the close relationship between the nature of a power structure and its outward symbolic manifestations: "investigations into the symbology of power and into its nature are similar endeavors." This similarity between the nature of power and its symbols is especially clear in political regimes in which power is legitimated through a charismatic leadership, as was the case with Peronism. According to Geertz, charisma, far from being a quality inherent in the leader, is a cultural phenomenon, historically constructed through a symbolic apparatus.[8] In political movements that, like Peronism, have the desire to construct themselves as political religions, this is particularly relevant.[9] An analysis of how the Peronist government carried out the manipulation of symbols and the creation of political rituals therefore provides an interesting point of departure for an investigation into the nature of Perón's power and charisma.

The regime created a political imagery, centered in the glorification of the personalities of Perón and Eva,[10] which was essential for the creation and maintenance of the charisma of both. Political rituals also played a fundamental role in the creation of this political imagery. In his book, *Conducción Política*, Perón acknowledged the importance of political liturgy. He wrote that, unlike other political parties, Peronism had only two fixed dates during the year when it took the people to the streets: the Seventeenth of October and May Day.[11] Perón's regime turned both dates into highly formalized celebrations, during which the government could publicly show off the popular support it enjoyed and at the same time recreate the direct contact between the leader and "his" people. This direct contact was one of the symbolic bases of its legitimacy.

The process of transforming both dates into Peronist celebrations, however, was quite complex. May Day and the Seventeenth of October both originally meant different things to different sectors of society. Moreover, both had histories that preceded their transformation into official celebrations, but the history of the Seventeenth of October had been very short (only a year), and it had been closely linked to the origins of Peronism and Perón's leadership. Certain adjustments gave it a meaning that would adequately fit into the emerging Peronist political imagery. Consequently, the government reinvented the history and meaning of the Seventeenth of October. On October 17, 1945, the unionized working class spontaneously mobilized with the aim of forcing the military government to free Perón and to respect the social benefits granted by him. In successive commemorations, however, the day became an annual ritual of communion between Perón and his "people," rechristened by the Peronist regime as "Loyalty Day."

The manipulations of the meaning and history of May Day were more complex, since that celebration had a longer history, and one completely independent of the origins of Peronism. While Peronist propaganda could simply invent a short history for the Seventeenth of October, it had to reformulate a long and already existing one for May Day.[12] The Peronist regime created the myth that, after Perón took power, a peaceful and patriotic May Day replaced the bloody and revolutionary celebrations of the previous period. However, not only had May Day festivities been peaceful and patriotic long before the coming of Peronism, but even the myth of previously violent May Days predates Peronism.

In this instance, as in many others, Peronism appropriated a group of symbols and a tradition already in existence and reformulated them. As Mona Ozouf claims, "The new festival is always based on the old one that it claims to replace, and accounts that set out with the intention of drawing contrasts end up sounding much the same."[13]

The important differences between the natures of May Day and the Seventeenth of October affected the way both dates were celebrated at the official level. Although May Day was turned into a Peronist celebration with profound symbolic content, it never acquired the semireligious character that the Seventeenth of October had. The pre-Peronist tradition of May Day could be redefined, but never totally erased. Still, important similarities in the set of symbols linked the two days. On both (although not always on May Day), people gathered under the balcony of the Casa Rosada (government palace) in the Plaza de Mayo, which became the geographical space most clearly associated with Perón's charismatic leadership. In the Plaza de Mayo, Perón and his people, in direct contact, ritually renewed their pact of cohesion and loyalty. In order to reinforce this image, Perón had to appropriate a mythical version of the past in which the Plaza de Mayo had always occupied a central place in the important events of the national history.

Pierre Nora defines what he calls a *lieu de mémoire* as a historically constructed space in which collective memory crystallizes. "Contrary to historical objects, however," Nora tells us, "*lieux de mémoire* have no referent in reality; or rather, they are their own referent."[14] The Plaza de Mayo, where the events that led to the Revolution of May 1810 took place, already was a *lieu de mémoire* par excellence in the historical liberal tradition. Perón simply appropriated that tradition and transformed the plaza into a Peronist *lieu de mémoire*.

The process of generation of a Peronist political liturgy, in general, and of "Peronization" of both celebrations, in particular, can be divided into three periods. The first, roughly from 1943 (1945 for the Seventeenth of

October) to 1948, is characterized as a period of struggle for the monopolization of symbolic space. During this period, Perón tried to appropriate the significance of the two celebrations, assigning them a new meaning aligned with the official version of *peronismo*. By 1948 the two dates, which originally had had distinct meanings for different sectors of society and therefore had been commemorated in different ways, had acquired one single meaning, while official propaganda either suppressed or rendered irrelevant alternative celebrations.

The second period, from 1948 to 1950, represented the institutionalization of the official symbolic apparatus. The Peronist regime, having unified the meaning of both celebrations, generated a new mythology and invented a new tradition for them. This period coincides with the tenure of Dr. Oscar Ivanissevich as the secretary, and later minister, of education, who had a large influence on the design of the official political liturgy. As he had done in the area of education (Part III), Ivanissevich tried to associate these political rituals with certain "transcendental values." The regime eliminated, in this period, the spontaneity that had marked the first celebrations carried out during the Peronist regime, particularly on the Seventeenth of October.

Finally, the third period, from 1950 to the end of Perón's regime in 1955, saw the crystallization of the Peronist rituals. In these years the regime achieved a definitive monopoly of the public symbolic space and eliminated all traces of spontaneity in both celebrations. After the removal of Dr. Ivanissevich from his ministerial post, the regime's strategy of generating the illusion of unanimity took other forms. Peronism lost interest in associating the "doctrine" with other transcendental values that had given it legitimacy. After 1950, the "doctrine" itself, along with the figures of Perón and Eva, became objects of public worship. By 1953, Peronism had become a true political religion.

The Celebration of May Day before Perón: The Taming of a "Revolutionary" Festival

The well-known history of the origins of May Day will not be repeated here in detail.[15] In Argentina, the German socialist club Vowartz adopted May Day as the Día del Trabajo in 1890. From the outset its celebrations had the same peaceful, law-abiding, and ambiguously festive character that May Day had in other countries of the world. As in France, for example, the conservative press described the early celebrations in Argentina with a mixture of irony, contempt, and praise for the order and "culture" shown by the workers.[16] As also occurred in other countries, Argentina's May Day celebrations from the beginning became associated with patriotic symbols. The "Manifiesto" published by the group organizing the first May Day praised the country and its institutions that had preserved liberty. At the end of the 1890 celebration, participants shouted, "Long live Socialism! Long live Liberty! Long live the Argentine Republic!"[17]

During the early years, May Day was essentially a Socialist celebration. The Socialist Party organized public demonstrations, which became a tradition after 1897. Some unions did take part, but they always constituted a small minority of the participating groups. Workers, of course, were not a minority among the demonstrators, but they appeared as Socialists and not as members of unions.

After 1901, Anarchists abandoned their policy of rejecting the celebration and began to organize their own demonstrations, although they gave them a different tone from those of the Socialists. For the Anarchists, May Day was not a festive day but one of mourning for the Martyrs of Chicago. Moreover, the May Day celebrations gave them the opportunity to exercise a sort of "revolutionary gymnastic."[18] Not surprisingly—considering that the government had concrete plans to halt the infiltration Anarchists were making into the working class—the police made the Anarchist demonstrations the preferred target of repression.[19] In any case, Anarchist demonstrations soon lost impact, while those organized by the Socialists, always peaceful and law-abiding, recovered their preeminence, especially after 1911, making them once again the only significant parades.

The reaction of the bourgeois press to the May Day celebrations is significant. The papers emphasized the peaceful character of the demonstrations, comparing them favorably with other instances, located in a mythic past or in other countries, in which May Day had endangered the social order. The point of comparison for the first May Days was usually Europe or the United States. "Among us," as *La Nación* opined in its April 30, 1890, edition, "the event cannot have a great importance, because there is neither a 'labor question' nor the principal causes which give [May Day] importance in Europe and the United States."[20]

Later, the bourgeois papers added another point of comparison. The peaceful and law-abiding May Day celebrations of the time were compared with others occurring in an ill-defined past when May Days had had a violent character. Against this violent past, the peaceful character of the present demonstrations provided evidence of the success of the government's social policies. Especially after 1910, the press asserted that May Day celebrations no longer constituted a threat to social order because workers were content.

The Socialists rapidly adopted this myth. For example, in a 1926 May Day speech, Socialist leader Adolfo Dickmann said that "decades ago, this festival of the workers was among us . . . a day of terror, a day of sad premonitions, [a day] of angry protest and repression. Today, the First of May is celebrated in a climate of general sympathy, and even with the cooperation of the Executive Branch, which issued a decree declaring it a holiday."[21]

Socialist celebrations always followed a similar pattern. The party machine organized local concentrations of supporters in the neighborhoods, where participants formed into columns. These columns converged at the Casa del Pueblo (the Socialist Party headquarters), whence the participants marched, now in a single column headed by party leaders and Socialist congressmen, toward the site where the main celebration took place. After the ususal speeches, an "order of the day" was read, in which the special meaning given to that year's celebration was expressed. The speakers usually linked this special meaning to the current domestic or international political situation. Another celebration took place on the night of April 30 in a rented theater where popular artists performed short allegorical or folkloric plays.

By the 1920s the celebration of May Day had been totally incorporated into Argentine political culture. Not only were different political groups (with the exception of the Anarchists, who were already clearly in decline) trying to appropriate the meaning of the legitimized celebration but the state was as well. In 1925, for example, the year in which President Alvear had decreed May First to be a national holiday for civil servants, the municipality of the city of Buenos Aires inaugurated the Plaza Primero de Mayo.[22] In the same year, the director of the Military Academy invited Professor Carlos Groussac to deliver a special presentation on the meaning of Workers' Day in the academy headquarters.[23]

A series of coincidences eased the "preemption" of May Day by the State. In Argentina, May First not only commemorates the Día del Trabajo, but also the anniversary of the *Pronunciamiento de Urquiza* of 1851, which marked the end of Rosas's dictatorship. In addition, and as homage to the *Pronunciamiento*, the National Constitution was sanctioned on May 1, 1853. This Constitution established the First of May as the day the president opened the regular session of the legislature. The "discovery" of this "happy coincidence" during the 1920s provided groups, apart from workers, with the opportunity to give a more patriotic flavor to the May Day celebration.[24]

After 1927 the Independent Socialist Party, which had separated from the main Socialist Party in that year, began to organize its own demonstrations commemorating May Day. The Independent Socialists introduced the novelty of including the Argentine national flag in the parade along with the traditional red flags.[25] By the end of the 1920s, Catholic worker groups also began to celebrate May Day, incorporating religious messages into their celebration. By the beginning of the 1930s, then, diverse groups celebrated May Day, each giving its own significance to the day. However, the traditional parades of the Socialists continued to be the most highly attended. Only the demonstration organized by the Independent Socialist Party approached it in importance, particularly in years such as 1930 when the Independent Socialists also celebrated their recent triumph in legislative elections.

During the 1930s, with the exception of the short interlude of the Uriburu government, May Day celebrations underwent important changes as a result of what may be described as a process of "double contamination." On the one hand, various political groups with distinct and sometimes incompatible ideologies were "using" May Day, incorporating their own symbols into it and giving the celebration a broader meaning. On the other hand, the patriotic symbols incorporated by other groups also deeply penetrated the Socialist celebrations, an occurrence spurred in part by the international situation. The emergence of totalitarian regimes in Europe during the thirties forced the Socialists to incorporate new elements into their traditional celebrations, elements that were used more and more as a way to reaffirm the democratic and patriotic spirit animating the party. In 1932, Socialist deputy Jacinto Oddone could still see fit to complain about the attitude of certain groups that were trying to place the emphasis of May Day on the commemoration of the *Pronunciamiento de Urquiza* and the ratification of the Constitution.[26] Only two years later, however, Enrique Dickmann would repeatedly emphasize the patriotic aspects of the day.[27] May Day was losing its original character as an international celebration and was becoming, well before Perón, a "national" festivity.

In 1936, May Day took on a new character. That year, the crumbling Popular Front organized the main parade with the participation of the Confederación General del Trabajo (CGT), the Socialist Party, the Communist Party, and the UCR, along with other "bourgeois" political organizations. For the first time, the national anthem was sung at a May Day meeting, and national flags flew everywhere. The presence of patriotic symbols became a permanent and invariable characteristic of May Day celebrations from this point forward. In addition, from 1934 on, the government had banned the display of red flags in the demonstrations. The Socialist Party itself, voluntarily, had also eliminated red flags from its demonstrations, and national flags had taken their place. As one reporter on the May

Day celebrations of 1938 noted, "Only the Argentine flag led the demonstration, and it was the only one to be seen on the speaker's tribune."[28] Far from complaining about this prohibition, Socialist leader Mario Bravo publicly expressed pride that the national flag was the only one flown at the celebration.[29]

By 1940 the transition of May Day from a Socialist to a semipatriotic celebration was complete. The government of President Ramón Castillo had prohibited not only the display of red flags but also of the national flag during May Day celebrations. Nevertheless, a journalist from *La Prensa* noted the enthusiastic and emotional way in which the crowd sang the national anthem and the absence of "exotic salutes," which had predominated in previous years when the national anthem was sung.[30] Although several unions organized independent celebrations, the one sponsored by the Socialist Party continued to be the most important and best attended. However, from 1939 on, the CGT competed with the Socialists, albeit without success, for the organization of the event.[31] In 1942 the CGT organized parades for workers in the interior of the country.

By 1943, then, the celebration of May Day had two important characteristics. First, the Socialist Party no longer had a monopoly on the symbolism of May Day, even though its parades remained the most important. Other political groups, and even the state itself, were celebrating May Day in their own ways. Second, the Socialist celebration was permeated with patriotic symbols, and the Socialist May Day was becoming, contrary to General Sosa Molina's recollection, a patriotic festivity.

Perón and May Day: The Reinvention of an Invented Tradition

After the Revolution of 1943, Perón began the process of "unifying" the meaning of May Day. In December 1943 he had been named secretary of labor and welfare. May Day 1944 was the first celebration under the new military regime. Although all public independent demonstrations celebrating May Day had been prohibited by the government, the day had been declared a national holiday.[32] The government replaced the usual variety of demonstrations by organizing an official celebration to which representatives of a number of unions were invited.[33] Present at this event were President Edelmiro Farrell and Perón (both of whom delivered speeches) as well as other senior officials of the regime.

Perón began his speech by making clear the new meaning he intended to give to May Day: "In this celebration, I want to inaugurate a new custom: that the secretaries of labor and welfare, each First of May, report to the country on what they have done for the welfare of the workers of the fatherland, and that this date not be wasted any longer in empty political speeches." May Day would become, according to Perón, a date on which the "special" relationship between the working class and the government, represented by the secretary of labor and welfare, would be made manifest. The only two participants in the festival, therefore, would be the government, in the role of provider of benefits, and the unionized working class, playing the role of recipient. Perón also took advantage of the opportunity to clarify the new type of relationship that he personally wished to have with the workers. He announced for the first time a detailed program of benefits that would be granted to the working class, a program that closely resembled the Programa Mínimo of the CGT.

In Perón's May Day 1944 speech, there are many elements that would come to form an essential part of his discourse: the idea of replacing class struggle with class collaboration, the denunciation of "bad politicians" who had in the past exploited workers for their own gain, and a warning against "exotic" ideologies.[34] In 1944, Perón was still trying to attract both workers and business leaders. In his speech, to the former he offered a program of reforms and to the latter, the benefit of having the state act as a barrier against social conflict.[35] His success in attracting both sectors, however, was far from complete. His famous speech before the Bolsa de Comercio de Buenos Aires in August 1944 was probably his last serious attempt to court the business sector, while, as late as November 1944, union enthusiasm for Perón was at best lukewarm.[36]

In 1945, May Day was again monopolized by the state. All other public demonstrations, apart from the Catholic Workers' Masses, were once again prohibited. Perón's speech on this occasion showed clearly the precarious situation of the military government in this moment. Forced by domestic and international pressures, the military government had liberalized its policies somewhat and tried to reach a rapprochement with the opposition. Although Perón's speech contained firm and even threatening words for "speculators" and those who opposed the social policies of the secretary of labor and welfare,[37] portions of his speech more resembled his 1944 speech to the Bolsa de Comercio than the tone of his discourse later in 1945. On this May Day, Perón chose to emphasize his respect for the rights of employers and his rejection of radical reforms, presenting himself as an enemy of social disorder. The only way to prevent social conflict, which would certainly hurt businessmen above all, was through a controlled policy of social benefits. Perón, moreover, defended himself from accusations of being a social agitator: "I know how to distinguish the line that separates a worker's claim of the socioeconomic kind, and another [claim] that aspires to the domination of society by the proletariat."

Organized labor's support for Perón was still weak at the beginning of 1945. Although many union leaders were present at the official May Day celebration, the organ of the CGT, called *CGT*, published an editorial note in its May Day issue recalling that workers' triumphs in obtaining social justice had been secured as a result of hard struggle. No mention was made of either the Secretariat of Labor and Welfare or its policies.[38] The article also emphasized the "democratic faith" of the workers.

In 1944 and 1945 it is possible to perceive the beginning of a process that would lead to the creation of a Peronist May Day after 1946. In the official discourse the political parties were deprived of legitimacy as contenders in the political realm; it was a discourse fashioned by a government that, in reality, denied the validity of the political realm itself. May Day was no longer a festival of "empty political speeches." It was now the moment in which the "apolitical" state, represented by the secretary of labor and welfare, could renew its direct contact with the organized working class—without the need of any kind of intermediary—and inform workers of the social benefits they could obtain through this direct relationship. Political parties, for their part, had lost their vitality as channels for the expectations of the opposition, a tendency that reinforced this process.

This "peculiar" relationship between the military government and the working class, however, was severed at the beginning of October 1945, only to be restored, in a very different fashion, on the Seventeenth of October.

The Seventeenth of October as the Symbolic Birth of Peronism

Both the chain of events leading to the massive gathering of workers in the Plaza de Mayo on October 17, 1945, and the nature of this mobilization have been studied by many authors.[39] In this chapter and the following one, the events of the Seventeenth of October are approached from a different perspective. Our attention focuses on an analysis of the process through which the Peronist state appropriated and reformulated the memory and tradition of both this day and May Day, in order to make them fit within the Peronist imagery then being constructed. But first, what happened on October 17, 1945?

As a result of strong domestic and international pressure, Perón was forced on October 9, 1945, to resign from all three of his official posts—vice president, minister of war, and secretary of labor and welfare. Perón's position, however, remained sufficiently strong to enable him not only to keep his closest associates in important positions within the government but also to obtain permission to deliver a farewell speech to the workers. At the suggestion of union leaders, this speech was even broadcast over the official radio network.[40] The CGT, realizing the possible consequences of the fall of Perón, organized a meeting so workers could hear the speech live and also demonstrate publicly their support for the colonel.[41]

Perón's farewell speech is important because he used several "discursive tools," which he would use again on October 17, creating the illusion of a "rite of passage."[42] In addition, the interpretation of the events from October 9 to 17 would become an essential part of the Peronist mythology built around the Seventeenth of October. He began his speech in the usual way, recalling the social policies carried out by the secretary of labor and welfare during his tenure. But it is possible to identify an important difference between this speech and his previous ones. As Emilio De Ipola points out, in Perón's speeches delivered between 1943 and 1945, there was a certain ambiguity in his self-identification. In earlier speeches, Perón introduced himself variously as a member of the government and as "one of you" (the "you" signifying whichever audience he was addressing at the time). In the same way, the Secretariat of Labor and Welfare was presented alternately as both an official institution and as the *casa del pueblo*.[43]

There was no ambiguity in Perón's farewell speech. He spoke "as a citizen" who was deeply involved in the working-class struggle for social benefits: "We shall win in a year, or we shall win in ten, but we shall win." Perón was clearly trying to distance himself from a government to which he had belonged until the previous day. As he recalled in his speech, one of the first measures he had taken as secretary of labor and welfare was to abolish the union regulations issued by the military government he now characterized as totalitarian. According to Perón, during his term as secretary, no workers had been persecuted, no unions closed down. On the contrary: "When possible, we always requested from the authorities [to which he, as vice president, minister of war, and secretary of labor and welfare, undoubtedly belonged] the freedom of workers who had been arrested for various causes." Although Perón had always claimed that he belonged to "the people," only now was he going through the rite of passage that would make his identification with "the people" complete, and this rite was completed on October 17.

Perón ended his speech by appealing to the workers to keep calm. He repeated, once again, his usual slogan, "From Home to Work, and From Work to Home." He also told the workers that President Farrell had promised that the government would honor all the social benefits granted by the secretary, and that therefore no further violence or mobilization was required.

There was, however, a second underlying message in his speech, which was probably directed to a wider audience (recall that the message was transmitted through the official radio network). This second message was a clear warning: the hopes of the workers must not be frustrated by anyone, because if that should happen, the results for the country would be tragic.[44] And to make sure the message was clear, he ended his speech thus: "I now request order, so we can go ahead in our triumphal march. But should it be necessary, some day I might request war."

In this farewell speech, Perón managed to link the fate of the workers with his own. Although he now lacked effective power, having been stripped of all official duties, his relationship with the working class was not abrogated by his fall, but redefined. Perón was now ready to continue the struggle from any position in which he found himself. However, even though he claimed to be ready to join a trade union and "fight from below," he also managed to make it clear that in fact he had reserved for himself a special position vis-à-vis the workers. It was up to him to decide when to request peace or war. Perón implicitly declared that he was better qualified than the union leaders to decide what was best for the working class.

Perón's resignation further weakened the government. The fact that most of Perón's associates remained in their positions was not only considered an offense by the opposition, which became more vocal and radical in its demands, but also by the military in the powerful Campo de Mayo garrison. On October 12 the government was forced to announce publicly that general elections would take place at the beginning of 1946. On the same day, several senior officers met at the Círculo Militar to evaluate the situation. At the same time, a group of opponents to the government gathered at the Plaza San Martín to demand the immediate surrender of the government to the Supreme Court. This incident generated a violent clash with the police in which the crowd beat up an army officer.[45] Finally, the "Peronist cabinet" was dismissed and Perón was arrested and sent to Martín García Island.

Meanwhile, the unions were deeply divided. The secretary of the CGT, together with the leaders of other independent unions, approached the government in an effort to open negotiations. It seemed obvious, even to Perón, that his political career was over.[46] On the other hand, the rank and file, particularly the meatpacking unions of Berisso led by Cipriano Reyes, and the sugarcaners' union (FOTIA) in Tucumán, demanded immediate mobilization and the declaration of a general strike. Although President Farrell assured the unions that the benefits obtained during Perón's term as the secretary of labor and welfare would not be revoked, it soon became clear that this was not totally true. The program the new secretary of labor made public was very different from Perón's. In addition, employers refused to obey the provisions of some decree–laws issued during Perón's tenure.[47] At the same time, the government attempted to appease the opposition by arresting Perón's closest associate, Lieutenant Colonel Domingo Mercante.[48]

Between October 14 and 16, the Board of Secretaries of the CGT met several times without reaching any decision as to what to do. On October 15 the government announced that Perón was no longer under arrest, but in the military hospital. Although the news calmed the union leaders, the pressure from the rank and file was so strong that, on October 16, the leadership of the CGT, after a heated debate, declared a general strike for the eighteenth.[49]

The debate of October 16 was important because it made explicit several issues that would become crucial in the definition of the relationship between Perón and the unions. Néstor Alvarez, deputy secretary of the CGT, made the point that the CGT could not, "as a matter of principle," declare a strike to demand the liberation of Perón. In what were almost prophetic words, he said that this "would imply the alienation of the future of the CGT."[50] Ramón Tejada, on the other hand, was perhaps more realistic in delineating the relationship between Perón and the unions. He said:

> However we look at it, if we declare a general strike, it will be for the freedom of Colonel Perón, because by demanding his return to the government we are in fact defending our achievements, since he was the only one who has done justice to the workers' aspirations. If the CGT demands and attempts to secure the freedom of Perón, it will not weaken union principles because we can now say that Perón is one of us. . . . The only thing that was necessary for the revolutionary authorities led by Colonel Perón to start their work of social justice . . . was for the workers to wake up from their lethargy and come in mass to the unions, from where we had been calling for many years.[51]

Although the strike had been called for October 18, the rank-and-file agitation within some unions on the sixteenth had become too hard to control. As a result of this mobilization, on the seventeenth huge masses of workers, coming primarily from the province of Buenos Aires, marched toward the Plaza de Mayo to demand the immediate release of Perón. Perhaps the workers gathered in the Plaza de Mayo simply because it was the closest public space to the government palace, and not for any special symbolic reason. At the same time, other demonstrations, anticipating the same passivity shown by the police in Buenos Aires, took place in La Plata, Berisso, Rosario, and other cities in the interior. Daniel James has emphasized the highly symbolic content of these demonstrations in which the workers literally "took over" the public urban space for the first time in the history of the country. These gatherings had, in many cases, a festive and even Carnival-like atmosphere—people dancing and drinking in the streets—that continued until the eighteenth. In many aspects, the events of October 17 and 18 implied a temporary subversion of the existing social order.

In some cases, the demonstrators committed acts of violence against opposition newspapers, students, upper-class clubs, and other symbols of economic or social power.[52] Anti-Peronist groups also initiated some of these violent incidents. A march by the right-wing, pro-Perón organization, Alianza Libertadora Nacionalista, was fired on from the building of the opposition newspaper *Crítica*. At least one of the supporters of the Alianza died in that incident.

Meanwhile, the strike committee began negotiations with the government in order to free Perón. By the evening of the seventeenth, it was clear that the government was in an untenable situation, and negotiations with Perón were opened. After some initial indecision, Perón realized the powerful position he was in and demanded the resignation of the entire cabinet and the formation of a new one composed of members loyal to him. When the government accepted his terms, he, in turn, agreed to address the masses gathered in the Plaza de Mayo in order to calm them. He did so later that night.

In the speech given by Perón on the seventeenth, he closed the circle that he had started with his farewell speech of the tenth by first announcing his retirement from the army: "I leave this glorious and sacred uniform that the fatherland granted me in order to wear the civilian jacket and to blend myself with the suffering and sweating masses. By doing so, I give a parting embrace to this institution that is one of the pillars of the fatherland: the army. And I also give the first embrace to this great mass that represents the synthesis of a feeling that had died in the Republic: the true civility of the Argentine people. You are the people." The rite of passage begun on the tenth was now complete: Perón was undoubtedly part of the people, remaining, at the same time, above them. From this privileged position he could announce the coming of the Peronist millennium: a time of peace that would be possible, thanks to the union of the three pillars of the fatherland: the people, the army, and the police force. Perón identified the working masses with the nation.

Finally, Perón, as "a big brother," asked the workers to spend the strike day, which had been declared by the CGT for the eighteenth, by celebrating "the glory of this meeting of men of good will and of work." Toward the end of his speech, Perón asked the workers to remain in the Plaza for fifteen minutes more so that he "could keep this great spectacle of the people in [his] sight."[53] As De Ipola points out, Perón fixed the place of each of the participants on that seventeenth of October: his, at the balcony of the government palace; the people's, in the Plaza de Mayo. In other words, he turned the event into a spectacle.

In his now-classic study of Brazilian carnivals, Roberto Da Matta distinguishes between "rituals of inversion" and "rituals of reinforcement." The former imply a disruption of the system of social classification, joining what is usually separated, and integrating elements that are otherwise excluded from a particular social space. "Rituals of reinforcement," on the other hand, tend to reinforce the validity of the existing mechanisms of social classification, making clear each one's place in society.[54] On October 17, 1945, Perón took the first steps toward the transformation of what originally had been a "ritual of inversion" (the workers "taking over" urban spaces from which they had been excluded) into a "ritual of reinforcement" (confirming his own place above the workers and transforming the event into a spectacle).

The Seventeenth of October, by its own nature, also fixed the nature of the relationship between Perón and the workers. After all, the first time that the working class mobilized by taking over the urban space and making its presence felt was for the liberation of Perón.[55] The Peronist propaganda would turn the events of the day into Perón's original source of legitimacy. The working class had mobilized not only to rescue him, but also to place him where he rightfully belonged: on the balcony of the government palace. Perón, on the other hand, detached himself completely from the military government in order to become the candidate of the people. Following Geertz, we can say that Perón generated his own "charisma" by putting himself at "the heart of things."[56]

How were these events evaluated by the different social sectors and by the press in the days following? According to *La Época*, the only paper then loyal to Perón, the protagonist of the events of the seventeenth had been the people who spontaneously mobilized to rescue Perón, "the greatest leader of the Argentine people."[57] The movement lacked leaders, and its participants were the "true people," representing "the true nation."[58] For *La Epoca*, the people were moderates, which explained why, according to the paper, there had been no acts of violence.[59] These people were, moreover, the exact antithesis of those groups—obviously also part of the people—that had participated in the September Marcha de la Constitución y la Libertad (March of the Constitution and Freedom, see Chapter 2) and in the gathering at the Plaza San Martín on October 12. According to the paper, "What an abyss separated these people, the true people, from those 100 'families' of the plutocracy who had camped out in the Plaza San Martín days ago! There, perfumed and heavily made-up women hurled insults at the military and government officials; there, effete 'gentlemen,' aided by their Communist friends, seriously hurt an army officer . . . ; there, 'girls' wrote insulting words on the walls of the military club just like whores, possibly acting under the influence of drugs."[60]

The version of events presented by the papers of the opposition, which then included all but *La Epoca*, was exactly the opposite of *La Epoca*'s. The word "people" had been used freely both by *La Prensa* and *La Nación* when these papers covered the events of the Marcha de la Constitución y la Libertad and those of the gathering in the Plaza San Martín. Both papers carefully avoided the word, however, when describing the participants of the seventeenth. In this case, it had been "rioting groups,"[61] "isolated groups which did not represent the authentic Argentine proletariat,"[62] "completely drunk individuals,"[63] and other such characterizations. In the most favorable cases, the participants of the events of the seventeenth were described as "workers," a word which only meant that they belonged to that social group, and therefore did not represent the whole "people."[64]

The events of October 17 and 18 puzzled more groups than the "oligarchy."[65] The Socialist paper *La Vanguardia* and the Communist *Orientación* shared their perception of the phenomenon. The occurrences of the seventeenth had been, for both those papers, organized by Perón from behind the scenes; he also had manipulated the lumpenproletariat. The people of the seventeenth were not, and could not have been, workers but were a strange combination of criminals and people of the lowest moral and social strata.

The following is the characterization found in *Orientación*:

> These people too ingenuous or too self-interested, who wish to believe that the working class supported the strike of the 17th, should know that organized workers in this country had never:
> - cheered the name of a Fascist colonel
> - thrown stones at the buildings of democratic newspapers

• attacked the houses of professors at democratic universities
• delivered death threats to the first Socialist congressman who designed the bases of our worker legislation
• robbed businesses
• insulted women in the street
• assaulted local Communists
• shouted or written with chalk, "Perform a patriotic act, kill a student!"
• shouted and written on the walls, "Perón, yes; books, no!"
• gotten drunk after attacking a beer warehouse
• cheered the police forces.

La Vanguardia, for its part, published the following under the title "The Strategic Plan of Colonel Perón":

> [The Seventeenth of October] for the citizen, without distinguishing classes, was the reverse reflection of the March of the Constitution and Freedom. What Argentine worker would join a demonstration to recover his rights as if it was a Carnival parade? What Argentine worker breaks, depredates, robs, and steals under the pretext of this recovery? What Argentine worker is moved against culture and civility to maintain his rights for a dignified and better life? What Argentine worker attacks an unguarded pedestrian because he is wearing boots and a shirt?[66]

For both papers the Seventeenth of October did not have a place in the legitimate historical development of the country. *La Vanguardia* compared the events to the terror provoked by the *candombes* in the era of Rosas.[67]

The events of the seventeenth took everyone by surprise. Even the CGT was astonished. Certainly, the CGT had played an influential role in defining the outcome of the process leading to the release of Perón. However, it is also true that the mobilization of the seventeenth had escaped its control. The issue of its journal, *CGT*, published after the events, mentioned neither these nor Perón. All emphasis was placed on the strike called by the CGT for the eighteenth.[68] The eighteenth, according to the journal, "would forever be in the workers' minds." However, Perón had already changed the meaning of the strike of the eighteenth. Instead of a day of protest, it became one of celebration, which in successive commemorations would be called the day of "San Perón."[69] The CGT and Perón were both trying to appropriate the meaning of what had happened. This was the beginning of a struggle over the symbolic meaning of the Seventeenth of October, which would be resolved in the following years.

4

THE STRUGGLE FOR SYMBOLIC SPACE

In February 1946, Perón won the presidential elections, defeating the Unión Democrática, an odd coalition of the main political parties including the Unión Cívica Radical, the Socialist Party, and others. Perón did not have a party of his own and was supported by a newly formed Labor Party, organized by the loyal unions and the UCR Junta Renovadora, a dissident sector of the radicals. Even before assuming the presidency, Perón wanted to discipline the forces that would take him to power. In May 1946 he issued an order dissolving all the parties that had supported him and creating instead an umbrella party, the Partido Unico de la Revolución, later renamed Partido Peronista.

In 1946, Perón, as president-elect, presided over the official celebration of May Day. As the country was again in transition toward a democratic system (at least formally), the government allowed the traditional celebrations—in contrast to the previous two years. The Socialists, as was conventional, organized a gathering in front of the Casa del Pueblo, while other political groups held meetings in various public spaces. For the first time, the main parade was organized by the CGT together with autonomous trade unions and with the support of the Partido Laborista (Labor Party) and the UCR Junta Renovadora.[1]

Perón, Eva (Juan's wife and the First Lady), Mercante, and Secretary of Labor and Welfare Russo led the parade, giving the celebration an official touch. In contrast to the Socialist demonstrations of earlier years, the workers, at least in theory, participated in the procession as themselves rather than as members of a political party. Although Perón and Mercante had been invited to lead the parade as guests of the organizing committee, they were not scheduled to speak. Surprised for the moment by the request to do so, they had to improvise.

For the first time, Perón openly associated May Day with the emerging Peronist movement. He said at the beginning of his address that May Day 1946 was the jubilee of the people's victory in the Plaza de Mayo the previous year on October 17.[2] By linking the traditional Workers' Day to the founding date of Peronism, he was taking the first steps toward the "Peronization" of May Day. In a somewhat moderate tone, Perón went on to promise that his government would promote the economic emancipation of the workers.[3]

The attitude of the CGT toward Perón was still ambiguous. For May Day, *CGT* published a manifesto making clear the independence of the CGT from the government.[4] Union leaders Silverio Pontieri's and Luis Gay's speeches, although they included praise for Perón, also contained the classic themes of the CGT's traditional discourse: the importance of unity within the workers' movement and its independence from the government and from politics in general.[5]

The first serious steps toward the reformulation of the meaning of May Day were taken by the Peronist press. Both *El Laborista*—the newspaper of the Labor Party[6]—and *La Epoca* began to publish articles about the organization of the May Day celebration toward the end of April. In these articles, its new character was emphasized: "For the first time in the history of the country, the Argentine workers await May Day, their day, with a promising future for their legitimate aspirations. It will be an authentic celebration of labor. It will be even more so because the workers are celebrating [May Day for the first time] since the man who galvanizes the confidence and sympathy of all the Argentine proletariat, Colonel Perón, was confirmed in a popular plebiscite as the first magistrate of the Argentine people."[7]

Following the cue given by Perón on May Day 1944, both newspapers emphasized the "apolitical" character of the celebration: "this time [it] will not be spoiled by *politiqueros* [low politicians]."[8] On the contrary, May Day would give the workers the opportunity for "honest happiness and a true rest for their muscles."[9] Above all, the First of May was to be a celebration of worker unity.[10] *El Laborista*, which still reflected the interests of the traditional trade unions, emphasized the working-class character of the festivity. *La Epoca*, however, more in line with what would later become the official Peronist version, emphasized social reconciliation, comparing the present celebration to a mythical past in which May Day had always had a "class" content.[11]

The Peronist press placed special importance on the festive character of the celebration. In an editorial, *El Laborista* presented its own version of the history of May Day in Argentina. Three periods were differentiated: a first period marked by police repression, a second one marked by contempt for the proletarian content of the festivity, and a final period of "true" celebration, which, as expected, began with the June Revolution.[12] In an editorial of May 3, the history became even simpler: the proletariat had always been repressed by a "bullying police." This had happened, in part, because the pre-Peronist May Days had been occasions for insulting the government and the upper classes. Now, in contrast, the president-elect received only praise from the people.

The Peronist press did not especially emphasize the patriotic aspects of the date (by stressing the connection to the *Pronunciamiento de Urquiza*, the Constitution, etc.). *El Laborista* nevertheless published an editorial on May 1, 1946, commenting on the "double character" of the celebration and pointing out the importance of the *Pronunciamiento*, which had ended Rosas's tyranny and cleared the path for the passing of the Constitution. *La Epoca*, for its part, noted that under Perón's government, May Day would have a more "national" meaning because the working class was itself now more "national." "Before," the workers gathered around a red flag and sang "The International." "Now," only Argentine flags were to be seen, and the National Anthem had replaced this "foreign song."[13]

The myth that contrasted a peaceful present with a never well-defined past in which the First of May had been violent, was not new and had been in place when Perón got to power. This myth, bear in mind, had been used not only by the conservative sectors but by the Socialists as well. The Peronists redefined this myth and reached different conclusions. According to Peronist propaganda, the working class, as a consequence of its new patriotism, no longer needed to be represented by the Socialist Party or any other type of political mediation. Such mediation had been replaced by a direct contact with the leader.[14]

According to the Peronist version, the frightening characteristics of the pre-Peronist May Day had two fundamental causes. On the one hand, May First had been violent before Perón because the governments of the ancien régime were oligarchic and repressive. But on the other hand, the essence of the celebration had been different before Perón. May First had been an occasion for protest by a working class made up, overall, of foreigners who held antinational ideologies. Now, as a result of the triumph of Peronism, a working class purged of its alien elements was the standard-bearer of national sentiment.[15]

While prior to May Day, most of the Peronist press's articles on the topic centered their attention on the CGT and the organization of the celebration, in the days following the festivity the accounts made clear that

Perón had been the main protagonist of events. The May 1 cover of *El Laborista* bore a full-page portrait of Perón.[16] *La Epoca* noted that it was the first time in history that a president-elect celebrated May Day with his people.[17] Certainly, the process of appropriation of the symbols and meanings associated with May Day, although far from complete, had begun. This tendency did not escape notice by the Socialist Party. On the cover of *La Vanguardia* for April 30, they complained that the day's meaning was being usurped by the "pirates of social redemption."

On June 4, 1946, Perón was sworn in as the constitutional president. Quickly, the heterogeneous coalition that had brought him to power began showing its first rifts.[18] Although Perón's position was quite solid, he was not totally in control of the situation. His first objective, then, was the disciplining of his own party while placing the institutional mechanisms of the state under his control. As already noted, even before he was sworn in, Perón had dissolved and reorganized the various forces that had supported him, merging them into the Partido Unico de la Revolución (Sole Party of the Revolution), later renamed the Partido Peronista (Peronist Party). Some members of the Labor Party (the main political force that had supported Perón), led by Cipriano Reyes, did not obey the order and formed an autonomous Labor bloc in the House of Representatives. Perón worked to consolidate his power at the symbolic as well as at the material political level. Slowly at first, the Peronist propaganda machine began to lay the foundations for what would become the Peronist political imagery. One of the first opportunities for doing so was the celebration surrounding the first anniversary of the Seventeenth of October.

In July 1946, Peronist deputy Eduardo Colom, a former *yrigoyenista* radical and now owner of *La Epoca*, introduced a bill declaring the Seventeenth of October a national holiday, the Día del Pueblo (Day of the People).[19] In August the Labor deputies Cipriano Reyes and Carlos Gustavo Gericke sponsored a similar bill.[20] The legislative debates generated by these two proposals signaled the existence of divergent perceptions of the meaning of the Seventeenth of October. Peronist Deputy Albrieu pointed out that the Seventeenth of October should have the same status as May 25, since 1810 marked the beginning of a nation and 1945 the beginning of a new social class. Radical Deputy Absalón Rojas, on the other hand, argued that there was nothing to celebrate, since on October 17 nothing important had really happened. According to Radical Deputy Nerio Rojas, who echoed the argument that the participants of October 17 had been lumpenproletariat and not authentic workers, "On that day we saw workers in the streets, granted, but we also saw people who . . . got paid only on that day."[21] After a debate full of irregularities, the bills were passed and the Seventeenth of October became a national holiday.[22]

The main celebration commemorating the first anniversary of the Seventeenth of October featured a gathering of workers in the Plaza de Mayo organized by the CGT, with full support from the government, to whom Perón gave a speech. However, there were other celebrations organized by different groups. The Seventeenth of October did not yet have a single meaning. On the morning of the seventeenth, there was a *misa de campaña* (open-air Mass) in the Plaza de Mayo organized by the Union of Intellectuals. Perón, Eva, and high government officials attended. Later, Perón and Eva solemnly laid a wreath of flowers at the tomb of San Martín. At the same time, another Mass was celebrated in the Church of Santo Domingo, this one sponsored by the Unión Popular Demócrata Cristiana, at which the president was represented by a military aide-de-camp. At midday, from the balcony of the government palace, Perón and Eva watched a parade in their honor made up of 1,000 bus drivers in their buses.[23]

The dissenting faction of the Labor Party also organized its own celebration under the name Día del Pueblo (significantly, the official festivity was baptized "Día de la Lealtad" [Loyalty Day]). The Laborites emphasized the difference between "their" Seventeenth of October and the official one. Cipriano Reyes, the main orator in the Labor celebration, pointed out that, in contrast to the CGT, the Laborites were celebrating the anniversary in a truly popular way, without any official sponsorship.[24]

The right-wing group Alianza Libertadora Nacionalista also tried to commemorate October Seventeenth in its own way. A group of people belonging to this far-right organization walked by the offices of *Crítica* and, despite police attempts to stop them, laid a wreath close to the tree where a year ago one of their militants had been shot and killed.

At the official level, October Seventeenth was celebrated with pomp. The buildings around the Plaza de Mayo were decked with the national colors and illuminated. In addition, the Buenos Aires municipal government on that day cleared all citations and pardoned those arrested for municipal offenses, while Perón solemnly inaugurated the sports pavilion in the national prison. As if that had not been enough, a public school was officially named "Seventeenth of October," and a directive from the Ministry of Justice and Public Instruction ordered all teachers to use schooltime to explain the meaning of the date being commemorated.[25] The students of public schools were given a leaflet published by the government that explained what had happened on October 17, 1945. "The people," the leaflet read, "full of patriotic fervor and inflamed by civic passion, flooded the streets of all the cities and towns of the Republic in a way never before seen. They demanded the return of a man whom dark forces had unjustly tried to remove from his position, a position he deserved because of his merits and his struggle."[26]

During the week prior to October 17, the official radio network broadcast a series of speeches connected to the celebration by trade union leaders. Eva Perón, whose role in the celebrations had not yet acquired the prominence it would have in future years, officially opened the series. Eva also inaugurated a succession of popular events that took place in the Colón Theater. After the meeting in the Plaza de Mayo, the crowd attended several "popular dances" in the streets, organized and sponsored by the city government. The image of the workers dancing in traditionally upper-class streets served as a symbolic recreation of the "takeover" of the city and its symbols of power that the *descamisados* had carried out the year before.

On that first anniversary of the Seventeenth of October, different groups commemorated different aspects of the previous year's events in different ways. The unions, however, tried to make it clear that it was "their" celebration, as shown in the new version of the events presented by the CGT.[27] The leader of a parade by members of the Unión Obrera Metalúrgica (Metalworkers Union) asked for police intervention to remove a group of "Peronist Committee" members who were trying to join their parade. Although the members of the committee argued that since they shared a similar ideology with the workers, they should be allowed to march with them, the metalworkers insisted they did not want "politicians" in their group. Finally, the "politicians" were invited to leave by the police.[28]

As expected, the official celebrations of Loyalty Day were centered on the figure of Perón. He began his speech by addressing his "dear *descamisados*."[29] According to Perón, the purpose of the celebration was to commemorate how the year before, "the humble people saluted my liberation after the escape of the traitors." In his 1945 speech, Perón had taken the first decisive steps toward redefining the meaning of what had happened on the seventeenth of October, turning a day of protest into a festivity. Now this transformation was complete. The people had been mobilized on October 17, 1945, to celebrate the liberation of their leader—not to demand his liberation, as had actually happened. Perón also took advantage of the speech to highlight the charismatic character of his connection to the people: "I want to tell the Argentine people that I do not wish to govern based on any other bond . . . than the union that is born from our hearts. I do not wish to rule over men, but over their hearts, because mine beats together with that of each *descamisado*, whom I understand and love above all things."

Toward the end of his speech, Perón again introduced a reformulated version of the past. Initiating what would later become an essential component of the October Seventeenth ritual, he announced a holiday for the following day, the eighteenth (which would come to be known as "San Perón" Day). He intoned: "Just as on the last seventeenth of October, being only a *descamisado*, I ordered the eighteenth to be a holiday, I want the people to enjoy themselves in their innocent celebrations tonight." Perón, needless to say, had "ordered" nothing of the sort. He could not have done so, because at the time he held no official position at all. What he had done was to ask the workers to use the strike day already declared by the CGT to celebrate the events of the seventeenth, an action that undermined the relevance of the CGT.

According to Perón, there had been three essential actors who determined the outcome of events on the original seventeenth of October: he himself at the center of events, the traitors, and the *descamisados*, whose only role had been to celebrate his liberation. Again, Perón reaffirmed his privileged position with respect to the workers: "I, as the first *descamisado*, shall remain vigilant from this place, and shall pay attention, just in case I have to call our *descamisados* back again to this Plaza de Mayo."[30]

On the first anniversary of October 17, several new elements were introduced. These would later form part of the rituals associated with the celebration. Some of these elements had occurred spontaneously in 1945, but they now acquired a new character. One was the "dialogue" between Perón and the people gathered in the Plaza. In 1945 there had been a kind of dialogue when people from the Plaza had loudly asked Perón where he had been in the preceding days. Perón responded evasively, honoring an agreement he had made with the military authorities. Now the "dialogue" had a completely different meaning. Since the government "belonged to the *descamisados*" and Perón was the "first *descamisado*," he promised solemnly to ask the people each October Seventeenth if they were happy with his government.

Not all the ritual gestures emerged as a result of Perón's efforts or those of his propagandists. Some of them were the consequence of attempts by the audience to recreate certain events that had happened spontaneously during the original October seventeenth. In 1945, for instance, partly as a protest against the opposition newspapers and partly as a means of obtaining light, the crowds had made improvised torches with these papers. In 1946 people on the balconies of buildings surrounding the Plaza de Mayo threw newspapers down to the participants so they could use them for torches.[31] The provision of newspapers to use for torches was repeated in the following years.

Furthermore, the acts of violence that had taken place in 1945 were recreated in 1946. After the official festivities, a large number of demonstrators marched to the offices of the opposition newspapers (*La Prensa, La Nación, Crítica*, and *La Razón*, among others) and committed acts of vandalism. Significantly, *La Vanguardia* was not hit. The attackers not only threw stones or broke windows but also carried out symbolic takeovers of the buildings. A group of people, for example, from atop the neighboring buildings, climbed onto the roof of *La Nación*, where they planted a national flag, most likely to signal the "antinational" character of the newspaper.[32] This episode would be repeated in the following years.

Although the main celebration of October 17, 1946, was orchestrated by the state, there was still room that year for alternative forms of more or less spontaneous celebrations. The Peronist regime did not yet have a monopoly over the meaning of the Seventeenth of October. This could be seen even in the treatment given by the Peronist press to this issue. Although the narrative of events was similar in all newspapers sympathetic to the government, there were certain important points on which they disagreed. The fact is that during the first years of Perón's government, different Peronist newspapers represented different groups within the heterogeneous movement.

The Seventeenth of October, therefore, represented something different for each of these groups, as becomes evident from analyzing their various interpretations of the events. First, although Perón was obviously the unquestioned protagonist of the events of October Seventeenth and the hub around which all these events rotated, who had been the person closest to the leader? Who had given him the most loyal support? For *El Laborista*, which was now under the control of Mercante, it was logically Mercante himself. The October 17, 1946, edition of *El Laborista* is full of photographs of Perón, Eva, and Mercante in poses evoking images of a family. In one of these, for example, Perón can be seen seated at his presidential desk with Mercante beside him (both in uniform), while Eva, in a fur coat, serves them coffee. In another, under the caption "Patrician Legacy," Perón is pictured presenting the "Colonel's sword" to Mercante.[33] For *El Líder* (directed by Angel Borlenghi), the "second protagonist" had naturally been Minister of the Interior Borlenghi, who, during the seventeenth of October, "came and went imposing only one condition, which was the condition of the people: the freedom of Perón."[34] In Borlenghi's newspaper, Mercante was only mentioned in passing.

Another difference (undoubtedly the most important) in ways the various Peronist newspapers interpreted the events of the seventeenth of October was their characterization of the people: Who had mobilized in 1945, and why? Again, in 1946 the answer to this question depended on the group each newspaper represented within the movement. *El Líder*, the newspaper of the *empleados de comercio* [shopworkers][35] and therefore closest to the more traditional unionism within Peronism, emphasized the "worker" quality of the demonstrators of October 17, 1945. Although the paper did not explicitly spell out the role played by the CGT, it characterized the events as a "general strike" and made the CGT conspicuously present in its pages.[36] *Democracia*, a newspaper still directed by Manuel Molinari—who had supported *laborismo* from the beginning but who by this point was taking a more independent stance—staked out a more definite position.[37] According to this paper, it had been the CGT and the unionized working class (and therefore not Perón) who, on October seventeenth, "had saved the nation."[38] In fact, this paper claimed that Perón's only political party was the trade unions.[39] In their editorial, *Democracia* declared that "[October 17] could have been the triumph of Perón. This was what the oligarchy thought, and they have their reasons. But for us, it was the triumph of the people."[40]

El Laborista, for its part, characterized the participants in the events of October 1945 very differently. In their version, "the people" (it did not specify workers) had spontaneously mobilized, without waiting for a signal from the unions.[41] The reason for their mobilization had been to celebrate "social justice and the decision [by the people] to give their all to the service of the man who they feel liberated them and who embodied their highest aspirations."[42] In emphasizing the spontaneous character of the mobilization, *El Laborista* was underscoring the important part played by Perón in the events, while negating any central role for the trade union leaders. The "people" did not need union leaders to tell them to whom they should "give their all."

However divergent these characterizations of October Seventeenth were, there were many other points on which the various Peronist papers agreed almost totally. All emphasized the patriotic character of the day and, in an attempt to appropriate a glorious past, associated it with the May Revolution. In the week prior to the seventeenth all the Peronist papers published day-by-day narratives of what had happened the previous year during "October Week," in the same way that schools commemorated "May Week" (the week previous to May 25).

Another point of convergence among the papers was their failure to mention Eva Perón. The only references made to the president's wife were to emphasize her suffering and uncertainty during Perón's arrest. Official propaganda would only begin to give Eva a central role in the events of October after 1947. In that year, for example, *El Laborista* would publish a page-length article entitled "María Eva Duarte de Perón: Symbol of the Lineage of the Argentine Woman," in which Eva was characterized as one of the main organizers behind the mobilization of October Seventeenth. But it would be *Democracia* (after Eva took it over in 1947) that would reinvent the history of Eva's participation in the events of October.[43]

In 1946 the celebration of the Seventeenth of October was orchestrated by the state, but space nevertheless remained for vestiges of spontaneity, even in acts of ritual violence. This type of violence would be absent from the celebrations of May Day, which at the beginning of the Peronist regime still resembled their Socialist predecessors. In 1947 the process of the appropriation of May Day and the Seventeenth of October had significantly advanced. By the beginning of May, Perón had occupied the presidency for almost a year and had consolidated his power to a much greater extent. On April 13 the Senate voted to dismiss members of the Supreme Court from office. This gave Perón total control over the three branches of government. He had by this point also managed to discipline his own party and, above all, the CGT, removing independent-minded Luis Gay as general secretary and replacing him with the more docile Aurelio Hernández.

May Day was declared a national holiday and, as would become policy for the Seventeenth of October as well, newspapers were prohibited from publishing that day. Although the main demonstration was once again organized by the CGT, the old Socialist models were followed. Smaller parades formed in the neighborhoods and demonstrators marched toward the center of the city where they merged into one column. This column, headed by Perón, Eva, Vice President Hortensio Quijano, and other top officials, was led to the Plaza de Mayo. From the balcony of the government palace, the president gave his speech.

It seems clear that the Peronist unions had appropriated the celebration. This appropriation, however, highlighted some of the profoundly paradoxical aspects of the Peronist discourse and political imagery. The fact that the Peronist May Days were organized by the CGT suggests that, in contrast to the old Socialist meetings, workers now participated in the celebration (at least in theory) *as workers* and not as members of a political party, as noted earlier. It is therefore possible to say that, under Perón, May Day was essentially a working-class festival. However, both the government and the CGT emphasized May Day's character as a "celebration of unity" of all the people, and not just of workers. According to the CGT, since Perón's rise to power, May Day was above all a "celebration of brotherhood."[44] May Day's purpose was no longer to express the unfulfilled demands of the working class, but rather to "reaffirm Argentine identity, sovereignty, and liberation."[45]

Safekeeping the gains made in social benefits could only be assured through an unquestioning support of the government and through "order, work, production, and solidarity."[46]

As in the previous year, non-Peronist political groups organized their own meetings to celebrate May Day in 1947. Each of these groups tried to claim an important role in the development of the tradition of May Day, a tradition which was now in danger of being monopolized by the Peronist state. The Socialist Party issued a statement recalling that the celebration of May Day had been born as an eminently Socialist event. The UCR, for its part, published its own declaration of the social policies of Radical governments, which it portrayed as much more authentic than the "demagogic" measures taken by Perón's government.

Although the celebrations of "Peronist" May Day and October Seventeenth were similar in several aspects, there were also important differences. The Seventeenth of October commemorated a spontaneous mobilization by the working people in order to secure Perón's liberation. Although the meaning of this date was, as we have seen, redefined in part by the Peronist regime, the spontaneity remained an important component, at least during the first years of Perón's government. October Seventeenth also commemorated the workers' symbolic takeover of the urban space, and was portrayed as such by the opposition press.

May Day, however, had a long tradition deeply rooted in Argentine political culture and therefore the appropriation and reformulation of its meaning by the Peronists was not immediate. It is, therefore, not surprising that the first Peronist May Days were in many aspects very similar to the traditional Socialists ones and that only gradually were they transformed into something new. However, although the Peronist and Socialist celebrations of May First were similar, Perón's speeches during these celebrations, for reasons discussed immediately below, took important elements from the Anarchist tradition.

The Peronist propaganda machine attempted not only to invent a tradition for these two dates but also to link these invented traditions with a venerable past. Eric Hobsbawm points out that the aim of traditions, including invented ones, is to emphasize invariability and stability.[47] To construct a Peronist imagery it was necessary to define a past into which the "new traditions" could be inserted. For the Seventeenth of October this was simply the history of the country in its liberal version. The founding date of Peronism was nothing less than the recreation of the revolution of May 25, 1810. In both incidences, the people had made their voice heard in the Plaza de Mayo, thereby altering the course of history. In the case of May

Day, however, the past Perón would use was the Anarchist tradition of rebellion and mourning. As president, Perón could announce the beginning
of a new era of social justice and happiness, which implied a break with the
past.[48]

The manipulation of the past generated a paradoxical situation. As "first
worker," Perón was forced to proclaim himself the heir to the same tradition
that as president he was attempting to break away from. The Socialist tradition of peaceful and multiclass celebrations was not useful for Perón, since it
did not provide sufficient justification for a radical rupture. Precisely because of this peaceful character, Perón would adopt many of the rituals of
the Socialist celebrations. For his discourse, however, he opted for the Anarchist tradition of protest: "So many celebrations of May Day go through my
memory! Since 1910, as a student, I have witnessed the most tragic of the
celebrations of May Day in the history of Argentine labor. I see them [the
workers] rise up again in 1916, 1917, and 1918, and I see them also much
later, when the Argentine masses arrived at this plaza demanding justice,
disillusioned by their ungrateful destiny."[49]

This "discursive paradox" of sorts became evident toward the end of
Perón's May Day speech in 1948. When referring to the "rights of workers,"
which he claimed should be incorporated into the Constitution, Perón spoke
simultaneously in his capacity as the president who graciously granted those
rights, and as the "first worker"[50] whose brothers had fallen fighting for
those rights and who would fight to defend them.[51]

It is interesting to note that in the speech quoted above, Perón once
again placed the Plaza de Mayo at the center of events. We know, however,
that neither the Socialist nor Anarchist celebrations of May Day were held
there. Perón used this geographical space, already transformed into a *lieu de
mémoire* par excellence by the liberal tradition, in order to link this invented
image of a sinister past to one with a happy present.

In 1947, even more than in the previous year, the Peronist press emphasized the festive and "national" character of May Day. *La Epoca, El Líder,*
and *El Laborista* organized different contests among workers. *El Laborista,*
for example, planned one to choose the "Queen of Labor," a contest which
became a ritual part of the official celebration in successive years.[52] The
Peronist press characterized May Day as a "festival of liberty, progress, democracy, and justice."[53] It was also to be a celebration of nationality.[54] Only
El Líder, a newspaper that still had strong ties to the unions, mentioned the
"symbolic evocation of the first martyrs [of the working class]" as a principal aim.[55] This was also the only newspaper to emphasize the international

character of May Day.[56] But in 1947 it was also clear that May Day would have another meaning that would be even more important. It would serve as a show of "homage and gratitude to one who knew how to take the pulse of the worker's needs and bring happiness to his home."[57] May Day now became part of the list of national events that had led to the development of Peronism and that included June 4, 1943, October 17, 1945, and February 24, 1946.[58]

Like May Day, in 1947 the Seventeenth of October solidified patterns established in 1946. Beginning a trend that would deepen in the following years, the 1947 event resembled the official celebration of a national holiday. On the afternoon of the seventeenth, Perón solemnly received the salutes of civilian and military authorities. Also on that day, 24,200 employees of the postal service were promoted.[59] The efforts to convert the Seventeenth of October into a state celebration may be seen in that, from 1948 onward, diplomats from friendly nations would appear next to Perón on the balcony of the government palace. On October 17, 1948, for example, José Artajo, Spain's foreign relations minister, stood next to Perón in an effort to emphasize the friendly connections between the two countries. The "officialization" of the Seventeenth of October would have two consequences. First, it would serve to universalize its meaning: it would no longer be a Peronist celebration, but a state one. Connected to this was the attempt to give the date a patriotic content by symbolically linking it to May 25, 1810. On both these occasions, it was stressed, the people had gone into the streets to defend their rights. With this symbolic move, Peronism, implicitly, was also appropriating the May Revolution. Second, the "officialization" of October Seventeenth would also serve to domesticate and unify the meaning of the festivity. However, by 1947 this process was not yet complete, and there was a space—although unquestionably smaller than in the previous year—for divergent interpretations.

As in 1946, there was in 1947 a *misa de campaña* in the Plaza de Mayo. This time, however, a new symbolic note was added. The altar was placed under an arch depicting allegories of the Seventeenth of October, thus subordinating the religious celebration to the political one.[60] A new protagonist of the celebration was Eva Perón. Many demonstrators carried posters with her portrait. After Perón finished his speech, the people gathered in the Plaza de Mayo called on Eva to speak. She politely declined.

The Labor Party again tried to organize an independent demonstration, but they had to cancel it due to official pressure. Implicitly admitting their lack of political relevance, the Laborites gave bad weather as the excuse for canceling the celebration. There was no longer room for two parallel celebrations, and this would be their last attempt. The Seventeenth of October definitely belonged to the Peronist regime.[61]

Even more than in the previous year, there was in 1947 a strong tendency to ritualize certain gestures. Perón started his speech with his coat on, but people demanded that he take it off, which he did, symbolizing his status as a *descamisado*. *La Nación* ironically pointed out that certain people had taken to mimicking in their clothing certain aspects of the original Seventeenth of October.[62] Once again, even after Perón's calls for moderation at the end of his speech, acts of violence were committed against certain newspapers. This time, the vandals applauded the very police officers who had come at the request of *La Prensa* to disperse them.[63]

The Peronist press coverage of October 17, 1947, was much more monolithic than that of the year before. On at least one occasion, two different papers printed identical headlines.[64] In 1947 there were no longer references in the Peronist press to the role played by the CGT on October 17, 1945. *Democracia*, while still under the direction of Molinari, had in 1946 stressed the role of the unions in the mobilization. Now, under Eva Perón, this same newspaper declared that the *descamisados* of 1945 had gone to the Plaza "without leaders or directives."[65] Only *El Líder*, which still represented in part the traditional unions, mentioned (if only incidentally) the fact that the trade unions had played some role in the events of October. The expressions "working class," "*descamisados*," and "people" became synonyms for the Peronist press.

The Peronist press also reformulated the history of events leading up to October seventeenth. In this new version, not only had his resignation been voluntary, but Perón was portrayed as a martyr, having saved the lives of those who had betrayed him by advising the workers to remain calm in his farewell speech.[66] In 1947 the celebration of the Seventeenth of October had more to do with honoring Perón than with the commemoration of the historic event. People gathered in the Plaza de Mayo to show their support for the Peronist regime, while Perón was presented as the embodiment of national identity.

Another important characteristic in the Peronist press's version of the events of October was the reformulation of Eva's role. While her role had been characterized the year before—in a version closer to reality—in terms of the suffering of a woman for the uncertain destiny of her partner, this new version of history showed her as a more active participant in the organization of the mobilization.[67] Although in 1947 it was possible to perceive a trend toward the standardization of the celebration of May Day and October Seventeenth, this standardization would only be completed in the following years.

Toward the "Nationalization" of May Day and the Seventeenth of October

In the period from 1948 to1950, new patterns developed in the celebration of Peronist political rituals. The figure of Perón became absolutely central to both days, and Eva's role became more prominent in both festivities as well. Moreover, during these years the government "tamed" October Seventeenth, suppressing all evidence of spontaneity, particularly in the acts of violence against opposition newspapers. The Seventeenth of October was definitively becoming a "ritual of reinforcement."

At the beginning of 1948, Dr. Oscar Ivanissevich, who was to exercise a large influence over the formation of the political symbolism of the regime, was appointed secretary of education. Ivanissevich attempted to link Peronism to transcendent values and to turn it into a true "political religion." The Peronist rituals progressively came to monopolize the public symbolic space. Ivanissevich collaborated in the organization of the regime's liturgy through his participation in the committee that organized the celebrations of May Day and the Seventeenth of October. He was also the author of the lyrics for the hymn "Marcha del trabajo" ("March of Labor")—which was to be sung at all official celebrations—and possibly of the "Peronist March."[68] His particular style and his unlimited devotion to Perón and Eva can be clearly perceived in the celebrations organized during his tenure.

Throughout this period, both May Day and the Seventeenth of October became much more ritualized. May Day 1948 is a case in point. The celebration started, in fact, on April 30 with an immense gathering of primary and secondary schoolchildren in front of the Monument to Labor. Perón and Ivanissevich delivered speeches, after which they freed doves whose wings had been painted with the national colors. The official program for the celebration of May Day was very detailed and included performances by the orchestra and ballet of the Colón Theater, as well as a parade of floats depicting allegories that carried the provincial winners of the "Queens of Labor" contest.[69] One of the high points of the day was the selection of the national "Queen of Labor" by a jury composed of Perón, Eva, Mercante, Cardinal Copello (Archbishop of Buenos Aires), members of the cabinet, and members of the secretariat of the CGT.[70] Later, the original version of the "Rights of the Worker" was carried solemnly to the official stage in a crystal urn covered by the national flag. José Espejo, general secretary of the CGT, in the name of the workers, formally requested that these rights be included in the Constitution. There were also other ceremonies that included the participation of public schoolchildren.[71]

There are several things worth noting about the organization of May Day 1948. First, it was from beginning to end an official celebration. Although it was still, at least in theory, organized by the CGT, it is not difficult to see the heavy participation of official bodies and institutions, including the presence of the military.[72] Second, the intense symbolic and allegorical content of the celebration matched the patterns established by Oscar Ivanissevich. Third, the active participation of the Church hierarchy was remarkable. Not only was Cardinal Copello part of the jury that selected the Queen of Labor, but he also ordered the bells of all the city churches to ring in homage to May Day. Fourth, Eva was an important protagonist in the celebration, and delivered a speech. Finally, Perón, unlike previous years, did not lead the "workers' " parade.

In 1948, Perón felt that his position as "first worker" was secure and he did not need to claim for himself the heritage of a combative tradition. This was evident in his speech at the official celebration, which avoided references to the Anarchist tradition. Perón was not speaking this year in the name of those who had been killed in defense of their rights. May Day 1948 was "the festival of a government and of a nation of workers, a festival of brothers who come together . . . in a sincere embrace of all Argentines, with no distinction of position, caste, or class."[73] Eva, on the other hand, after pointing out the differences between the "old" and the "new" May Days, assumed the role as "bridge" or intermediary between Perón and the people. She spoke to Perón in the name of the people, and to the people in the name of Perón. On that occasion, Eva said, "I, who have the full spiritual power of all the humble people in my country, tell the General: 'Thank you, Mr. President; your people support you because they know that you, in the Casa Rosada, are one more *compañero* who dreams and works for the happiness of all the *descamisados*.' And as the wife of the leader, remembering how the people returned Colonel Perón to me and the nation, I tell you, that if my life were necessary for the benefit of the people, I would give it up with all my heart for our *descamisados*."

The official celebration of the CGT was not the only one Perón attended in 1948. The Unión Obrera Metalúrgica (UOM) had organized another celebration to commemorate the Tragic Week of 1919. This meeting was a working-class event, and its tone was different from that of the official celebration. Once again, when addressing this working-class audience, which met to remember the events of the working-class struggle, Perón opted for claiming the Anarchist heritage as his own. In the Plaza de Mayo celebration, Perón no longer needed to introduce himself in his double role as president and as "first worker." His position vis-à-vis the unionized working class was sufficiently assured. But in the UOM celebration, in which Perón seemed to be uncomfortable—he was late and Eva did not attend, even though her presence had been anticipated—things were different.[74] Only as "first worker" could Perón justify his presence in a purely working-class meeting. Perón began his speech by stating that as president he wanted to attend the commemoration of the Tragic Week. However, he immediately put himself at the end of a chain of events that started with the Tragic Week. According to him, the cause begun in January 1929 "with a bloody flag" had ultimately come to fruition on February 24, 1946. When facing a totally working-class audience commemorating purely working-class events, Perón still had to use his old discursive script. It should not come as a surprise that, although the UOM continued holding similar celebrations in the following years, Perón did not attend these meetings.

In a manner similar to that of May Day, the Seventeenth of October also definitively lost its commemorative character. The aim of the celebration was clearly to give Peronist supporters the opportunity to reaffirm their devotion for their leader and to recreate the fundamental basis of the regime's legitimacy: the charismatic leadership of Perón based on his contact with the people without any intermediaries. Eva explicitly pointed this out in 1949: "This is the unsullied origin of our leader. It is necessary to say it and highlight it. He did not emerge from the manipulations of a political committee. He is not the result of the delivery of political favors. He did not, does not, and will not know any way of conquering the will of the people other than using the clean channels of justice. That is the root and the reason for the existence of the Seventeenth of October. That is its birthmark. It was born on the farms, in the factories, in the workshops."[75]

Perón, in his "dialogues" with the people, also contributed to the re-creation of his direct contact with the masses as the source of his legitimacy. In 1948, for example, after asking the crowd if it was satisfied with his government, Perón said: "I ask this question because my authority emanates from the people, and therefore I am accountable only to them."

From 1948 onward, the Peronist symbology began to expropriate spaces formerly dominated by symbols not wholly controlled by the government in order to further legitimate itself. In 1948, for example, the *misa de campaña* in the Plaza de Mayo, which in the previous years had opened the celebration, was held for the last time. The Mass, however, began formally with the raising of the national flag by General Secretary of the CGT José Espejo, while other union leaders stood guard. From this year on, unlike previous years, no representative of the president would attend Masses organized by the different Peronist Catholic organizations. This marked the end of a process.

From the beginning, Perón had sought to legitimize his discourse by linking it to the social doctrine of the Catholic Church. In 1946, Perón had been the Catholic candidate, so it is not surprising that he sought to validate his power by permeating his political discourse with Catholic symbols.[76] Progressively, however, Peronism created its own political imagery that gradually monopolized the symbolic space, pushing the Catholic symbols out. Owing to a complex host of factors I do not discuss here, the relationship between the Catholic Church and Perón showed the first symptoms of cooling around 1948.[77] This process was reflected in the evolution of the celebrations of the Seventeenth of October.

In 1946, Perón had attended a *misa de campaña* organized by a group of Peronist intellectuals and had sent representatives to other Masses. In 1947 this was repeated with one addition: the altar in the Plaza de Mayo was adorned with Peronist allegorical motifs. In 1948 the Mass played a much less important role in the celebration, and no presidential aides were sent to represent Perón at other Masses. In 1949 the *misa de campaña* was completely eliminated from the list of activities, and other political symbols replaced it. *La Prensa* commented, ironically, that near the Pyramid of May (a monument in the Plaza de Mayo), there now stood "a monumental figure which represented—according to the explanation given later—the people protecting a flag hoisted on a pole . . . and holding up a placard with the name of the president."[78]

In 1948 measures were taken to prevent acts of violence against the opposition newspapers. Toward the end of his speech, Perón explicitly asked that no acts of violence be committed. Police and CGT guards stood in front of the buildings of *La Nación*, *La Prensa*, and others in order to avoid such incidents. There were also no attempts on the part of the Alianza Libertadora to lay flowers in front of the *Crítica* newspaper building as had happened in previous years.

On the Seventeenth of October in 1948, Perón for the first time presented the Peronist Medal, in recognition of the recipients' outstanding records of service to the country and the party. By awarding the Peronist Medal to military personnel and policemen for their heroic actions, or to sports figures who had successfully represented the country in official competitions, Perón was erasing the line between the state and the party. Being loyal to the nation meant being loyal to the movement and vice versa. The fact that these medals were handed out on the Seventeenth of October contributed to the blurring of these lines. In 1948 the official celebration was much better organized than in previous years. The newspapers for making the ritual torches were now distributed by the organizers themselves, and stalls selling food and beverages were set up. The CGT distributed free train tickets to the workers, and the government canceled all celebrations in places located on the main rail lines in order to ensure that workers traveling by train would arrive at the main celebration in the Plaza de Mayo on time.[79] Furthermore, different official departments and the CGT organized a large number of cultural events. These included the play *Octubre Heroico* staged in the Cervantes Theater.

For the first time on May Day, military troops were not quartered on that day in 1949, so that the soldiers could (and were invited to) attend the meeting. Establishing a pattern for the following years, the government ordered that all non-Peronist May Day celebrations had to be held on April 30, so that they would not interfere with the official gathering. In this way, the Peronist regime assured its symbolic monopoly over May Day without necessarily banning alternative celebrations. There was to be no other May Day but the Peronist one. This "Peronization" of the day was recognized by *La Nación*: "In homage to the First of May as the Día del Trabajo, a celebration of Peronist reaffirmation took place in the Plaza de Mayo. A large crowd gathered there to express their solidarity with the President of the Republic and his wife, whose names were enthusiastically applauded."[80] As further evidence of the "Peronization" of May Day, the song "Los Muchachos Peronistas" was included in the program.

In the coverage of both dates given in the Peronist press, it is possible to detect the extension of patterns established in previous years. Peronist newspapers presented May Day as a national celebration in which not only workers but all sectors of society could participate. *Democracia* also emphasized that the new character of the celebration was not due only to the new government, but also to the "new" masses: former May Days had been opportunities for subversive demonstrations in which the red flag had expelled the national one and "The International" had replaced the National Anthem.[81] The "new" Peronist masses were not coming to the Plaza de Mayo to demand their rights, but to give thanks to Perón for having granted them.[82]

As could be expected, only *El Líder* stressed the eminently working-class character of May Day. But this newspaper would also show a strong tendency to homogenize events, much as the rest of the Peronist press did. In 1949 the headline of an April 28 editorial read: "The First of May, a

Universal Date," which stressed the working-class and international aspect of the celebration.[83] But on the next day, the headline read: "A National Date: Our First of May,"[84] and finally, on April 30, it had become "Perón and the First of May."

By 1950 the Peronist regime had imposed an official meaning and significance on both dates. There was no more space for alternative celebrations or interpretations. The Peróns were now the undisputed center of both, a fact that contributed to the reinforcement of their image as charismatic leaders. Moreover, by exalting the "national" character of these two obviously Peronist celebrations, the regime implicitly identified nationality itself with Peronism.

The Crystallization of Peronist Rituals

In 1950, Ivanissevich was removed from his position for reasons that are still not clear, but were probably related to an increasing animosity between him and Eva. From that moment on, the person in charge of handling the Peronist propaganda would be Secretary of Information Raúl Alejandro Apold. After 1950, the attempts by the regime to "Peronize" the state and society accelerated. The Peronist "doctrine" became a leitmotiv of official propaganda, while programs of indoctrination were established in schools and official bodies. The boundaries between the party and the state became increasingly diffuse. The regime became progressively wrapped up in a symbolic dynamic whose focus was centered on worshipping Perón and Eva. There would be no place for "second protagonists." After 1950, Mercante's star began a rapid descent, and a year later there was no longer any mention of him.[85]

The effects of the new tack taken by the regime became evident during the celebration of the "Year of the Liberator General San Martín" in 1950. In that year the CGT modified its statutes and transformed itself clearly into a "branch" of the Peronist Party.[86] Moreover, as the regime's ability to provide concrete benefits became limited by the economic crisis that began in 1949, the emphasis was placed more and more on symbolic exchanges. This situation also forced Perón to take a more authoritarian path. The official discourse became more aggressive toward the opposition, while the regime's policies turned more repressive and restrictive concerning freedom of expression. Nineteen-fifty was not only the "Year of the Liberator," but also the "Year of the Visca-Decker Commission," which, according to *The Economist*, had closed more than 150 newspapers by the end of April.[87]

These new tendencies evident within the regime, due partly to the intensification of already-existing patterns, were highlighted in the managing of symbols and in the way in which the regime celebrated its political rituals. Attacks on the opposition became more open and speeches regained the aggressive tone that had moderated, in part, in earlier years. With the celebrations analyzed here, the tendency during this period was toward trivialization. The election of the "Queens of Labor" is a good example. During the years from 1948 to 1950, the event had symbolized the virtues of the "New Argentina's" youth. The juries were made up of distinguished figures, such as Cardinal Copello. After 1950, the contest was turned into a mere beauty contest. Small wonder, then, that after 1951 all the "Queens of Labor" were elected from among the representatives of the union of "variety artists" and by a jury made up of popular film stars and CGT leaders.

In the previous period, the symbolism of the rituals was only in part explicitly Peronist. It was also possible to find more general allegorical elements that evoked broader values such as nationalism or justice. May Day was, for example, characterized as the "national celebration" of the people's unity. After 1950, Perón, Eva, and the "doctrine" became the sole focus in the articulation of the Peronist political liturgy. As Perón explained in his speech of October 17, 1950, if there was still opposition, it was "because there are idiots who still do not understand us." Peronist rhetoric was now saturated with religious elements. Peronism needed "apostles" to "preach" its doctrine, which Perón summarized in his "twenty fundamental truths of *justicialismo*." These he read to a crowd on October 17, 1951.[88] *Democracia* characterized the Seventeenth of October as a "lay Mass" and kept repeating that "God is a Peronist."[89]

October 17, 1951, was particularly important. In August and September of that year two crucial events had taken place. In August, Eva Perón, already gravely ill, had publicly renounced her nomination to the vice presidency. In September, loyalist forces thwarted an attempted coup d'état led by General Benjamin Menéndez. These two events occupied a central place in the celebration of the Seventeenth of October. On this occasion, besides the official celebration at the Plaza de Mayo, there was another gathering in the Plaza San Martín, which included a military parade. There, Perón awarded medals to those military men who had distinguished themselves during the crushing of the attempted coup. Workers representing the CGT and wearing their workclothes also awarded the CGT medals to those servicemen.[90]

By choosing the Seventeenth of October to reward the military's loyalty to the government, and by allowing the union representatives to present their own medals, Perón was taking a step even farther in erasing the line between the state and the party.

The celebration of October 17, 1951, was officially dedicated to Eva Perón, whose illness was growing more and more serious. That year, instead of calling the Eighteenth of October "San Perón" Day, it was declared the day of "Santa Evita." She received a special medal from the CGT and a Peronist Medal from Perón himself.[91] Perón's speech was devoted to the exaltation of his wife: "Eva Perón, standard-bearer in the struggle for this second independence . . . gave up everything without asking for anything in exchange. [She gave up] everything: her youth, her health, even her life."[92]

After Eva's death in 1952 the Seventeenth of October became a ceremony with a well-established program. It had entirely lost its original carnival-like character as well as all traces of spontaneity. The program for October 17, 1952, for example, began at 8:30 A.M. with the raising of the Argentine flag at CGT headquarters. Immediately afterward, the directors of the CGT marched from the Ministry of Labor and Welfare, carrying the "Peronist flame" up to a votive lamp located at headquarters. At 8:45, there was a minute of silence for Eva, and at 9:00 the leaders of the CGT went to the Plaza de Mayo where they raised the national flag at 9:20. Another minute of silence was observed at 10:00, and a commemorative plaque was uncovered at the Casa Rosada. The main demonstration at the Plaza de Mayo began at exactly at 5:00 P.M.[93] On October 18, at 7:00 A.M., Perón went to the CGT building to pay homage to Eva. The program included a torch-lit march and other tributes to her memory.[94]

In the context of an increasing authoritarianism, the denunciation of the opposition became even more virulent. While in 1948 Perón had promised to defeat the opposition "as one defeats others in a democracy: with ballot boxes and votes," in 1950 the weapon was "the strength of Justicialist action."[95] The fierce attack on the opposition was also carried out in the official press, which became less interested in stressing the social aspects of Peronism. In this context, Perón recovered, once again, the combative Anarchist tradition for May Day. *Democracia* reminded its readers that May Day was a tribute to the "precursors of Chicago," to whom Perón referred in his speeches.[96]

After the period of "Argentinization" of May Day, Perón had once again embraced the heritage of a more combative tradition.[97] Today's opponents were none other than the descendants of yesterday's oppressors. The name of U.S. Ambassador Spruille Braden began to reappear in the Peronist press.

Although it was materially irrelevant, it could still be used as a symbol of the enemy. The enemy, of course, was not only Braden but "all the Bradens" who operated both inside and outside the country.[98]

Toward the end of Perón's regime the process that had begun in 1946 was complete. May Day and the Seventeenth of October were no longer popular festivals, but highly ritualized celebrations organized entirely by the state. What originally had been a "ritual of inversion" was turned into a "ritual of reinforcement." Moreover, the Seventeenth of October lost its character of common oration and became a moment of communication between the leader and his people. May Day was a totally Peronist celebration, while the Seventeenth of October had lost all traces of spontaneity. The process through which both days were incorporated into the Peronist liturgy was not immediate, but the result of an intense effort to reformulate collective memory.

The redefinition of the meaning of both days, however, followed different patterns. The Seventeenth of October had been born as a Peronist event in 1945. It was relatively easy, therefore, to absorb it into the official imagery by redefining the role of the protagonists. By 1952, it resembled a semireligious celebration centered around Perón and the memory of Eva. May Day, however, had had a long tradition preceding, and completely independent of, the emergence of Peronism. The process of its incorporation into the Peronist liturgy was therefore more complex. It was not possible to invent a tradition from scratch. Instead, it was necessary to reinvent an existing one (which, as we have seen, was also invented). The Socialist tradition of a multiclass, peaceful, and patriotic celebration fit well into the patterns of the Peronist political rituals. This, however, was not enough. Peronism presented itself as a complete rupture with the past. In order to break with the past, therefore, Perón was forced to define from which past he would break away. He chose the Anarchist tradition of mourning and violent protest.

At the beginning of the Peronist regime, by claiming to be at the same time the heir to and conqueror of an (almost entirely fictitious) bloody May Day tradition, Perón tried to reinforce his legitimacy as "first worker." He was the brother of those killed defending their rights. But at the same time, as president, Perón could announce the beginning of a new era in which those rights would be granted and defended by the state. After the interlude of 1948 to1950, in which the regime tried to establish consensus by linking its doctrine to universal values, and in which May Day was characterized as a celebration of unity, Perón returned to his combative discourse of the years from 1946 to 1948. This time, however, he was addressing a different audience. His relationship with the working class was well established. After 1950, and in the context of an increasing authoritarianism, Perón used his radical discourse in order to threaten his opponents.

By manipulating symbols and establishing rituals, Perón was able to reinforce his image as a charismatic leader. Political rituals were moments in which Perón could physically place himself and the symbols associated with him and his movement at the center of events. Meanwhile, the official Peronist propaganda presented a vision of the past and an interpretation of events consistent with the regime's imagery. Perón also used political rituals to recreate periodically the mythical basis of the legitimacy of the regime: his direct contact with the people.

III

EDUCATION AND POLITICS: THE POLITICAL SOCIALIZATION OF YOUTH

In its preoccupation with achieving "spiritual unity," the Peronist regime used the educational system as a mechanism for the political socialization of Argentine youth. Political socialization is defined here as the process through which the population acquires the values and beliefs that define their political culture.[1] We have seen that the concepts of "indoctrination" and "spiritual unity" were at the core of Perón's ideas about managing society. The educational system provided an efficient channel for the indoctrination of the new generations. The Second Five-Year Plan explicitly established that "school texts will be structured in accordance with the principles of the national doctrine [and] will include special reference to the goals that the present plan establishes for each activity of the nation."[2] The Peronist regime used education as a tool for the creation of a Peronist mystique.

The following two chapters analyze the ways in which Perón's government used the educational system at all levels of learning, but the focus will be on elementary school education. This emphasis flows not only from the abundance of available sources at this level, but also from the fact that it was the level on which the attempts to manipulate the system were most evident. Chapter 5 analyzes the general tendencies in the organization of the educational system during the period from 1943 to 1955 and supplies the general background for the specific discussion in the succeeding chapter. Chapter 6 studies the changes introduced in primary school textbooks during Perón's regime and traces the continuities and ruptures in the way pre-Peronist and Peronist textbooks presented formative themes in political culture, such as the role of the state, national history, charity, work, and society. Analyzing the message conveyed by the school texts provides a

83

starting point for understanding the kind of change Peronism attempted to introduce in the political culture of the country.

The Peronist regime tried to replace the image of society linked to the liberal tradition in the textbooks (as in other areas of culture) for a new vision based on Peronist doctrine. However, given the limitations of the Peronist doctrine (see Chapter 2), the final product was a strange combination of tradition and modernity. This mixture also permeated other aspects of the Peronist discourse and seems to be one of the defining characteristics of populist discourse in general.[3] Indeed, Peronism began to modernize the material presented in syllabi and school texts. Textbooks from Perón's period were the first to emphasize the importance of economic and industrial development and the first to introduce the notion of rural and urban modernization. These texts also presented a vision of society that was more realistic and less static than the one presented by pre-Peronist texts. Still, Peronism also introduced, or sometimes reintroduced, more traditional elements in the vision of society linked to topics such as religion, the principle of authority, and the importance of discipline.

5

THE REORGANIZATION OF THE EDUCATIONAL SYSTEM

The Argentine educational system, like many other public services, was organized by the liberal governments in the last decades of the nineteenth century and grew rapidly in the first decades of the twentieth century. In 1884, after a heated debate, the federal government passed Law 1420, which established gradual, compulsory, and secular education in the city of Buenos Aires and territories under federal jurisdiction. The primary schools supported by the federal government were placed under the supervision of the Consejo Nacional de Educación. Secularism became the official ideological principle of the educational system—a system that became a powerful force for the maintenance of the liberal consensus discussed in Chapter 1.[4]

During the period of massive immigration, the educational system was also used as a mechanism to instill patriotic feelings in the children of immigrants. It was hoped that this patriotism would also function as a barrier against the "dissolvent ideologies," in particular, anarchism. To this end, Dr. José María Ramos Mejía, president of the Consejo Nacional de Educación, in the 1910s began a program of "patriotic education" based on the creation of patriotic rituals and the teaching of national history.[5] In using the school system as an agent for the generation of national feelings, Ramos Mejía attempted to replace the influence of families, in particular, those of immigrants, whom he saw as incapable of instilling the necessary love for their new fatherland in their children's minds. Although "patriotic education" continued to be a preoccupation for educational authorities, it lost momentum after Ramos Mejía stepped down in 1913.

In the late 1930s and early 1940s, particularly after the beginning of World War II, the educational authorities renewed their interest in patriotic education. Throughout the 1930s, inspectors from the Consejo Nacional de Educación discovered the existence of German schools that were openly spreading Nazi ideology. In reaction, much of the authorities' efforts centered on stressing the importance of defending democratic institutions and the principles of popular sovereignty at school.

Although during the 1910s as well as in the late 1930s, the purpose behind these programs of patriotic education was to reinforce broad nationalistic feelings in the minds of the students, there were certain situations in which the educational authorities attempted to transmit a more precise political message. In 1932, for instance, schoolteachers were ordered to prepare special classes to promote the "patriotic loan," the bonds the government was issuing. The *Monitor de Educación Común* (official publication of the Consejo Nacional de Educación) published a long article in which one schoolteacher explained how she had devoted a whole day to promoting the government-issued bonds, which would bring "peace, work, and progress."[6]

Education and the Revolutionary Government of 1943

The government emerging from the Revolution of 1943 placed the reform of the educational system high on its list of priorities. The social vices that the revolutionary colonels led by Perón claimed it was their mission to correct were viewed in part as the result of an educational system described as "atheist and cosmopolitan," which had contaminated the minds of several generations of Argentines. On September 25, 1943, Minister of Justice and Public Instruction Admiral Elbio Anaya issued a resolution restructuring the bases of the educational system. The new system had to respond to the "noble objective of bringing nationalism back into all aspects of Argentine social life, in accordance with the goals which inspired the movement of the 4th of June." The resolution stressed that the final objective of public education was "the formation of character and the inspiration of the individual and the family in social and patriotic behavior, and in the austere principles of Christian morality."[7]

Breaking an old tradition of secular education in the schools under federal supervision, the government appointed well-known militant Catholic nationalists to top positions in the school system. The new minister of justice and public instruction, Gustavo Martínez Zuviría, was a right-wing writer who, under the pseudonym of Hugo Wast, had written several popular and openly anti-Semitic novels. Manuel Villada Achával, another noted militant Catholic nationalist, was appointed undersecretary of education, and in 1944, José Ignacio Olmedo, also a militant Catholic, was appointed administrator of the Consejo Nacional de Educación. One of Olmedo's first actions was to place all teachers under temporary suspension until each teacher's ideological affiliation could be determined.

For the first time, non-Catholic schoolteachers and officials were persecuted and dismissed for ideological and religious reasons. For the new authorities, the Catholic nationalist ideology was one of the pillars of the nation. The appointments made at other levels of the educational system followed the same pattern. The supervision of the University of Buenos Aires was entrusted to Dr. Tomás Casares, a known member of the Argentine Catholic Action organization. Another ultraright-wing ideologue, Jordán Bruno Genta, was appointed administrator of the University of El Litoral, and later dean of the Instituto Nacional del Profesorado. University student associations, such as the Argentine University Federation or the University Federation of Buenos Aires, were declared illegal.

On December 31, 1943, the military government issued a decree introducing Catholic education in public schools under federal jursidiction.[8] All liberal groups, including many teachers' associations, opposed this decree.[9] Later, other important sectors of Peronist workers would oppose this decree's becoming law.[10] Catholic education (and religious education in general) had been excluded from the regular curriculum by Law 1420. However, Law 1420 applied only to schools under federal jurisdiction, that is, to schools in the city of Buenos Aires, national territories, and the federal schools established in the provinces.[11] In the educational system of the provinces, Catholic education had either persisted, or, in many cases, had been introduced in the first decades of the twentieth century. In 1936, Governor Manuel Fresco introduced Catholic education in the schools of the province of Buenos Aires. In 1937 similar measures were taken in the provinces of Mendoza and Catamarca. By that year, moreover, the provinces of Corrientes, San Luis, La Rioja, Jujuy, Santa Fé, Córdoba, and Salta all had some form of Catholic education.[12] However, what was acceptable in the provinces was not necessarily so in modern and cosmopolitan Buenos Aires. In spite of the fact that during the 1930s a friendly relationship between the state and the Church had emerged, the introduction of Catholic education at the federal level was seen by many sectors of society as an assault on a long tradition of secular public education.

Although the 1943 decree provided alternative courses on morality for children of non-Catholic families, according to official sources, participation in the courses offering religious instruction was massive. In 1946, for example, 97.49 percent of students enrolled in schools dependent on the Consejo Nacional de Educación received religious education. In the city of Buenos Aires, according to a source from the Consejo, only 4.6 percent of the students enrolled in official schools received alternative instruction on morality.[13] Between 1944 and 1946, the percentage of students in the first and second years of secondary school attending religious classes throughout the country went up from 91.10 percent to 93.19 percent.[14]

Although the success of Catholic education could be attributed to the process of the "re-Catholicization" of society (see Chapter 1), two points should be kept in mind when looking at these figures. First, the quantitative sources from the Ministry of Justice and Public Instruction during the period under consideration are not reliable. Different sources often provide different figures for the same factor. Second, the massive enrollment in religious classes might also be explained by the way in which these courses were instituted. Although nonreligious classes in morality had been made available by the 1943 decree, it was assumed that Catholic education was the norm. Until 1944, parents who did not want their children to receive Catholic instruction had to go in person to the district's Consejo Escolar and register their children on a special list. This process was not only time-consuming for the parents, but it could also have exposed their children to discrimination from overly vigilant school authorities. After 1945, parents could mail in their request for exemption from religious instruction. From the beginning, however, the rules made it difficult for parents to enroll their children in the alternative classes on morality.[15]

Although most pupils attended the religious courses, and most teachers agreed to teach them, it was possible to detect some lack of enthusiasm on the part of the teachers. Over the years the ministry sent many memoranda reminding teachers and school authorities that religious education *was indeed part* of the official curriculum, and therefore should be taken seriously. Apparently, there was a general tendency to relegate religion classes to the end of the day, when students were already too tired to be expected to pay adequate attention.[16]

Another area of reform in the educational system into which the military authorities ventured was that related to technical education. Argentina lacked an organized system of technical education. The revolutionary colonels placed great confidence in the industrial and technical future of the country. This confidence was evident in the report of the Ministry of Justice and Public Instruction for the year 1943, which suggested including such courses as airplane mechanics, radio communication, and metallurgy in the curriculum of the technical schools. According to the report, technical education should be "eminently nationalist for two reasons. First, because it will educate future generations of technicians in the traditional principle of love for one's country . . . [and second, because] it will set the stage for the technical emancipation of the nation, by nationalizing the industry through the substitution of national for foreign technical equipment."[17] In 1944 the government established the Dirección Nacional de Aprendizaje y Orientación Profesional, which answered to the secretary of labor and welfare.

Another preoccupation of the military government's education authorities was to create a body of loyal teachers who would be indoctrinated in the ideology of Catholic nationalism. Acting on this concern, authorities created the Escuela Superior del Magisterio in 1944. The school was designed to serve as an antidote to the education provided in the Escuelas Normales, characterized by the military leaders as "materialistic, positivist, and cosmopolitan," besides suffering from a "frivolous encyclopedic breadth." In order to be admitted to the school, the applicant had to take an oath "to faithfully serve the fatherland, and to recognize the Greco-Roman tradition of Western culture to which we belong, and the Hispanic-Christian culture of our illustrious origins, as the only authentically Argentine ones."[18]

The curriculum of the Escuela Superior, which included such courses as "Metaphysics and Its Regulating Function for Scientific Intelligence" and such subjects as theology, was prepared by a team of well-known militants of the Catholic right. These included Jordán B. Genta, who was also appointed dean, Lila Losada de Genta, Father Leonardo Castellani, Joaquín Llambías, and others. J. Olmedo and J. Genta presided over the official opening of the school in August 1944. The opening speech by Genta was a veritable catalogue of antiliberal sentiments. He condemned with equal fury both "quantitative democracy, which requires the suppression of all traditional institutions, privilege, and responsibility," and the "progressive pedagogy," which he said should be replaced by an undefined "national pedagogy." Genta also made clear his ideas about how the nation's history should be taught. "The idea," he exhorted, "is to replace the falsified history of the liberal doctors, [which is] anti-traditional, anti-heroic, [which] denies our illustrious Hispanic origins, and which is founded on an explicit or implicit historical materialism, with a true history, traditional, heroic, and proud of its origins." Olmedo, for his part, chose to focus his attention on the ominous consequences of free thinking.

The Escuela Superior was short-lived. At the beginning of 1945, under growing international and domestic pressure, the military government was forced to expel the staunch nationalists from cabinet positions and other high posts. This purge was also extended to the area of education. Olmedo and Genta were dismissed, and Catholic nationalism, although still the dominant ideology in the education field, showed a lower profile. No provisions were made for the Escuela Superior in the national budget for 1945.

When Perón took power, the educational system was already on its way to becoming a tool for the indoctrination of youth in the ideology of Catholic nationalism. The following sections show how Perón deepened and redefined various aspects of the educational system reforms already tackled by his immediate predecessors.

The Redefinition of the Role of the Public Educational System

During his administration, Perón paid particular attention to education. His two main goals were the expansion of the public educational system and its use for political purposes. In both respects, his achievements were impressive. Between 1946 and 1952 the number of elementary school pupils rose from 1,267,459 to 1,512,184. Moreover, according to official sources, the government built over 1,000 new elementary schools and created over 150 new secondary schools. Similarly, the number of students enrolled at the University of Buenos Aires increased from 17,742 in 1941 to 41,325 in 1951, and the number of high-school students also grew from a total of 38,868 in 1946 to 46,942 in 1951.[19]

In terms of the second goal the development of Perón's education policies can be divided into three periods, each coinciding with the tenures of his three ministers of education. The first period runs from 1946 to 1948, when Belisario Gache Pirán was minister of justice and public instruction. During this period, Perón succeeded in converting into law the 1943 decree that had instituted Catholic education. This was an important step in securing the legitimacy of the regime, since the passage of such a law had been an electoral promise that guaranteed Perón the semiexplicit support of the Catholic Church. The second period, from 1948 to 1950, coincides with the tenure of Dr. Oscar Ivanissevich in the position of secretary, and later minister, of education. During this period, significant reforms in the structure of the educational system took place. After the passing of the Constitution of 1949, the Ministry of Public Instruction was separated from the Ministry of Justice, and education became an autonomous area. The creation of the Ministry of Education formalized and legalized a situation that had, in fact, existed since 1948, when Perón created a semi-independent secretary of education under the leadership of Ivanissevich. During this second period the syllabi for elementary education were reformed. The third period coincides with Minister Armando Méndez de San Martín's term. This was certainly the most polemic period, in which "Peronist" texts were introduced in primary schools and open political indoctrination of pupils and teachers took place. Toward the end of this period, as well, the conflict between Church and state, latent for many years, finally exploded with violence.

The First Period, or, the "Democratization" of the Educational System

When Perón took power, he had four priorities in terms of educational policy. First, he sought to legalize, through an act of Congress, the decree which had introduced Catholic education into the schools. This first objective was achieved in 1947 after an intensive campaign led, ostensibly, by Eva Perón. In addition, Congress passed a law that same year known as the "Statute for Private-School Teachers," which, in fact, was an undercover subsidy for private schools, most of which were Catholic. Second, Perón wanted to extend control over the universities, still a stronghold of opposition, by passing a law that would eliminate their autonomy and the principle of tripartite government. These rights, however, had already been suspended by decrees passed by the military government. Third, Perón wanted to centralize the educational system. This goal would be totally fulfilled when, after the reform of the Constitution, he was allowed to create an independent Ministry of Education. Fourth, he wished to foster the expansion of education at all levels, particularly the technical system begun by the military.

Perón's enthusiasm for technical education was related, on the one hand, to his plans for industrial development, for which he would need a qualified working class. But, on the other hand, much like the preceding conservative governments, he saw schools as an instrument for disciplining the working class: "The social danger of the present community resides in the fact that men do not have possibilities, or, if they have them, those possibilities are very limited. Men with an uncertain future are the most dangerous because they feel attracted to bizarre theories and attitudes. No young man who has a secured future can afford to waste his time on such theories. Rather, he spends his time thinking about his future and trying to reach it."[20]

In the speech in which he introduced his First Five-Year Plan before Congress, Perón emphasized his belief in the importance of democratizing the educational system at all levels. Social justice should also extend to education. According to Perón, of the 2.5 million children who went to primary school (a rather exaggerated figure), only 3,500 would be fortunate enough to graduate from universities. The state, he claimed, had the responsibility to provide an adequate education for the huge majority of students who would not end up in university classrooms. One possible alternative was to enlarge the system of technical education.[21] The expansion of this area was therefore presented as an important step forward in the democratization of the system.

The First Five-Year Plan also included a proposal for a university law. This law would not only eliminate the autonomy of the universities, but also prohibit political activity in them. The bill included, as well, a proposal for the reorganization of the Consejo Nacional de Educación, which would extend its jurisdiction to secondary and technical education. According to Perón the fact that the universities were autonomous did not guarantee that they were democratic, since "the people and the university go in different directions." Actually, he asserted, the government not only had the right, but the moral obligation to intervene in university affairs, since the government authorities had been democratically elected by all the people (by all the male population, to be exact), while university authorities had not. The duty of the government was, then, to force the universities to be more popular and, thereby, more democratic.

Although it is clear that Perón's most important motive for eliminating the autonomy of the universities was that they were in the hands of the opposition,[22] this was not his only reason. As a precondition for obtaining "spiritual unity," Perón, like some of his predecessors, was particularly interested in integrating all the levels of education into one system under the direct control of the state. In 1947 the government issued a decree "with the agreement of the ministers" which established the general goals for education at all levels.[23] The tone of the decree was familiar, and it stressed the importance of "spiritual unity." Its preamble read:

> Although the Executive branch acknowledges the serious merits of the argument that the science of education should be an autonomous discipline, and the difficulties in reconciling the demands of the pedagogic ideal with those of the political ideal, it is indisputable from the point of view of the national interest in present times, that schooling should contribute to the forging and consolidation of the unity of the people, morally, economically, politically, and culturally. . . . In order to oppose deviant spiritual attitudes . . . doctrinal coordination in primary, secondary, and

higher education is essential for the formation of the Argentine man. It is up to the State to achieve the cultural harmonization of the Nation.[24]

The first article of the decree established that "the goal of national public schools will be the formation of the Argentine man with full consciousness of his roots, an authentic vision of the great destiny of the nation, and a fervent historic will to serve his fatherland and humanity."

According to the projects included in the First Five-Year Plan, all levels of education were to be free for those who could not afford to pay tuition. The plan also stipulated measures to motivate the private sector, in particular, big industrial companies, to finance a system of fellowships for students who could not otherwise attend technical schools without financial help.[25] The university law was passed by Congress with only minor modifications, while the project to reform the Consejo Nacional de Educación, like many other laws included in the First Five-Year Plan, was never debated in Congress.

Technical education would remain an important feature of Perón's educational policy. In 1947 a new system of "technical missions and of cultural extension" for males, and a similar one of "domestic culture missions" for females, resembling the Mexican system of "cultural missions," was established. In 1948 the Universidad Obrera Nacional was set up by Congress, which would open its doors in 1952. The Universidad Obrera represented the highest level in a system of technical education for working-class students under the jurisdiction of the Comisión Nacional de Aprendizaje y Orientación Profesional (CNAOP).[26]

In spite of the official discourse, which emphasized the democratic character of the system of technical education, it was never, in fact, integrated into other parts of the educational system. The technical education provided by the institutions under CNAOP was a parallel system aimed at furnishing practical education to young men of working-class origin. The students enrolled in the technical schools of CNAOP would later attend the Universidad Obrera, but, in practice, they had no access to secondary schools, let alone universities. In this sense, the parliamentary opposition by deputies from the UCR was right in stressing the reactionary character of the system of technical education promoted by Perón, since it divided the educational system along clear class lines.[27] Although Perón expanded access to higher education, it is also true that, in a certain sense, he achieved what the conservative governments before him had attempted without success: to create a system of technical education for the working class without connections to the regular education system.[28]

As others had before him, Perón tirelessly expressed the need to create a truly nationalist educational system that would inculcate patriotic feelings and love for the country's traditions in the minds of the students. In this sense, the Peronist discourse on education was not notably different from that of the military government. In a speech given in February 1948, when Dr. Ivanissevich was sworn in as the secretary of education, Perón said: "It is necessary to confront, without wasting time, educational reform, . . . which will allow us to create, maintain, and permanently encourage the new Argentine philosophical school. Without an Argentine soul, without an Argentine thought, without an Argentine feeling, the people would be an amorphous mass whose destiny would be entrusted to the audacious, to the evil, and to the liars. This reform has to be faced and made. And if it is necessary to fight in order to impose it, we will do so."

The idea of inculcating nationalist feelings through the schools was certainly not new. But if, in previous decades, this nationalism had been defined generally in negative terms, as a barrier against what was perceived as social danger, the "dissolvent ideologies," or the massive presence of immigrants, for Perón, nationalist education had a positive connotation. According to him, it was necessary to generate nothing less than a new philosophy that would bring about a new society. Although he preferred to keep the definition of this philosophy shrouded in vague terms, Perón himself would make the meaning of this project explicit years later. As he would pronounce later, the masses had to be prepared before they could be led; if not, he would unintentionally repeat the mistake made by President Yrigoyen, who had been deposed by his own "ill-prepared masses." The educational system would play a central role in the "preparation of the masses."

Unlike the military authorities before him, and in order to avoid irritating the opposition, Perón did not appoint well-known militant nationalists to the most visible positions within the educational system. In the beginning, in fact, the officials nominated for the highest positions in the educational bureaucracy were people of obscure origins. Belisario Gache Pirán, minister of justice and public instruction, was a thirty-eight-year-old lawyer without any kind of experience in the field of education. At the time of his nomination, he was a federal judge appointed by the military government (without the approval of the Senate, naturally). Earler, he had been a federal prosecutor and a judicial clerk. The person who was really in charge of education, however, was Jorge Arizaga, who, in a less visible position than Gache Pirán, had been a long-time bureaucrat in the educational system. He had been secretary of the committee on pedagogy for the Consejo Nacional de

Educación and a member of the Consejo Escolar for the twelfth district for eleven years. Ideologically, he was a Catholic nationalist, and he had coauthored the educational reform bill of the province of Buenos Aires under Governor Manuel Fresco. Another important official was the administrator of the Consejo Nacional de Educación, Miguel Mordeglia. He was a medical doctor characterized by the nationalist newspaper *La Tribuna* as a "resolute and energetic partisan of religious education."[29] For the middle positions within the educational bureaucracy, Perón appointed longtime civil servants of Catholic nationalist ideology, who were not difficult to find within the structures of the educational system. In this system, as mentioned in Chapter 1, it had once been possible to find people of the most diverse ideological affiliations. The purges carried out by the military government in 1943, however, created an excellent opportunity for Catholic nationalists to fill the vacated middle positions in the ministry.

The Consejo Nacional de Educación had been taken over by the military authorities and placed under the direct jurisdiction of the Ministry of Justice and Public Instruction. In the presentation speech of the First Five-Year Plan, Perón claimed he intended to end this intervention as soon as Congress passed his bill for the reform of the educational system. Gache Pirán repeated these same words when he swore in Mordeglia as the government representative in the Consejo.[30] Mordeglia's tenure was short. In January 1947, Perón passed a decree that not only failed to restore the autonomy of the Consejo, but placed it permanently under the direct control of the Ministry of Justice and Public Instruction. Given these facts, Mordeglia resigned his position and was replaced by Paulino Mussachio.[31] This was a decisive step toward the centralization of the educational system.

During the first phase of his government, Perón continued the reforms begun by the military authorities of the June Revolution. Although there were no major changes in curricula, Perón took the first crucial steps toward the centralization of the educational system, a precondition for transforming it into an efficient mechanism for political socialization.

The Ivanissevich Years, or, the Beginning of Peronist Education

A radical change in the structure of the educational system came when Perón created the office of secretary of education and appointed Dr. Oscar Ivanissevich to the post in February 1948.[32] The 1853 Constitution had established a fixed number of ministries, and an amendment in 1898 had raised that number from five to eight. Therefore, before the reforms of 1949, no separate Ministry of Education could be established. The secretary of education in fact operated as a ministry without the constitutional formalities.

Dr. Ivanissevich was a renowned surgeon who had been close to Perón very early on. From the beginning, Ivanissevich had supported the university policies of the June government. When Perón came to power, Ivanissevich was named administrator of the University of Buenos Aires and was later appointed ambassador to the United States. As Ivanissevich recalled many years later, one of his tasks as ambassador had been to study the American educational system in order to use it as a possible model for a reform of the Argentine system. He stamped the office with his very personal style. He always wore to work the same white lab-type coat that was the required uniform for Argentine teachers and had the habit of writing some of his speeches in verse.

During Ivanissevich's term as secretary (and later minister) of education, the Peronist regime attempted to link its "doctrine" to transcendental values such as nationalism and religion. The creation of a Ministry of Education was in part the result of Ivanissevich's influence, which spread beyond the realm of education. The eclectic character of Ivanissevich's ideology became evident from the first, as is apparent in the speech he delivered when he took office. He defined himself as a revolutionary in all the areas in which he had participated. However, he also made it clear that his "revolutionary spirit" was based on "the Christian faith inspired by my mother. This faith was and is today, more than ever, both armor and a battering ram, defense and attack, reason and force." Ivanissevich ended his speech by exhorting the teachers, "those civilian heroes of the cross and the book," to "follow the civilizing steps of our motherland Spain" and to work for the "Great Argentina which Sarmiento dreamt of, and Perón is making true." Under Ivanissevich, the centralization of the educational system begun in the preceding years continued. The Consejo Nacional de Educación, now named the Dirección Nacional de Enseñanza Primaria, was finally absorbed by the Ministry of Education.[33] The Undersecretariat of Education was also done away with.

Ivanissevich tried to emulate many of the pedagogic methods and institutional organization that he had seen in the United States. He created offices for vocational counseling and an office of academic advisers called "The Teacher Is a Friend." Moreover, the new minister created a system of "student clubs" in an attempt to bring the school closer to the community,[34] and he started a program of "useful vacations," which kept schools open to the community the whole year long. During his term, Ivanissevich also made the expansion of the preschool educational system a priority and reformed the curricula for the first time since Perón took office.[35]

Concerning his orientation to education, Ivanissevich stressed the importance of feelings over thoughts. The role of education was, according to him, to form "good" students, rather than "wise" ones, and to inculcate respect for the country's traditional culture, one aspect of which was the Catholic religion. Schools should prepare "ordinary people to be ordinary people: healthy, honest, hard-working, loyal, and, above all, altruistic." According to Ivanissevich, the objectives of the existing school system were the antithesis of those he was pursuing.

Although the official discourse on education stressed the importance of feelings and spontaneity, the three values most frequently mentioned in the syllabi for primary schools in 1950 were discipline, piety, and nationalism. The preface to these syllabi, found at the archive of the Ministry of Education and written by Ivanissevich, noted in his peculiar style that "our boys should learn to know and love God, the central axis of our moral life; to know and love the nation, the base and foundation of our civil life; and to use with confidence the elemental techniques of knowledge for the development of intellectual life."

The most important virtue teachers were supposed to instill in their students was "civility." Ivanissevich provided an exhaustive catalogue of the behaviors that had to be taught:

> The teacher should pay constant attention to all things related to "civility." It is necessary to practice all times, as a habit of life, those norms of respect, cleanliness, elegance, and gentlemanly manners in boys, and refinement and femininity in girls. . . . How they should behave toward one another, friends, and classmates, with their superiors, parents, and other members of the family . . . how they should behave in the classroom, in school, in the streets, at church, at the movies, at public spectacles, when going out, in sports; how they should introduce themselves, greet others, take leave; how they should behave at the table, when they can talk, when to keep their mouths shut; when they should stand, and when they should sit down.

Ivanissevich organized an unprecedented mise-en-scène as a tool with which to achieve his ambitious goals in education. Patriotic celebrations were turned into dramatic and well-prepared theatrical scenes in which thousands of students, together with workers and soldiers, paraded at night with torches, in order to symbolize the unity of the Argentine people.[36] Every year, the Ministry published a calendar of festivities clearly stipulating how each (in accordance with its status) should be celebrated.

Perón spelled out the new character he intended to give education in his opening speech to Congress in 1949. This was the first time Perón mentioned in Congress the philosophical principles the government wished to imprint on education. Some of the themes covered, such as those referring to the importance of spiritual unity, were almost identical to those in the decree of 1947 mentioned above. This time, however, Perón added other themes that revealed Ivanissevich's unique touch. The school had as a basic objective to inspire the will of the students to serve God, the fatherland, and humanity. Education had to inculcate such principles as justice, virtue rather than materialism, and national consciousness, while making it clear that the human conflict was a conflict between believers and nonbelievers. "The aim of our crusade for the general welfare, inspired in the truth, is the recovery of faith."[37]

Ivanissevich put into practice many of the ideas mentioned in the 1947 decree. But if the basic orientation had been already established by 1947, why was the curriculum not changed until 1950? We can only speculate about the answer to this question. Probably one of the reasons was the new energy injected by Ivanissevich into education reform as secretary (and later minister) of education. However, it is also important to remember that education had been, since the beginning, an area of conflict within the general policies of Perón's government. Furthermore, it was only by 1950 that Perón had managed to place all institutional mechanisms of power under his control. By that year, Perón had already replaced members of the Supreme Court with staunch defenders of the regime, had gained firm control over Congress, and had tamed the labor movement. Nineteen fifty was also a highly symbolic year for the regime. The Centennial of the death of José de San Martín gave Perón the opportunity, on the one hand, to tighten his control over the media through the parliamentary Visca-Decker Commission, and, on the other hand, to create a new source of legitimacy by linking the figure of San Martín with his own. This association would be obvious in the textbooks approved for 1951 (see Chapter 6). The new direction given to education was thus accompanied by an open exaltation of the regime.

Although the student homages to Perón and Eva did not have the institutionalized character they would under the tenure of Méndez de San Martín, Ivanissevich did not miss a single opportunity to show his loyalty to the president and his wife. This was exemplified in a speech he gave on October 18, 1949, for the opening of a student dormitory in the National Institute of Physical Education. Ivanissevich reminded his audience, "Today, on

San Perón Day, as an homage of loyalty to his doctrine, we gather to remember, with concrete accomplishments, Your Exellency, Mr. President of
the Republic, and the Lady President." This unconditional loyalty was sometimes presented in a more picturesque manner. In a talk broadcast on the
national radio channel, Ivanissevich explained that among the superlative
virtues of the president, not the least important was that General Perón "is
very careful with his clothing. You will never see a spot on his suit, not even
the ashes of a cigarette." Of course, he would add, this was not because
Perón had servants cleaning his suits, but because he himself was very careful never to stain them.

Ivanissevich turned the Ministry of Education into one of the most
visible institutions of the state. The minister frequently spoke on the radio,
and the actions of the Ministry were publicized through "education news"
clips shown in movie theaters. Both primary and secondary students were a
constant presence in the streets, as they were often taken out of the classrooms to participate in parades and celebrations and on excursions organized by the Ministry.[38]

While Ivanissevich was in charge of education, his influence was felt in other
areas as well. The regime attempted to link its imagery and "doctrine" to the
principles of nationalism and the Catholic religion. The difference now was
that it was less a question of "Catholicizing" or "nationalizing" Peronism,
and more a question of the "Peronizing" of nationalism and Catholicism.
According to official propaganda, one of the virtues of Peronism was precisely that it had perfected and surpassed these principles. The role of education was to engrave these ideas onto children's minds. At the same time, it
cannot be denied that Ivanissevich contributed to the modernization of the
system's structure. Many of his reforms survived not only his removal in
1950 but outlasted the Peronist regime as well. This seems to be another
example of the tension between modernity and traditionalism that permeated other areas of Peronist discourse and policies.[39]

The Méndez de San Martín Years

In 1950, Ivanissevich was forced to resign from his post. The reasons
for his dismissal are not clear, but it has been said that it was related to a
growing hostility toward him on the part of Eva Perón. Ivanissevich was
replaced by another medical doctor (although a less prestigious one),
Dr. Armando Méndez de San Martín, who had close ties to Eva and had

actively participated in the events of October 17, 1945. In September 1946 he had been appointed administrator of the Sociedad Argentina de Beneficencia, and in 1948, director of Asistencia Social.

Both Ivanissevich's dismissal and his replacement by Méndez de San Martín were unexpected. Apparently Méndez de San Martín himself was surprised and could not provide the press with the names of his staff because of "the unexpected nature of this appointment."[40] The new minister changed decisively the style imposed by Ivanissevich on the Ministry of Education. Méndez continued the centralization process, but dismantled most of the reforms introduced by his predecessor to bring the school closer to the community. The "student clubs" and "useful vacations" were suppressed, much to the delight of schoolteachers who had been forced into extracurricular— and mostly unpaid—duties on weekends and during vacations.[41]

Méndez de San Martín's tenure was marked by two important, interrelated issues: the "Peronization" of textbooks in particular and education in general (see Chapter 6); and, partially linked to this first development, the conflict between the state and the Catholic Church. Between 1950 and 1955, the Peronist government explicitly tried to turn the official school system into a center of political indoctrination of youth. After Eva's death in 1952, this tendency became more marked. Homage to her memory became compulsory, and her autobiography, *La razón de mi vida* (The reason for my life), was declared a mandatory textbook for all levels of education by congressional law.

If, during the first years of Perón's government, emphasis had been placed on the need to democratize the educational system and, during Ivanissevich's tenure, on inculcating certain universal and transcendental values in the minds of children, during Méndez de San Martín's years the key value seems to have been "indoctrination." On a more general level, after 1950 "doctrine" became one of the most important components of the Peronist political imagery. In a speech delivered in 1953, Perón defined himself as the first indoctrinator of the nation who "delegated to the Argentine teachers and professors the responsibility of inculcating [the Peronist doctrine] in the children and youth of the New Argentina."[42] The Second Five-Year Plan of the government explicitly established that each school should be a "*unidad básica* of propaganda for the plan," and that education should be based on the foundations of national doctrine. A decree of 1953 established that the teachers' objective should be to spread among the students and outside the classroom "the national doctrine, its foundations, its achievements, and its scope."[43]

What were the foundations of the national doctrine? In 1952 the Ministry of Education published a series of "Handbooks for the Argentine

Teacher," which were intended to provide guidance for teachers' duties. In the second issue of this series, an article entitled "Observations on the Primary School Curricula" noted:

> The syllabi for elementary education bring to school the thought of General Perón, a thinking that has crystallized into a doctrine, *justicialismo*, national in scope and destined to clarify in the collective Argentine soul the high ideals of the Nation. The school, as an instrument created by the state to assure its projection into the future, and the teacher, as the agent of the state, should both adjust their work to the postulates of that doctrine. General Perón has said, addressing the high officials of the national administration, "Those who don't follow the doctrine which has been created for the Nation, are against the Nation . . . social justice, economic independence, and the sovereignty of the state cannot be denied by any Argentine; . . . they cannot even be discussed." On the other hand, it is up to the state and not to the teacher to set the goals of education.

This passage shows how Peronism displaced the meaning of certain familiar concepts. "Spiritual unity," not mentioned but implicit in the text above, which at the beginning of Perón's regime found its expression in loyalty to the nation, now implied loyalty to the state. Once the state replaced the nation, it was a logical leap to make Perón the embodiment of the state and, therefore, of the nation.

The indoctrination and co-optation of youth would take place not only in the classrooms, but also through less formal venues. These included children's magazines published by the regime and sporting events for children, and other institutions, such as the Unión de Estudiantes Secundarios (UES), set up to "frame" youth. The UES had two branches, one for male students and one for female students; the latter was located in the presidential residence. Although the UES was presented by the regime as a kind of sporting club for students in high school, it was in fact a political center of indoctrination. In theory, participation in the activities of the UES was voluntary, but the students who failed to join could be penalized. The government also offered strong material incentives to students who took part in the UES.

These attempts to ally youth with the Peronist regime served to deepen the already-existing tensions between the state and the Catholic Church, which were especially evident at the end of the period under consideration. During Perón's second term, it became clear that the state and the Church were involved in a struggle for the control of symbolic space. Peronist political imagery was acquiring the characteristics of a true political religion, which did not accept alternatives. A memorandum issued by the Ministry of Education in February 1953, for example, required all teachers of religion to adjust their teachings to the Doctrina Nacional Justicialista.[44] In November 1954, positions for "spiritual counselors" were created within public schools, to be provided by the Fundación Eva Perón. Finally, in 1955, when the conflict between the Church and the state began to take a violent turn, the religious education established in 1943 was eliminated.[45]

Méndez de San Martín gave new impetus to the centralization of the educational system. A decree passed in 1953 gave the federal government a monopoly over the granting of schoolteachers' degrees. This was also a potentially conflicting issue since, traditionally, most of the private normal schools were part of religious Catholic organizations. Moreover, during Méndez de San Martín's tenure, the system of technical education was enlarged, and the Universidad Obrera Nacional finally opened its doors.

The universities also suffered the consequences of the new directions in education policy. The university law, which had been passed in 1947, was modified in 1953. The new law (No. 14,297) had no precedents in modern Argentine legislation. For the first time, the state would not only regulate the internal administration of the universities but it was also granted the right to issue directives concerning the content of the courses offered. According to Law 14,297, the courses offered at university level should reaffirm national consciousness in the manner ordered by the Constitution of 1949. The first article of the law made clear that higher education should be "humanistic . . . with a preference for technical specialization, and [had] to inculcate [in the minds of students] the notion of social responsibility and the conscientiousness to serve their people." The second article went a step farther by making mandatory in the academic curricula of universities courses devoted to students becoming versed in the national doctrine and the fundamentals of the Constitution of 1949. The new law granted student representation in the academic administration of the university, provided that student delegates were part of any "recognized union body," that is to say, one accepted by the government (Article 59). Perón's goal was clearly to obtain control of the universities. As Tulio Halperín Donghi points out, unlike other levels of education, "the university for Perón represented a political problem rather than an ideological one."[46]

During his administration, Perón dramatically expanded the public educational system and progressively transformed it into a gear of his regime's enormous propaganda machinery. Schools became centers for the indoctrination of youth. This tendency became particularly clear during the period of Armando Méndez de San Martín's ministry.

In his first years, Perón had continued with the ideological tendencies in educational policy established by his predecessors. By 1950, however, the Peronist regime was embarked on a dynamic of self-glorification that required the monopoly of the social symbolic space by the state. Perón gradually redefined the components of the ideological pattern established in 1943 in order to make them fit the vague directives of "the doctrine." In this way, within the official discourse, the idea of loyalty to the nation was transformed into loyalty to the state, and gradually into loyalty to Peronism and to Perón as the embodiment of the idea of the nation-state.

6

"PERONIST" TEXTBOOKS FOR PRIMARY SCHOOLS

The tendency toward the transformation of the educational system into a machine for political indoctrination and the contradictions inherent in its discourse can be clearly seen in the contents of primary school textbooks published after 1951. Textbooks play an important role in the transmission of ideas and values for at least two important reasons. First, the material in the textbooks is more difficult to manipulate than the contents of the syllabi. Although the latter specify more or less precisely the orientation a teacher should give to a course, the teacher still has some freedom within the course to stress certain topics or give them a more personal touch. Textbooks, however, are "there," and it is difficult to avoid the meaning the author wished to give its contents. Second, texts are the tools with which students learn their first words during a very receptive stage in their lives. What they read in their textbooks has a profound impact on their lives. The importance of textbook content in the process of the political socialization of children has been acknowledged by a wide range of political regimes, and certainly by Perón's. This chapter analyzes the contents of the textbooks published after 1951, a year in which a new series of books was introduced into the schools that had to comply with the guidelines set out by the Peronist government, and compares them to textbooks published earlier.

Evolution of Textbook Policy

When, throughout this chapter, I refer to the Peronist texts, these are the texts published according to the regulations passed in 1951. The books published before that year (in fact, before 1952) will be considered "pre-

Peronist," as they followed the guidelines established before Perón came to power, even though they were actually published during his tenure. Peronist textbooks were therefore only used for four years. Their study is valuable not so much for any concrete impact they may have had on the formation of Argentine youth during Perón's government, but because they offer a privileged insight into the discourse with which Peronism tried to socialize future generations. It is then possible to compare this discourse with the one that dominated in the years before Perón. The focus is on the changes introduced in certain areas that I consider crucial in the formation of a political culture and that fit a specific vision of society. These themes include the perceptions of the relationship among social classes, the role of the state, the concept of the fatherland, national history, religion, and the place of women in society. To this end, I have analyzed thirty-three primary school texts published between the 1920s and 1955 by two of the most important Argentine publishers, Estrada and Kapelusz.

Even more than course syllabi, textbooks in Argentina had remained unchanged for a long period of time. Books approved at the end of the nineteenth century were still used with only minimal changes in the 1940s. Many of these texts were even put into use again by the Liberating Revolution after Perón was overthrown. No changes were made in the contents of the texts from the beginning of the century to the coming of Peronism. Educational authorities were, of course, aware of the problems derived from the outdated texts. The regulation for the approval of school textbooks passed in the 1910s required texts to be revised every five years. This rule, however, was never enforced. During the 1930s, teachers and authorities on numerous occasions complained of the large quantity and poor quality of the texts that had been approved. Articles published in the *Monitor de Educación Común* even suggested the establishment of a single text system, "as in the most advanced countries."

When educational authorities complained about the poor quality of some texts, they were, in fact, expressing their concerns about two different issues. First, they were worried about the poor technical quality of some texts, which even contained grammatical errors. Second, they were uncomfortable with the content of some of the books.

To those who were in charge of designing educational policy, the political importance of school texts was clear. An ad hoc commission appointed by the Consejo Nacional de Educación in 1939 to review the contents of textbooks stressed this point: "The textbook, aimed at deeply engraving the most transcendental notions of life in the memory and heart [of each pupil], is the instrument of the State to shape the citizen's consciousness." The commission recommended restricting the number of texts and enforcing the regulation prescribing the revision of texts every five years. In 1940, as an indirect result of these recommendations, a "patriotic pamphlet" was added to all texts; it contained the national symbols, the lyrics to the National Anthem, a political map of the country, portraits of the founding fathers, and some articles of the Constitution. Finally, in 1941, the Consejo Nacional de Educación passed a new regulation for the approval of school textbooks. The regulation specified the patriotic illustrations that the books for each grade had to include, and although it did not take effect until 1943, it remained in force until 1950.

The idea of establishing a single textbook published by the state that would serve as the mandatory text for all schools was again considered at the beginning of Perón's tenure. In July 1946 several Peronist senators, including Admiral Alberto Teissaire and Ramón Saadi, introduced a bill to this effect in the Senate, according to which the book would be selected from among submissions put forward in a public competition. This bill, which never became law, was nevertheless the topic of a heated public debate and was vigorously opposed by the newspaper *La Prensa*.[1]

Although the proposal was never debated in Congress, the use of a single textbook for the first grade was established through a resolution by Minister Oscar Ivanissevich at the end of 1949. The book, entitled *Florecer*, was written by Emilia Dezeo de Muñoz, a career official of the ministry, and it certainly was not selected through any public competition. The liberal press opposed the book. *La Nación* expressed its hope that the "introduction of *Florecer* into the Argentine primary schools does not mark the beginning of a pedagogic regime foreign to the education needed for democratic life."[2] As expected, publishing companies also opposed the plan, seeing it as a form of unfair competition by the state. However, this attempt to establish a single text was short-lived, and it is not clear whether *Florecer* was ever used in the classrooms. I discuss some of the characteristics of the book below.

Apart from the brief experience with *Florecer*, students in primary schools continued using the texts approved before the beginning of the Peronist government until 1951. In September 1950 the Ministry of Education created a commission to draft a new regulation for the approval of textbooks. The new standard, which was not markedly different from the one passed in 1941, nevertheless introduced some substantial changes in the general orientation required of the books. Whereas the regulation of 1941 prescribed that books had to be inspired by a patriotic orientation, defined in very general terms, the regulation of 1951 was more precise in its requirements.

The books should "be inspired by the spiritual, philosophical, political, social, and economic orientation of the New Argentina, in order to strengthen in the Argentine child the will to serve the fatherland, the family, and humanity."

At a very general level, both regulations required a patriotic orientation, but the concept of nationality was not necessarily the same. For the 1951 regulation, the real meaning of nationality was essentially that which fit the directives set by the state in Perón's New Argentina. At the same time, the ministry started a campaign of indoctrination for schoolteachers. A resolution dated October 10, 1952, authorized the publication and distribution of a series entitled "Handbooks for the Argentine Teacher." The resolution began: "That the content of the first of these handbooks, *Justicialismo*, presents the doctrine elaborated by General Perón and some of the main achievements inspired by it, in order to educate the teacher and to facilitate his compliance with his obligations as an agent of the state." Again, General Perón was identified with the state.

Although many drafts of books were presented for approval after the new regulation came into force, in the eyes of the ministry none of them had managed to interpret correctly the "spiritual, philosophical, political, social, and economic orientation of the New Argentina." In light of this, on July 4, 1952, the Ministry of Education granted an extension of forty-five days to the authors who had submitted drafts of textbooks in order to give them more time to adjust their textbooks to the requirements of the regulation. Finally, a new resolution issued in September canceled the competition, because none of the texts, even after the extension, seemed adequate. From then on, the Ministry of Education would accept for review any book presented at any time if it complied with the requirements. Apparently, some publishers were reluctant to adapt their texts to the new directives and were punished as a consequence. This was the experience of the publisher Editorial Estrada, whose textbooks for third, fourth, and fifth grades were banned by the educational authorities because they "ignored the realities of the New Argentina."

Law 14,126 of 1952, which ordered the use of Eva Perón's biography *La razón de mi vida* as a textbook for all levels of education under the jurisdiction of the ministry, represented a step toward the Peronization of the educational system. *La razón de mi vida*, by law, had to be used as a text in all grades in the primary schools and would also be used as the single text for the fifth and sixth grades. The law established that the book also had to be used in secondary and technical schools for different courses ranging from literature to civics. Moreover, other books of openly Peronist orientation, such as Enrique Pavón Pereyra's official biography of Perón, *Perón, 1895–1942: Preparación de una vida para el mando*, were also approved as texts for various courses.

An important feature of the textbooks published after 1952 was the ubiquitous presence of the images of Perón and Eva. In some, the phrase traditionally used for beginning reading in the first grade, "Mommy loves me," was replaced by "Eva loves me." The cult of personality was one of the central components of the Peronist political imagery, although this characteristic will not be central to my argument.[3] Instead, attention will be focused on the presence and development of other types of content related to the visions of society and political culture.

The "Peronization" of Textbooks

As mentioned above, the new Peronist texts, apart from *Florecer*, were approved after 1951. Some of them were completely new, as their titles suggest (*Justicialismo, Evita, Privilegiados*). In general, their contents were highly propagandistic in nature, and in some instances, they lacked any pedagogical value. A good example is *Evita*, a reading textbook for the first grade, written by Graciela Albornoz de Videla, who was the author of other similar texts. The first two words presented in the text were "Eva" and "Evita," replacing the traditional "*mamá*" and "*mamita*." On page thirty-three, the following reading on female suffrage appeared (keep in mind that as a book for first grade it was for pupils who were just learning to read): "Mommy and Daddy voted yesterday. It was the first time Mommy did so. They have done a good thing in allowing women to vote. When I grow up, I will also vote. Eva Perón defended with enthusiasm and energy the achievement of women's suffrage." *Evita* is probably an extreme example. Other texts approved after 1951 were adaptations of old texts already in use.

A curious example is the books written by Luis Arenas, *Tierra fecunda* and *Tiempos nuevos*. He had authored several texts before Peronism for the Estrada publishing house. *Tierra fecunda* was a draft submitted to the ministry for approval in 1951. The copy I was able to examine was very primitive; it looked like a rough draft and was covered with handwritten corrections, probably made by some ministry official. Most of these corrections were later incorporated in *Tiempos nuevos*, published in 1953, which thus seems to be a corrected version of *Tierra fecunda*. A comparison between these two versions allows us to detect the dimension of the changes required by the educational authorities in the content of the textbooks.

In *Tierra fecunda*, there were allusions to Perón, Eva, and the Fundación Eva Perón, but they were not explicit. For example, a reading on "Evita Children's Soccer Championships" noted that the games had been coordinated by "the organization." In *Tiempos nuevos*, however, it was made clear that "the organization" was the Fundación Eva Perón. In the same way, the chapter entitled "The New Country" in the first version came to be called "The New Argentina" in the corrected version, following a handwritten suggestion by an evaluator. Even more interesting are the alterations introduced in certain references to national history and to the place of Argentina in the world. The chapter in *Tierra fecunda* mentioned above ended:

> Incorporated one century and a half ago into the concert of free nations, our country has charted its course through the channels of progress and technology, and today advances along the steep paths of the sciences and the arts. We have not achieved the same degree of excellence in all fields, but in our hearts there is a will to constantly better ourselves.

The revised version, however, read:

> Incorporated one century and a half ago into the concert of free nations of the world, our country has charted its course through the channels of progress and technology, and today advances along the shining path of *justicialismo*. Led by the firm hand of General Juan Domingo Perón, the New Argentina is heading with a clear sense of direction to the shores of its finest destiny. The people have trust in their leader, because he has shown that he possesses both great ability and patriotism.

What in the original version was presented as the still-incomplete result of a century and a half of evolution, in the corrected version was condensed into the "achievements" of Perón. This condensed version of the past can also be seen in the passage devoted to "national unity." The original version read: "To these two names [Urquiza and Mitre] we must now add in the gallery of the great builders of our nation [the names of] Domingo Faustino Sarmiento, Nicolás Avellaneda, and Julio Argentino Roca. All of them laid the foundations of Argentine greatness which today is our pride as children of this land" (p. 123). The new version, however, ran as follows: "A century has passed since then, a century of slow progress and painful efforts for the country. Today, after a tenacious struggle, we can say that the dream of those great men has been achieved. The dawn of *justicialismo* shines in the sky of the fatherland" (p. 171).

Even what could be characterized as essentially Peronist topics, such as the Seventeenth of October, suffered changes at the hands of the anonymous evaluator. In the original version, the "loyalty" shown by the people in 1945 was framed in the context of other examples of historic loyalties, such as the Reconquest (after the English invasions of 1806 and 1807), or the heroic death of Sargento Facundo Cabral while saving San Martín's life. In the corrected version of *Tiempos nuevos*, all the attempts at contextualizing the founding date of Peronism were eliminated. Instead, the text points out that it was a question of "a hopeful people making an act of faith" (p. 63). The intention was to stress both the mythical and unique character of an event that did not admit of historical comparison.

The readings on the extension of political rights to women show similar emendations. While *Tierra fecunda* stressed the progressive character of the measure, in the corrected version it was made clear that the granting of women's suffrage had been the result of Eva Perón's lobbying. In the original version there were nine readings that can be characterized as openly propagandist; in the corrected version, there were more than twenty.

Luis Arenas was also the author of numerous other texts used during the Peronist period. All of them appear to be adaptations of previous texts in which he incorporated Peronist "touches" to comply with the requirements of the ministry. In a passage about ambulance service and public assistance, which had been included in almost all his pre-Peronist textbooks, Arenas added this final paragraph in the version included in *Agua clara* (1954): "at any time of day or night, the services of Public Assistance and the Fundación Eva Perón are ready for any emergency" (p. 99).

Another interesting case is that of *Florecer*, mentioned above. This book (although it is not clear if it ever was used) can be considered a transitional text, and the contents identifiable as "Peronist" are suggested rather than made explicit. The first topic related directly to the Peronist government is introduced on page forty-nine—the nationalization of the railways. However, other themes indirectly linked to Peronism, but which would become very important in Peronist texts after 1951, were already present in *Florecer*. These include the emphasis given to tradition and the figure of San Martín— the book was, in fact, dedicated to San Martín—and the specific references to Catholic symbolism. Although neither Perón nor Eva is named explicitly, the Fundación Eva Perón was introduced implicitly on page fifty-two: "A block away from my house I find a very old woman who can hardly walk. . . . Old people should be taken care of. Last night, Dad told Mom: 'Now old people can live in peace, they have their rights.' Why did Dad say that?"

On the following page there is a picture of an old couple with a portrait of Eva behind them.

Peronist Texts and Political Culture

Although the introduction of openly Peronist topics was one of the most evident characteristics of the texts approved after 1951, the most relevant changes were, in fact, of another nature. The following section analyzes how Peronist texts changed the presentation of values relevant to the formation of political culture. These texts tried to break away from the traditional vision associated with the liberal discourse that presented society as composed of independent individuals. Moreover, they introduced new social actors and reformulated the traditional image of the role of the state.

Charity versus the State:
How Class Relations Became a Public Matter

In pre-Peronist texts the concept of poverty was generally linked to moral precepts. Poor people were always "good" people. Giving money to the poor was an individual act and a moral duty for the rich. When a poor person performed a charitable action, the moral reward was doubled. This portrayal of poverty in textbooks seems to have been common not only in Argentina, but in other countries as well.[4]

The message of the readings in pre-Peronist books was that the social order could not be changed, and that poverty was an inherent element of the social order and not the possible result of its injustice or imperfections. In fact, the existence of poor people had a positive value, since it gave rich people the chance to improve (and show off) their moral qualities through charity. As a reading in *El sembrador* declared (1st edition, 1926; republished in 1956): "Where there are rich people who take care of the poor, [there are] wise and philanthropic people who practice charity with nobility."

Poor people, besides being poor, were usually children, the elderly, or women, which stressed their weakness and dependency. However, in Argentine texts, unlike the Italian texts studied by Umberto Eco, the poor always worked or, if elderly, had worked.[5] When in *Por nuevos caminos* (14th edition, 1949), a boy mistreated a female beggar, his mother reprimands him with the following words: "Think about the fact that [this woman] might have a child like you; she might work to support her family, and her wage is probably not enough. Respect other people's misfortunes, and within your means to give, give always, but without making other people feel you are giving."

Notably absent from the pre-Peronist readings dealing with poverty or charity was the state.[6] Acts of charity, in order to be valid, had to be individual and required a personal relationship between the donor and the recipient. In *El forjador* (1st edition, 1932, quote from 1942 edition), for example, Luis Arenas included a reading in which it was made clear that:

> When I give to an old people's home, it seems as if I am trying to get rid of all the elderly that life can put on my shoulders. . . . When I donate money to a hospital, it is as if I am freeing myself from the care of all its sick. When I donate money for the children, I ignore their education and support. . . . True charity is when I care for the elderly in my life, for the old servant in my house, if I cannot provide her with her own; charity is when I get involved in the education of the orphan left behind by my neighbor who is poor, and help him find a job.

This concept of charity, omnipresent in pre-Peronist texts, completely vanishes from the Peronist texts. The charitable act is replaced by the action of the state or, more frequently, that of the Fundación Eva Perón. It was no longer charity but "social justice." Moreover, in Perón's New Argentina, poverty (according to the texts) was not a serious problem. *Tierra fecunda* illustrates this point. Luis Arenas reminds us, in a reading on the rights of the elderly, that "no older person feels lonely or abandoned in our country. Even in the poorest families, the old are protected by their younger children. Why? Because in Argentina the young earn good salaries and there is no misery. . . . When the old have no families, they live in houses supported by the Fundación Eva Perón, an organization of social work subsidized by the state and aided by private donations."

This novel version of the nature of social relations is also manifested when compared to two somewhat similar readings, one from a pre-Peronist text, and the other from a Peronist one. Luis Arenas, in his pre-Peronist text, *El forjador*, tells the story of a queen who organized a contest to determine who in her kingdom could perform the greatest act of charity. After many people appeared and presented their charitable work, the queen rejected them all on the grounds that, rather than acting on truly altruistic motives, the participants had other motives in mind: namely, to show off their kindness and riches. Finally, the queen awarded the prize to a poor beggar who had shared her bit of bread with an equally poor child (pp. 275–76).

In this story we find all the classic elements associated with poverty and charity. A poor woman performs a completely disinterested charitable act and is rewarded for it. The participation of the queen in the good deed is only the granting of the prize. Charity is presented as a totally private action and doubly worthy if it is performed by a needy and dependent person (the fact that it is a woman beggar reinforces this aspect).

Very different is the message transmitted in *Alma de América* (1955) by León Benarós, author of Peronist texts for the primary and secondary schools. The reading entitled "The Three Wise Men of Arabia" tells the story of three sages who organized a contest to find out who was the wisest of the three. In the end, the man who wins the contest is the one who claimed to have studied how to solve social problems. In this example, what was being rewarded was not a charitable deed, but the ability to eliminate social problems—which, incidentally, are here recognized as such for the first time in a textbook. "Social problems" had been absent from pre-Peronist texts.

However, the appearance of the state and the Fundación Eva Perón in the texts did not necessarily imply a more progressive vision of the social order. In many openly Peronist books, the Fundación too easily became a sort of almighty benevolent entity that would hand out all kinds of benefits to a passive population whose members had only to open their hands to receive them. "The Fundación," says Luisa de García in *Obreritos*, "is like a friendly hand which helps without humiliating; it delivers food and aid to the needy; it is the artificial leg of the little lame boy and the sewing machine of the grandmother." On the one hand, the Fundación's work in some readings could be identified with such institutions as halfway houses, where poor people (in fact, unwed mothers, although this was never mentioned in the textbooks) could stay until they found a job (*Cajita de música*). On the other hand, the Fundación (and Eva) could also be presented as an example of classic charity taken to its extreme expression: boundless charity. Albornoz de Videla, in her book, *Evita*, offers the following "poem":

> Thank you, Evita. A job for my dad,
> Toys for me
> Medicine for my grandpa
> And a happy mom. . . .
> We owe this all to you
> And I want to tell you so.

The replacement of classical charity by the Fundación and the state as the means for dealing with poverty provided some authors with the chance to present a somewhat more progressive vision of society, one that included the perception of certain improvements in living conditions as "rights." This vision also recognized, although metaphorically, the existence of social problems, stripping poverty of its moral content. Poverty, in Peronist books, was no longer the natural consequence of the social order. However, these potentially progressive characteristics were neutralized in some texts whose authors merely shifted the old concept of charity from the individual to the institutional level.

Society and Social Classes: The Introduction of New Social Groups

The protagonists of the stories in pre-Peronist texts always belonged to the upper class. In a story from *Pan* by Juan Manuel Colla (1937 edition), for example, one can read (and this is typical): "The new maid is busy today. She says she has never seen so many people coming. . . . Dr. Alvarez Núñez, from Santa Fé, arrived at 6:00 P.M. Traveling in the same train with her was His Excellency, the President of the Nation, of whom she is an acquaintance." Most of the protagonists of the pre-Peronist texts would go to exotic and interesting places on vacation, their families had weekend homes, and they owned land in the countryside (*Actividad plena* and *Sé bueno*). When there were illustrations of aspects of family life, these would show an unequivocally middle- or upper-class background.

The Peronist texts involved an interesting paradox. The illustrations were generally similar to those of the pre-Peronist texts, showing some kind of middle-class environment (although in the text *Justicialismo*, the father does wear work clothes and a tie). However, the protagonists are not necessarily (in fact, they almost never are) members of the upper classes. A new actor also appears: the worker. The protagonist of *Patria justa* introduces himself with the following words: "My father is a stonemason. . . . He belongs to a union, where he meets with his fellow workers. All of them defend their rights and know that, in this New Argentina, the fair petitions of the workers are heard."

Similarly, the father of the protagonist in *Obreritos* is a carpenter. Of course, the appearance of manual workers in textbooks was not new. But their roles in pre-Peronist texts had always been that of "the other." In general, they were there to show the morality of work, but they were observed by the protagonists in the same way poor people were. They were never part of their families or the immediate environment. In a city such as Buenos

Aires, which, according to Miguel Angel Cárcano, had 35,000 undernour-
ished children in 1932, pre-Peronist texts presented a totally unreal vision
of society.[7] In it, the protagonist of the readings, with whom children were
expected to identify, belonged to a social class and had access to a series of
goods and services that were out of reach for the majority of the students.

In Peronist texts, workers and, less frequently, the unions through which
workers defended their rights became part of the everyday universe of schoolchildren. The protagonists of the stories presented in the Peronist textbooks
went on vacation to hotels belonging to the Fundación Eva Perón. This
kind of vacation was undoubtedly closer to the realities of most of the readers than the vacations in family country homes presented by the pre-Peronist
texts. Unlike the image of society told in most of the pre-Peronist texts, in
the *sociedad justicialista* of the Peronist texts, social mobility was a true possibility but only with the help of the state. Everybody could buy or build
a house with a loan from the Banco Hipotecario Nacional.

Society in pre-Peronist texts was composed of independent individuals,
following the vision linked to liberalism (particularly in the older texts).
The only possible contact between members of different social classes was
through acts of charity or good deeds. An example of this can be found in a
reading included in *Sé bueno* (1st edition, 1933), a story about a newspaper
boy who found a briefcase full of money on his way to school. Instead of
keeping the money, the boy found the owner and returned it. The owner
happened to be a high-level employee in the Jockey Club, and as a reward,
he offered the boy a job as a messenger in the club. Of course, the boy felt
that his best reward was the satisfaction of having done a good deed. In the
latest pre-Peronist texts, it is possible to find a more integrated vision of
society of a corporative sort, which employed the usual metaphor identify-
ing society with the human body and individuals with the cells. All individuals were necessary, although they obviously had different (and therefore
fixed) functions to perform (see *Promisión* or *Cielo sereno*).

Peronist texts presented a vision in which society was above the individual, and the concept of social solidarity was crucial. In *Obreritos*, for
example, there is a picture that shows a balance scale superimposed on the
figure of a man wearing a suit, probably a businessman, standing next to his
car, and shaking hands with a worker standing next to his bike. The obvious
message of this illustration is the equality of rich and poor. In the same way,
the concept of social justice and cooperation among the different sectors of
society is always present. The book *Cajita de música*, for example, reminds
us that "in today's fatherland, we are all equal. In this new fatherland there

is justice!" Social justice, however, is not necessarily associated with the autonomy of or protagonist role for the people. The leading force for social equality is always the state or Perón.

Peronist texts, in general, presented a vision of society that was in many aspects more real than the one presented by pre-Peronist texts. In this new vision, there was more flexibility and there were new social actors. Poverty was no longer seen as the natural consequence of the order of things. The state, on the other hand, was placed at the center of social transformation. This vision of society was, however, highly idealized. According to the texts, poverty had not just lost its moral character, but it was no longer even a problem in the New Argentina. Moreover, although the existence of social problems was implicitly recognized, social conflicts were left outside the picture, as in pre-Peronist texts. But if social harmony was the rule, this was no longer the result of individual charitable acts, but of a more global concept of social help under the eye of the state and the possibilities offered by the Fundación.

Work: How a "Sweet Burden" Becomes a Right

In pre-Peronist texts, work was presented as a burden that had to be borne cheerfully since it carried a moral content. Men, not women, had to work to support their families, and this was, in itself, enough of a reward. In *Rayito de sol* by Ruiz López, the father of the protagonist in one of the readings "goes proudly and happily to work, as he knows the sweet responsibility on his shoulders and cannot ignore that from his work comes the bread for those he loves . . . and since he thinks only of his wife and children, all work seems easy to him and all hardship is a rest for his conscience and happiness for his soul." Men worked hard but were happy because they could feed and clothe their families. No mention was made of things such as salaries, working conditions, or the impossibility of getting a job.

Of course, in pre-Peronist texts not only poor people work. In *Pan*, we are told that although people think that rich people do not work, nothing is further from the truth: "their job [rich people's] is surely not the same as that of the poor men who earn their daily bread. Theirs is different, and sometimes harder than that of others."

In Peronist texts, the issue of work is presented in a radically different way. It no longer was a "sweet burden" that had to be borne with happiness by those with a family to feed. Work was now a universal activity, and everyone ought to work in one way or the other: "Everybody works. God ordered men to work. Perón works. Daddy works, and Mommy too. I work. Everybody works."[8]

In the New Argentina, workers now toil happily, not because they must bear the "sweet burden" in order to feed their families, but because they earn fair salaries (*Obreritos*), because the new Constitution protects their rights (*Patria justa*), and because working conditions are better than they were in the past (*Cajita de música*). In addition, while in pre-Peronist texts work was presented as a moral duty to the family or one's conscience, in Peronist texts work was essentially a social activity. As a reading in *Luces nuevas* puts it, "They [the workers] deserve everybody's respect and consideration for being the ones who guarantee the greatness of the fatherland." In the case of the rich, the concept was the same. Compare the fragment from *Pan* presented above to the following from *Alma de América*, by León Benarós: "The owner of the business obtains his fair profit from sales. But could it be said that all the profit belongs to him? His customers arrive by roads that he did not build. . . . His company benefits from the common progress. The owner has, therefore, social duties. . . . The manufacturer should, therefore, try very hard to produce. His work will contribute to his own prosperity, but it will also promote the welfare of the people."

Rich and poor worked principally for a social duty: the betterment of the fatherland. In some texts, it is possible to perceive the usual displacement of concepts. The fatherland was equated with the state, and the state was identified with Perón. In *Niños felices*, a worker does overtime because General Perón asked people to "produce, produce, and produce!" In *Cajita de música*, a child is happy about the job he did during the day because Perón would be proud of him.

The State and Perón: Order and Progress

The absence of the state in pre-Peronist texts was notable in other areas as well. When the state was present, it was embodied in two institutions: the army, especially in pictures of military parades, and the school. School was viewed as a place where children went to be educated, instructed, and to learn to be useful (*Rayito de sol* and *Por nuevos caminos*).

In Peronist texts, the state had a broader presence, one not limited to the school or to a disciplinary role. As seen above, the state in Peronist texts supplemented the old idea of charity found in pre-Peronist textbooks, and it was also present in other aspects of social life. In *Patria justa* we read:

"Before, we were rich, but nothing was really ours. . . . Today it is the state who buys from the farmer." The state was present not just to discipline people, but also to help them by providing credit (*Patria justa*), to help the farmer (*Luces nuevas*), or to protect the population against speculators (*Abanderados*). The state, in addition, defined the limits of the right to property. In this sense, it is interesting to compare a reading on the *latifundios* (large estates) included in *Tierra fecunda* with the corrected version as it appeared in *Tiempos nuevos*. The original version read: "The *latifundios* were legitimate and legal, but they were an obstacle to the progress of the country. The government tackled the problem decisively and that is the reason the *latifundios* were reduced." The corrected version is more radical: "Things belong to the owner as long as they are useful to the community. And not just the water from the stream, but the land itself. If you do not work it, the state might take it away from you and sell it to somebody who would make it produce."

Of course, there is the usual identification of the state with Perón. In "Farmer," a reading included in the book *Evita*, we find: "The farmer sings . . . he is sure of his success, because he trusts his efforts and has the protection of God and the state . . . how happy the president of Argentina, Don Juan Perón, must feel for the work he has done!" Similarly, in *Abanderados*, we read about a boy who was so poor that he had not been able to go to school. Now, however, the situation was very different: "Before, he could not afford to study. Now, ever since Perón began to govern us, everything is within his reach."

Peronist texts included readings about the different official organizations such as the Banco de la Nación, the Banco Hipotecario, the Ministry of Agriculture, the recently created national airline, the merchant marine (whose creation is wrongly attributed to Perón in some texts), and Fabricaciones Militares. In some texts, the state replaced the individual effort of pre-Peronist texts. In the New Argentina, a worker could have a house because the Banco Hipotecario had lent him some money, not because he had been able to save enough to buy it.

In Peronist texts the state also has another important role: it is the sole agent of progress. This is particularly evident in the readings about the rural world. In pre-Peronist texts, the real rural world was also absent. Progress was generally identified with the urban world (*Cielo sereno* and *Promisión*). In a nation where most of the income was generated from the countryside, pre-Peronist texts presented an idealized and certainly anachronistic image of the rural world. The illustrations of rural activities in these books generally showed a primitive scene in which the farmer was working the land with animal-drawn plows (*Actividad plena*). There are no tractors or agricultural machinery of any kind, and the gaucho is still omnipresent. Life in the countryside was characterized as primitive but happy: "The rancho is the typical house of the gauchos, and it is very appropriate for different climates. This lovely shelter has taught the gaucho to be generous and hospitable."

The contrast between the primitive countryside and the modern and progressive city is expressed clearly in readings such as "Ranchos and Skyscrapers" in *El sembrador*. After describing the wonderful skyscrapers in Buenos Aires, the author compares them to the poor ranchos, reminding us that "each rancho . . . is a small temple to the past; each skyscraper . . . an altar to the future."

The image of progress presented by Peronist texts is, in contrast, truly complex. This complexity is consistent with the tension between what we could call as a traditionalist pole and a progressive one, which seems to have characterized most of the populist discourses.[9] From the traditionalist pole, all texts emphasize the importance of tradition (a "day of tradition" celebrating the anniversary of José Hernández's death was incorporated into the school calendar). Hernández's "Martín Fierro" (published in the 1870s) was considered the Argentine poem. The gaucho Martín Fierro, who during the Perón era had been elevated to a symbol of nationality, evoked a preurban and certainly preindustrial world. Martín Fierro is presented as the embodiment of a gaucho persecuted by "civilization" and escaping from it.[10] But, at the same time, the texts also stress both rural and urban progress.

The illustrations of country life in Peronist texts generally show a modern rural world with tractors and machinery. On the cover of *Comienza el día*, for example, one could see a rural landscape in which, while one farmer is serving maté, another one is lubricating the wheel of a tractor. But these images of rural progress are always associated with the action of the state (or more directly with Perón or Eva, who embodied the state). A drawing in *Justicialismo* shows a rural landscape full of modern machinery which, as the caption explains, had been acquired thanks to the Plan Agrario Eva Perón. In a reading from *Cajita de música*, a child visits his cousins' farm (it is relevant to compare this detail with pre-Peronist texts, in which the protagonists and their families were always landowners). One of the cousins takes the protagonist to a barn where the modern machinery is kept. The following dialogue ensues:

> "Now," says Ernesto, "we don't lose any part of the harvest as in past years. Each machine simplifies the job and helps us gain money and time."

"They must have cost a fortune, right?"
"We have them thanks to the help of General Perón. As he wants the rural workers to improve, he lends us the money we need."

As can be seen in this and in innumerable other examples, it is not the abstract state giving out the loan through an agency, but General Perón himself.

In pre-Peronist texts, urban and rural worlds are presented as the two poles in the tension between progress and backwardness. In the Peronist texts, on the other hand, a more integrated vision of the relationship between them is possible. While the countryside feeds the city, the city provides the countryside with the necessary technology (*Obreritos*). In depicting a renewed image of the rural world, and a more integrated vision of the relationship between city and countryside, Peronist texts showed the students a less anachronistic vision than the earlier texts. However, all improvements were presented as the result of state policy, and in most instances the state was identified with Perón or the Fundación Eva Perón. Yet the introduction of the state in texts became a characteristic that would persist in books published after Perón's fall in 1955. The 1956 edition of the *Manual estrada* made references, among other things, to the "rural laborer statutes" passed during Perón's government.

Concept of the Fatherland

In pre-Peronist texts, it is possible to find at least two concepts of "fatherland." One links it to the family, in which the fatherland is represented as a big family. In order to inculcate love for one's fatherland, therefore, it is necessary first to inculcate love for one's family (*Rayito de sol* and *Actividad plena*). The second concept of fatherland identifies it with the state and patriotic symbols. This is one of the few instances in which the state is present in pre-Peronist texts. In some examples, the two concepts are linked, as we see in a passage from *Por nuevos caminos*, by Pilar Salas:

The fatherland is, in relation to states and the people who make them up, as the parents in the home are in relation to their children: it dictates beneficial laws that rule over the whole territory and protect the life and property of everyone. . . . [It] keeps a powerful navy to protect the coasts and defend the country in case of war . . . and an army for the same purpose, which in times of peace patrols the country to help the government

maintain order and respect for the fundamental laws of the union, if anyone should rebel against them.

According to this fragment, the fatherland is the state which, in turn, is
analogous to the family. The most important functions of the fatherland–
state are to preserve order and to promote the general welfare. It is interesting to note the role assigned to the army here in times of peace.

The tension between a traditional pole and a modern pole that permeated all levels of Peronist discourse becomes clear in the conceptualization
of the fatherland in Peronist texts. On the one hand, the fatherland is associated with tradition. The figure of the gaucho was always included in the
readings about patriotic celebrations. In *Privilegiados* (a text for first grade),
for example, when the sound "tr" is introduced, the word *patria* (fatherland) is used as an example, and the illustration shows a young gaucho wearing
a ribbon bearing the colors of the national flag pinned to his chest. Peronist
texts repeatedly mention the importance of tradition, and in many cases
include quoted fragments of *Martín Fierro*. However, the concept of the
fatherland is also linked to the idea of material progress. In a reading on the
fatherland in the text *Mis amigos*, for example, the illustrations show a loco-
motive, an oil well, a paved road, a portrait of Perón, and another one of
San Martín. Of course, material progress was always presented as the result
of Perón's policies.

As with the presentation of the state, the fatherland was also identified
with Perón or Peronism. In the traditional iconography, *la patria* is depicted
as a sitting woman wearing a Phrygian cap, holding scales representing justice in one hand and the national emblem in the other. In *Comienza el día*,
the national emblem was replaced by the Peronist one. This association of
the Peronist emblem with the national one can also be found in *Cajita de
música* by Nélida Picollo.

In Peronist texts there is yet another element that defines the idea of the
fatherland. In a drawing in *Cajita de música*, a little girl is gazing at the "*tres
Marías*" (the stars in Orion's belt) and thinks: "I believe that one of those
stars is General Perón, the one in the middle is Evita, and the third one is
the Argentine people. These three stars that are always together make up my
fatherland." The introduction of "the people" as a defining element of the
fatherland is a crucial component of Peronist discourse and, in more general
terms, of populist discourse. However, it is interesting that the meaning
assigned to the word "people" in these texts is not immediately obvious.
None of them directly defines the meaning of the word "people." Yet it is
possible to find "the people" graphically represented in the pictures that

illustrate the readings on May Day and the Seventeenth of October. Most of the pictures show two clearly identifiable components of "the people": the workers and the army, the two pillars of Perón's power (see, for examples, *Alma de América*, *Mensaje de luz*, and *Abanderados*).

History and National Heroes: Toward the Homogenization of the Past

In general, Peronism is associated with a vision of the past linked to the historiographical trend known as "historical revisionism."[11] Although it is true that many of the followers of that trend were closely associated with Peronism from the beginning of the movement, it is also clear today that this revisionism, thanks to a combination of factors, became the official version of the past within Peronism only after Perón's fall.[12] In this section, the vision of national history to which students in primary schools were exposed during Perón's regime is limned, and its differences from previous periods are drawn out.

Pre-Peronist texts were characterized by the heterogeneity and eclecticism of their historical references. Even books published after 1941 (when the inclusion of a "patriotic pamphlet" was made compulsory) included different, and at times contradictory, aspects and perspectives of national history. In the book *Sé bueno*, by Juan Jáuregui, for example, Domingo Sarmiento is the only national hero included. San Martín, the greatest hero in the official history, did not appear, nor did the most important patriotic celebrations. *Gorgeos* features only a reading about the French exile of San Martín. *Actividad plena*, however, has various chapters, which cover practically all aspects of the "official history," and devotes quite a few passages to different aspects of the life of San Martín.

Other periods of Argentine or American history were also treated in different ways in different texts. Although the conquest of America, for example, was generally presented in positive terms, it was sometimes possible to find passages with ambiguous messages. The following passage in *Gorgeos* is one example: "The Indians fought tenaciously against the Spaniards to defend their lands, but were defeated."

One of the most interesting aspects of the way in which pre-Peronist texts presented national history was the treatment of Juan Manuel de Rosas. During the 1920s and 1930s, the traditional image of the national past linked to liberalism and originated by the generation of historians close to Bartolomé Mitre had begun to be revised. Throughout the years, even before the birth of "historical revisionism," Rosas gained a legitimate space in national history, as Diana Quattrocchi shows in her work. Carlos Ibarguren, who would become a notable revisionist historian, recollects in his memoirs the interest shown in Rosas by people in his classes (not just specialists) during the 1930s.[13] This tendency was also evident in the primary schools. In a two-part article entitled "The Teaching of History in Primary School," published in the *Monitor de Educación Común* in 1933, Natalio Pisano noted the following: "There is no doubt . . . that until recently, there were only a few people who dared speak about that time period [Rosas's] without showing the deepest contempt for the atrocities committed 'under the protection of fallacy.' This same contempt permeated most elementary school history texts. . . . But now is a good time to take a fresh look at that topic with more stringent criteria. Let us keep in mind that the vision given by the texts is the description which came to us from '*unitario*' sources . . . or from their descendants."[14]

Pisano had also prepared the draft of the new history curricula, and the word "tyranny," which had been used to refer to Rosas's government, had been eliminated. What in the 1910 syllabus had been termed "Rosas's tyranny," in those of 1936 and 1939 had been transformed into "Rosas and his times."

Although this revision of Rosas's image permeated syllabi and school texts, the most traditional vision, that of Rosas as a tyrant, was still prevalent. The presence of these two perceptions about his place in history generated an ambiguity in the treatment of the period, an ambiguity that becomes clear in the readings of pre-Peronist texts. Some texts, such as *El sembrador* by Héctor Pedro Blomberg (originally published in 1925 and reprinted without changes in 1956), portray Rosas in a favorable light: "Most Argentines, when they read the name Don Juan Manuel de Rosas, only think about the dark and tragic times of his tyranny. But the 'Restorer of the Law' was not only a dictator. . . . Before 1833, Rosas was an important landowner. During his youth . . . he understood the need for material progress. That was why, when his father made him responsible for the management of his lands, Rosas made them prosper extraordinarily."

Although Blomberg still referred to the Rosas period as "dark and tragic," by presenting a more humane picture of Rosas he was at the same time contributing to the removal of his evil image found in the liberal historiography. It is interesting to note that San Martín is not mentioned at all in the same text. A similar pattern was followed by Blomberg in *El surco*, which was first published in 1926. San Martín is absent from this text as well, although there are three readings on Rosas. The first is a fragment of a letter Rosas had written to his parents, in which he appears as a careful and devoted child. The tone, however, changes in the second passage entitled "Manuelita Rosas's Kiss," a story about how Rosas, tormented by the crimes that he committed, could not fall asleep until his daughter redeems him with a kiss. The negative tone of the third passage, actually a fragment by nineteenth-century liberal historian Vicente Fidel López, is more consonant with the liberal tradition.

Even more ambiguous is the image of Rosas portrayed by *Promisión* (10th edition, 1947). This book includes various pages devoted to "prototypes" and native characters. The eclecticism of these pages is remarkable. In the opening pages, we find Rosas, Bernardino Rivadavia, Vicente López y Planes, Miguel Cané, and José Manuel de Estrada. San Martín was relegated to a page dealing with "Prototypes by Province," which implicitly negated his status as a national hero. Other historical characters elevated to the category of "National Prototypes" were Justo José de Urquiza who overthrew Rosas, José María Paz (the caudillos' archenemy), Julio Argentino Roca, Estanislao López, and Facundo Quiroga (both caudillos against whom Paz fought), although the latter was referred to as "a terrible and bloody caudillo of the western region."

Peronist texts, in contrast, are very homogeneous in their treatment of history. History, following the official conception of the regime, was not presented as a process, but as a succession of crucial moments that changed reality and were related to equally crucial moments in the present. An interesting component of the "official Peronist history" was how events that had taken place during Perón's government ("achievements of Peronism") were linked to important events in the past. This was a mechanism that allowed government policies to enjoy an undisputed legitimacy in the symbolic arena. Peronists achieved this linkage by replicating historical events of the past. This was seen not only in official propaganda, but it also permeated (and that is its relevance here) educational materials. Thus, in the syllabi and texts for 1950, we are told that the "recovery of railroads" (their nationalization) was the culmination of the Reconquest of 1806–07 (railroads, like the invaders, were English). The Seventeenth of October 1945 was presented as similar to May 25, 1810. If the message had not been clear before, Perón, in a solemn occasion held on July 9, 1947, signed the "declaration of economic independence" in the same Tucumán house where 129 years earlier "political independence" had been declared. In Peronist schoolbooks the text of this declaration would always appear next to that of the declaration of "political independence" of 1816.[15] Perón himself, introduced in the texts as the "Liberator General Perón," recognized as an antecedent–replica only the figure of another liberator general, San Martín.

The purpose of this manipulation of the past was twofold. In the first place, the association of "achievements" of the Peronist regime with events of a glorious past provided legitimacy to those Peronist successes. Second, by viewing history not as a process but as a succession of relevant events, Peronism emphasized the uniqueness of each event, and thereby the achievements of the regime. These achievements, in turn, could only be compared to events from an equally unquestionable past. San Martín and Perón were generally presented together in the texts. In *Ronda del gran amor*, for example, one could read: "In the history of our nation, two figures stand out: San Martín and Perón. Although in different eras, they both appeared in difficult times for the nation. Both arrived with a marked destiny. . . . San Martín and Perón were the creators and keepers of the principles of the men of May. Perón, like San Martín, redeems the people."

In Peronist texts, Rosas was generally absent.[16] However, this omission should not be overemphasized, since it is part of a more general pattern. The period between the declaration of independence and the coming of Peronism was absent from official Peronist history. Thus, to stress Perón's glory, the entire period between 1816 and 1945 had to be eliminated. If Perón was able to achieve his three objectives of Social Justice, Economic Independence, and Political Sovereignty, it was because those who had governed before him had not wanted nor been able to carry out these programs. Perón had come to redeem the country from one hundred years (or thirty years, according to the version of his first speeches) of oligarchic government. Yet, there was no presentation of a critical and detailed vision of the preceding governments. This would have implied an open rejection of the liberal tradition and therefore open up another polemic front—something Perón was not willing to do, at least directly. What Peronism did was to ignore the preceding governments completely.[17] That is the reason that in Peronist texts, except for some references to Sarmiento (another of the "Peronist heroes"), the period known in traditional historiography as "national organization," although usually portrayed in a positive light, is given only marginal mention. The place of liberalism within Peronist discourse was ambiguous. Although Peronism presented itself as an alternative superseding liberalism, Perón never explicitly rejected the liberal tradition of the country. It was not by chance, then, that the railroads, recently bought by the state, had been named after the founders of Argentine liberalism. Moreover, Perón himself claimed to be the proud heir of this tradition as a military person from an army organized by Sarmiento and Roca (two nineteenth-century liberal presidents). This ambiguity, which permeated all aspects of Peronist discourse, becomes particularly evident in the treatment of the national past in Peronist texts.

Rosas, although practically absent from primary texts, was present in the 1950 syllabi. This, in fact, expresses more an existing tendency rather than a particular preference for his image. While "Rosas and His Times" had been an independent topic in the 1939 syllabi, and Justo José de Urquiza was part of a more "respectable group" that also included Mitre and Sarmiento, in 1950 the topic was "Rosas and Urquiza," and a bit later, "The Conquest of the Desert: The Civilizing Action of the Army: Rosas and Roca." The fact that Rosas was found together with Roca and the army in the fourth-grade syllabi suggests the continuation of an already existing tendency toward the incorporation of Rosas into the accepted legitimate history,[18] rather than a tendency to replace one official history with another, as the revisionists tried to do.

The Peronization of Catholicism

According to the December 1943 decree, made law in 1947, students in primary schools were supposed to receive (Catholic) religious instruction, unless their parents objected in writing. If parents objected, these students would take alternative "morality classes." However, although religious instruction had to be given in special classes, it is possible to see that Catholic imagery, generally associated with other traditional values (respect, obedience to authority, etc.), permeated most of the contents of the 1950 syllabi and, in a smaller measure, those of 1954.[19]

Although Catholic teaching was introduced in the schools in 1943, the issue had been discussed before the June 4 military coup. Religious references were present in pre-Peronist texts. However, those references were usually abstract. God was mentioned in general, but there was no reference to Catholic symbolism in particular. The Virgin Mary only appeared in traditional songs or legends (*Rayito de sol, Actividad plena*). In the same way, references to issues linked to charity, discussed above, also made oblique allusions to Christian morality.

In Peronist texts, as in the syllabi, references to religious topics abound. These references are, also, openly Catholic, and images of the Virgin (in particular the Virgin of Luján), Jesus, and the saints are used to illustrate the most diverse topics. A quick look at the 1950 syllabi shows us a similar pattern. In a section guiding the discussion of the advantages of bodily hygiene, teachers are instructed to remind students of the importance of baptism and penitence as examples of hygiene of the soul. However, there are two themes that were specifically linked to religion: Spanish colonization and Eva Perón.

The Spanish conquest and colonization were usually presented in pre-Peronist texts in positive terms. The role of missionaries was one of the many components of the structure of colonization. In Peronist texts, however, the role played by the missionaries in the conversion of Indians was highlighted. All the readings referring to the discovery and conquest of America were illustrated with depictions of priests and crosses. In the same way, the Catholic devotion to national heroes was stressed.

The other link to religion was Eva Perón. This topic was important since it resulted from the intention of the regime to change Peronism into a true political religion. By the 1950s, Peronism began to use and reformulate the meaning of Catholic symbols in order to link them directly to the Peronist political imagery; in other words, to "Peronize" them.[20] Therefore, the association of Catholic images and symbols with Eva's persona produces a paradoxical effect. On the one hand, it is true that Peronism introduced openly Catholic elements for the first time in school textbooks. But at the same time, this version of Catholicism was highly tinted with Peronist political elements. In other words, it was a Peronized Catholicism.

The relationship between Eva and religion was evident at two levels in the textbooks. On the one hand, her image replaced elements that in popular culture were linked to Catholic practices, such as the Three Wise Men or Christmas. In *Ronda del gran amor* (1953), for example, there is a story about children who had sent a letter to the Three Wise Men requesting toys. They receive the toys together with a note: "The Three Wise Men never forget nice girls. [signed] Evita." In *Abanderados* there is a reading suggestively called "La razón de su vida": "The entire population is celebrating the birth of Jesus, Our Lord. In all homes there will be cider, sweet bread, almonds, and nougat. The Fundación sends them. This is how Evita liked it, because the happiness of her people was the reason for her life."

The other level at which Eva was associated with religion was in her portrayal as a saint who in some cases had direct contact with God. In *Cajita de música*, for example, there is a passage in which Eva wanted to send a message of love but did not know how. She asked God what to do, and God answered that the message would be in the shape of a train full of doctors and nurses—a direct reference to the "hospital train" delivered by the Fundación Eva Perón, to which we will return later. In *Mensaje de luz*, we read: "[God decided] to end evil, and sent His favorite angel to the world . . . and on one day, God, seeing His desires fulfilled, ordered the return of the angel." As we can see, the figure of Eva Perón would serve as the articulating axis between two symbolic spheres—the Catholic and the Peronist—in a symbiosis in which Peronism became increasingly more prominent. The representation of Eva Perón takes us to another important element in Peronism, the role assigned to women in textbooks.

The Ambiguous Role of Women in Peronist Texts

The role assigned to women in society by the Peronist regime has been analyzed by many authors.[21] The extension of women's political rights and the central role of Eva Perón within the regime and within Peronist political imagery might suggest that the traditional role assigned to women in Argentina was being drastically reformulated during Perón's government. Yet several authors have shown that the coming of Peronism did not imply a change in the perception of women's place in society. However, this vision is only partially correct. Although the speeches and writings of Eva in this sense speak for themselves, the political practices in which women participated certainly contributed to a complex change in the perception of their place in society.

Catalina Wainerman and Rebeca Raijman have argued that, in the case of textbooks, there was a marked continuity between the pre-Peronist and Peronist texts when referring to the role of women. In both, the only legitimate space for a woman was the home. I believe that, although Wainerman and Raijman's analysis is valid, there are certain levels at which it is possible to see a rupture in the perception of the social place of women presented by the textbooks.

Pre-Peronist texts present women as mothers confined to the home. In *Rayito de sol*, for example, we read: "The mother is almost always in a room where she sews clothes or devotes herself to other domestic occupations . . . [the protagonist of the story] knows that his mother dresses him very well. . . . Next to his mother, he feels safe, protected, and happy." Women never worked outside their homes (nor did they need to: remember the social origin of the protagonists), and their job in the home was characterized as "chores" (as opposed to "work," which was what men did).[22] The only women in the texts who were not mothers and who worked outside their homes were teachers (who, it seemed, were never mothers).

Peronist texts, on the other hand, presented an ambiguous image of the social place of women. In *Al pasar*, for example, the new political rights of women are presented as an extension of their role in the home: "In the past, you governed the world from the sacred enclosure of the home because you rocked the cradle of the one who would be in power. Now, you are asked to continue, with your words and your advice, the work you thought was over; or take in your own hands the responsibility of leadership."

In some texts, the continuity among the visions of the pre-Peronist and Peronist texts is very clear: women had to remain in the home (*Al pasar*). Other books, however, stress the equality between men and women and women's capacity to study, work, and even govern (*Alma de América*). Moreover, Peronist texts introduce women workers for the first time. In *Ronda del gran amor*, for example, there is a passage about a mother who decides to earn more money for the family and to help pay the mortgage on their house. Significantly, the women workers in the texts are always manual laborers; there are no professional women. This is surprising because the percentage of women enrolled in universities increased during Perón's government.

Although the image of women in some Peronist texts is very similar to the one presented in pre-Peronist texts, the references to political rights, the appearance of women workers, and the like, in a sense questioned the traditional perception of the social place for women. This apparent paradox could even be seen in the quotes from some texts which make reference to *La razón de mi vida*, Eva Perón's autobiography, as the following passage from *Al pasar* shows: "Each day the world actually needs more homes, and for that purpose, [the world] needs more women ready to fulfill their destiny and mission. A first objective of the women's movement, if it's meant to improve women's condition as women and not change them into men, should be the home." While pointing out that the goal of a "good" feminine movement should be to send women back home, the text nevertheless implicitly recognizes the possibility of an alternative movement with other objectives. What in pre-Peronist texts was taken for granted, in Peronist texts was made explicit.

The Peronist government introduced a variety of new elements in the syllabi and school textbooks that went far beyond the mere incorporation of explicit political propaganda for the regime. The manipulation of the educational system by the Peronist administration was an integral part of a broader policy aimed at the generation of consensus—"spiritual unity"—through the indoctrination of the population. In addition, Peronism tried to perpetuate itself through the indoctrination of youth. The educational system was used as a tool for the generation of loyalty to the regime, but also for the reformulation of important aspects of political culture.

In some instances, Peronism introduced radically new ideas in syllabi and texts. More often, however, what it did was to redefine the meaning of already-existing concepts to make them fit the "doctrine." An example of this process is the reformulation of the idea of nationalism. What had originally been defined as the need to create loyalty to the nation was gradually replaced by the need to generate loyalty to the state as embodied in Perón.

As in other areas, Perón's government tried to replace the vision of society and the role of the state shown in pre-Peronist texts, a vision that was linked to the dominant liberal discourse, with another vision based on the "Peronist doctrine." Peronist texts stressed the importance of society over the individual, and introduced the state as an essential protagonist in the social web. However, due in part to the inherent ambiguities of the Peronist discourse and to the place assigned by Perón to the liberal tradition in his version of the past, Peronism was not able to establish a coherent alternative to the traditional viewpoint. The result was a mixture of traditionalism and modernity, which also permeated other areas of the Peronist discourse and seems to have been a defining characteristic of populist discourses in general.[23]

It is interesting to analyze a section called "Formative Aims: Values, Attitudes, and Habits," in the 1950 syllabus, which detailed the values that the syllabus was supposed to inculcate. These are classified under eight categories (the numbers indicate the frequency with which they appear): a) patriotic values: 52; b) values associated with religion: 91; c) values associated with discipline, sacrifice, virtue, and authority: 72; d) values associated with the concept of *hispanidad*: 11; e) values associated with tradition: 13; f) social justice, social help, and the exaltation of work: 35, many of these combined with religious references; g) progress: 12; h) democracy and popular sovereignty: 8. Eleven references are found to the place of women in society, of which seven assign women a traditional role in the domestic realm or in the area of charity. It can be argued that this syllabus stressed the importance of what I have referred to as the traditionalist pole in the Peronist discourse. But at the same time, as we have seen, the Peronist texts introduced new themes and content. The state and the trade unions became issues for discussion. The texts presented a more flexible and realistic vision of society than that presented in pre-Peronist texts. Moreover, Peronist texts and syllabi were the first to stress the importance of economic development and technical and industrial progress.

Peronism claimed to be a revolutionary movement that would establish true democracy in Argentina for the first time. It also claimed to be the first government concerned with the country's independent economic and social progress. At the same time, Peronism presented itself as a conservative ideology: it was the embodiment of the old union between sword and cross. The recovery of the true essence of nationality was among the regime's top priorities, according to the official propaganda. This essence was found in the myth of the gaucho.

We can only speculate about the actual impact of the introduction of "Peronist education." We have to keep in mind that the Peronist texts were used for only three or four years. Furthermore, it is not possible to ascertain how these texts were used by different teachers, whose presentations would depend on their commitment to Peronism. Should we consider significant the fact that the young people who became Peronists in the 1970s had received part of their political socialization during the Peronist regime? It is impossible to give a concrete answer based on the available elements, but I believe this question is worth revisiting in the future.

Finally, it is difficult to judge the educational policies of the Peronist government. Setting aside the manipulation and politicization of the contents transmitted through the educational system, there are other aspects of these policies that deserve to be taken into account. During Perón's governance, the educational system was greatly expanded. New social groups gained access to secondary and postsecondary education. There was also an increase in the number of women who enrolled in universities. Tuition fees were eliminated, and in this sense we can say that Perón democratized access to education. Moreover, some of the reforms introduced by the Peronist regime, particularly during Oscar Ivanissevich's term as minister of education, contributed to the revitalization of some archaic aspects of the official educational system.

List of Textbooks Analyzed

Graciela Albornoz de Videla, *Evita*. Buenos Aires: Luis Laserre, 1953.
Nélida Picollo, *Cajita de música*. Information not available.

Reading Books from Editorial Estrada

Clotilde Guillén de Rezzano Aglae and Matilde Chalde, *Mamita*. Text for first grade. First edition, 1942. Editions consulted: 1948, 1949.

Lila Blanca Deambrosi and Irma Freddi de Bedate, *Luces nuevas*. Text for second grade. Approved in 1954. February 1955 edition.

Prudencio Oscar Tolosa, *Al pasar*. Text for fifth grade. Approved by the Ministry of Education of the province of Buenos Aires in 1954. March 1955 edition.

Luis Arenas, *Cielo sereno*. No grade level given. Approved in 1942 and, with modifications, in 1945. 10th edition. Unless otherwise indicated, notes refer to the original text.

Matilde Emma Ortelli, *Nuevo día*. Text for first grade. October 1956.

Angela Gutiérrez Bueno, *Comienza el día*. Text for second grade. August 1954 edition.

Edgardo Raúl Derbes, *Mis amigos*. Text for first grade. Approved by the Ministry of Education of the province of Buenos Aires in 1954. February 1955 edition.

Luis Arenas, *Agua clara*. Text for second grade. Approved in 1954. August 1954 edition.

Gerardo Schiaffino and Cayetano P. Rimoldi, *Promisión*. Text for fourth grade. 10th edition, 1947.

María Alcira Robredo and María Lucía Cumora, *Tierra...!* Text for fifth grade. Approved in 1942. Editions of 1946, 1948.

Héctor Pedro Blomberg, *El surco*. First edition, 1926. Edition consulted: 1940.

_____, *El sembrador*. Text for fourth grade. First edition, 1925. Edition cited (without relevant changes from the first edition): 1956.

Pilar Chica Salas (Jorge de Andrada), *Por nuevos caminos*. Text for third grade. 14th edition, 1949.

Luis Arenas, *Tierra fecunda*. Text for fourth grade. Approved in 1951 under the title *Tiempos nuevos* and with substantial corrections for the period 1953–1958. Draft edition, 1951.

Elsa G. R. Cozzani de Gillone, *Mensaje de luz*. Text for third grade. Luxury edition of four copies. Approved and published in 1953.

Luis Arenas, *El forjador*. Text for higher grades. First edition, 1932. 13th edition, 1940.

Graciela A. Albornoz de Videla, *Justicialismo*. Text for fourth grade. Luxury edition, 1953. Approved in 1953.

Luis Arenas, *Tiempos nuevos*. Text for fourth grade. Luxury edition. Authorized in 1953. Edition of 1953.

Amalia Luisa Bruzzone, *Ronda del gran amor*. Text for third grade. 1953. *Manual de 4to grado* of 1956.

Books Published by Editorial Kapelusz

Angela Gutiérrez Bueno, *Privilegiados*. Text for first grade. 1953.
Luisa F. de García, *Patria justa*. Text for third grade. March 1955.
———, *Obreritos*. Text for second grade. February 1955.
María Alicia Domínguez, *Niños felices*. Text for second grade. 1953.
Fernando Veronelli, *Abanderados*. Text for first grade. January 1955.
Catalina B. Malatini de Gutiérrez and Rafael Gutiérrez, *Abejitas*. Text for first grade. First edition, 1942. Seventh reprinting, 1948.
Alberto Benito, *Orientación*. Text for sixth grade. 1957.
Miguel Angel Gómez, *Alma y Belleza*. Text for sixth grade. 1948. Presented for approval in Mendoza.
Roberto Parodi, *Gorgeos*. Text for first grade. 1935.
León Benarós, *Alma de América*. Text for fifth grade. Approved by the Ministry of Education of the province of Buenos Aires in 1955.
Juan Jáuregui, *Sé bueno*. Text for third grade. Approved by the Ministries of Education of the provinces of Santa Fe, Corrientes, and others. First edition, 1933. 16th edition, 1945.
Concepción de Prat Gay de Constela, *Actividad plena*. Readings for third grade. First edition, 1937. 13th edition, 1945.
Rafael Ruiz López, *Rayito de sol*. Text for second grade. 6th edition, 1931. No information available about the first edition.

IV

THE GENERATION OF
PASSIVE CONSENSUS

Thus far, we have discussed the ways in which the Peronist regime attempted to generate and utilize certain "formal mechanisms," with the objective of mobilizing and indoctrinating diverse sectors of society, and achieved a partial success. By "formal mechanisms" I mean those which required the extensive participation of the state apparatus and the formal structures of the regime, such as the Peronist unions. Those were the means for the politicization of the educational system and the use of the political rituals dealt with in Parts II and III. But in its search for a wider base of support, the Peronist regime also established a series of "informal mechanisms" aimed at the mobilization of sectors previously not directly integrated into its structure. Although the "formal mechanisms" were aimed at obtaining active support of the government through the direct mobilization and indoctrination of the people, the "informal mechanisms" attempted to secure what we may term "passive consensus." This "passive consensus" would be achieved through the politicization of certain aspects of daily life and popular culture.

By "passive consensus"—a concept introduced by Renzo De Felice in his monumental biography of Mussolini[1]—I mean the voluntary participation in regime-sponsored activities, a participation which did not necessarily involve active political support but which implied at least a benevolent neutrality toward it. These activities, such as the sports competitions for children organized by the Fundación Eva Perón, were surrounded by political imagery, and participants on many occasions were required to perform some political rituals in support of the regime. Such participation was not necessarily evidence of open support for the regime. Some of these activities were attractive enough in themselves to capture the interest of people of different political affiliations.

Unlike the totalitarian and authoritarian European regimes of the interwar period, the Peronist state did not establish a structured system for the political organization of youth, nor did it create formal mechanisms for the organization of workers' leisure time.[2] It did, however, attempt to create a network of semiofficial institutions that would contribute to the generation of patterns of social behavior that effectively blurred the distinction between the public and private spheres. In doing so, the Peronist regime sought to obtain the support of sectors of society that traditionally had been excluded from political life, such as women, who had recently been granted the right to vote, and the rural and urban poor. These attempts at politicizing (and ultimately "Peronizing") certain aspects of everyday life were a step forward in the creation of the "spiritual unity" that, as we know, was one of Perón's principal objectives.

The incorporation of new groups into political life also served as a political and social counterweight to the unions. The Peronist union system was one of the pillars on which the weight of the regime rested, and, for that very reason, Perón sought to create a balance in order to prevent the unions from becoming too powerful. Enlisting the support of new sectors as a counterweight against older and better-established ones had been a tactic of the regime from the very beginning. As Tulio Halperín Donghi points out, the less spontaneous the entrance of these new groups into political life was, the more docile they became toward those who had assured them of their newfound participation.[3]

In these two chapters, examples of Peronist policies intended to incorporate new sectors into the political structure of the regime and to generate "passive consensus" are studied. Chapter 7 analyzes the role played, in this sense, by the Fundación Eva Perón (FEP), which was instrumental in the mobilization of marginal social sectors and in the creation of Eva's charismatic image. Chapter 8 deals with the mechanisms created by the regime for the mobilization of women and children. These mechanisms were closely related to the work of the FEP.

Since the available primary sources on the FEP are scanty, very little is known about its internal organization, function, structure, or finances. A substantial part of Chapter 7 is designed to clarify some of these elements. Although the treatment of these issues might divert the attention of the reader from the main point, I believe that they are essential for understanding the role played by the FEP within the Peronist regime.

7

THE FUNDACIÓN EVA PERÓN

The FEP was, without doubt, one of the Peronist regime's most visible and controversial institutions. It was created in 1948 by Eva under the name Fundación de Ayuda Social María Eva Duarte de Perón in order to provide "social assistance" to those sectors of society which, for various reasons, were outside the scope of the state or trade-union welfare apparatus. Social assistance was broadly defined and included everything from medical services in the FEP hospitals to "direct social assistance" in the form of material benefits given personally to those in need. By the time of Eva's death in 1952, the FEP had become an extremely powerful institution that handled enormous amounts of money without any kind of external control. It was a true "state within the state."

To study the FEP is not an easy task. Almost no internal records of the FEP survived the fall of the Peronist regime, and those that did are in private collections. In addition, the indirect evidence available on the organization is so tainted with either Peronist or anti-Peronist propaganda that it is very difficult to separate myth from reality. This is probably why the FEP is one of the least studied aspects of the Peronist regime.[4] There is, however, a promising body of evidence, only partially explored, which provides good insight into the role of the FEP in Perón's government. In what follows, I show how the FEP was used to counterbalance the power of the unions and as a tool to incorporate sectors that were otherwise marginal to the official structure of the regime.[5] The latter purpose was achieved through the threefold character of the FEP: as provider of direct social aid, as provider of social services, and as an institution around which the regime could generate a mythology of Eva. In this third aspect, the FEP was instrumental in the creation of the Peronist political imagery.

In order to understand the role played by the FEP in Perón's regime, we must briefly examine the situation of the social welfare system in the country, and particularly in Buenos Aires, at the time of Perón's coming to power.

Social Services in Argentina before Perón

Prior to 1943, Argentina lacked a formal structure for the provision of social services and aid. Social legislation was limited to scattered laws that provided protection to workers under certain special circumstances. Pensions were based entirely on the so-called *cajas de jubilación* established for civil servants in 1888. During the following decades, other unions obtained *cajas de jubilación* through congressional laws. The funds for these *cajas* came from the contributions of employees, employers, and in the majority of cases from the state as well. In general, the *cajas* suffered from endemic deficits, largely due to misadministration.[6]

The *cajas* system drew complaints from various sectors. By some, it was seen as unfair, insofar as better paid workers belonging to rich and powerful unions, such as the Unión Ferroviaria or La Fraternidad, received more and better benefits than workers belonging to poorer unions. Among others, some industrialists saw the system of *cajas* as inefficient; in many instances it enabled the retirement of workers at an early age, when they were still productive. On the eve of the June Revolution, there was a consensus among diverse political and social groups—including Socialists, industrialists, and Catholics—that the system needed to be reformed and that the state should intervene to create some kind of centralized system for social welfare.

Public health services were not much better. The Argentine public hospital system had grown quickly during the last decades of the nineteenth century and the early decades of the twentieth, as a response to the accelerating growth of the population.[7] Rather than one single official health-care system, there were many systems with badly defined and overlapping jurisdictions. At the national level, there was the Dirección Nacional de Higiene and the Comisión Nacional de Asilos y Hospitales Regionales; on the municipal level, there was the Asistencia Pública; and there existed varied and complex provincial systems as well. Although on the one hand the federal state directly or indirectly funded most of the hospitals in Buenos Aires, it administered only 24.9 percent of the available beds. The city, on the other hand, administered 26.75 percent of the beds, and the Sociedad de Beneficencia de la Capital (SBC), 28.18 percent.[8] Throughout the first decades of the century, there were numerous unsuccessful attempts to create a more centralized system of public health.

At the core of the health-care and social assistance systems was the SBC, along with many other charitable institutions created in the last decades of the nineteenth century. The SBC was the oldest, created in 1823 by the liberal minister Bernardino Rivadavia in an effort to wrest away from the

Catholic Church the control it had traditionally exercised over charities and female education. The SBC's top officials were women from the elite of Argentine society, and the wife of the President of the Republic was traditionally appointed its honorary president.

The history of SBC is well known. It was closed by Juan Manuel de Rosas, and reopened when his government fell. In the following decades, the SBC went through a period of rapid expansion as a semiofficial institution. In the 1870s it was already quite powerful, sometimes disputing with the state itself, usually over the jurisdiction of the provision of certain public services.[9] The legal status of the SBC was ambiguous until the beginning of the twentieth century when, in 1908, Law 3727 finally turned it into an official institution under the Ministry of Foreign Relations and Religion. However, the SBC maintained a high degree of autonomy in the expenditure of its budget. By 1934, the SBC administered twenty-five health institutions in Buenos Aires, including hospitals, maternity clinics, and asylums, which provided more than 11,000 beds and doctors' offices.[10]

In addition to these health-related services, the SBC also organized charitable activities and awarded "virtue" prizes to poor people who met certain "moral" requirements. These moral qualifications were associated in general with values such as resignation, sacrifice, and submission. The awards ceremony was held in the Colón Theater, and was attended by the President of the Republic, various ministers, the archbishop of Buenos Aires, and other national and religious authorities.

Notwithstanding its character as a charitable institution, most of the resources of the SBC, like those of most private charitable organizations, did not come from private donations, but from government subsidies made through "annex M" of the federal budget. In 1935, for example, the SBC received a total of $12,018,094, of which only $385,344 (3.21 percent) came from private donations, and $8,715,750 (72.52 percent) came from direct subsides by the state. In addition, the state supplied the SBC with permanent sources of income such as the revenues of the national lottery and the fines for illegal gambling.

The SBC was essentially an elite institution organized along the traditional lines of social patronage. At certain times of the year, children from orphanages or other asylums were sent in special uniforms to the streets to beg. Through the SBC, the economic and social elites could maintain the facade of their interest in charities, while doing so with money from the state.

Throughout the 1930s and the beginning of the 1940s, there was a growing concern among social reformers and the state over the inefficiencies of the social welfare system. During these years, there were concrete attempts to establish control of the use of the public funds awarded to charitable institutions and social services. In 1941, the government created the Dirección Nacional de Subsidios under the Ministry of Foreign Relations and Religion, in order to ensure that official subsidies were not being duplicated.[11] Law 11,672 in 1943 established strict controls over the use of the public funds received by hospitals. In spite of such attempts, however, by 1943 the state was continuing to finance an inefficient system of social services over which it did not have complete control and which continued to operate under the guidelines of traditional charity.

The Revolutionary Government, Perón, and the Centralization of Social Welfare

The revolutionary government of 1943 moved quickly toward the centralization of the welfare system. As early as October 1943, the government created the Dirección Nacional de Salud Pública y Asistencia Social (DNSPAS), which not only absorbed the functions of the old Dirección Nacional de Higiene but also those of all organizations linked to the provision of charity, social assistance, housing, and health. This body, however, was shortlived. In August 1944, Perón's Secretariat of Labor and Welfare absorbed all official organizations dealing with charity, housing, and social assistance, and left the DNSPAS, now renamed the Dirección Nacional de Salud Pública (DNSP), in charge only of health issues.

The revolutionary government wanted to create a centralized system of social assistance, one which would eventually expand into a universal social security system, as Perón advocated from his position as president of the Post-War National Council.[12] This system would also replace the pensions provided through the *cajas de jubilación*. A step forward in this direction was the creation of the Instituto Nacional de Previsión Social (INPS) in October 1944. This new body was placed in charge of the administration and coordination of retirement plans and social welfare.

The creation of a centralized system, however, proved to be more difficult than expected. The main source of opposition came from the unions, particularly from the most powerful ones, which were not ready to surrender control of the *cajas* and place the provision of their members' social welfare in the hands of the state. Perón, on the other hand, quickly realized that the discretionary power to grant new *cajas* and specific social benefits to the loyal unions would provide him with an important tool for generating political support among the unions. Therefore, although Perón rhetorically supported the establishment of a centralized system of social security, his actual policies during his tenure as the secretary of labor and welfare were half-hearted. For example, even after the creation of the INPS—which was supposed to centralize the delivery of social benefits and gradually absorb the *cajas*—the Empleados de Comercio union, under Angel Borlenghi, bypassed the Secretariat of Labor and Welfare's bureaucracy and applied directly to Perón for a long-sought-after *caja*, which he granted. In this way, Perón secured the loyalty of the union and of its general secretary, who would later become his minister of the interior.[13] In 1946 the industrial workers also obtained their *caja* in a similar way.

This situation changed once Perón took power. He had already secured the solid support of the unions. Although he still needed to remain on good terms with them, establishing a state-controlled system of social security would provide the regime with an important source of patronage *outside* the control of the unions. During his government, Perón made serious efforts to create such a system but he could not overcome opposition from the unions, which continued to resist the plan. The First Five-Year Plan, for example, attacked the system of *cajas* on the basis of the old arguments that it was unfair to the poor unions and overly generous in its benefits.[14]

The reaction of the unions was immediate. In a workers' conference called into extraordinary session in 1947 in support of the First Five-Year Plan, the idea of a universal social security system was almost unanimously rejected.[15] Although the government never dropped the issue, the fact remains that the social security system was never implemented. In 1950, Perón still talked about the possibility of establishing universal social insurance in the long run and continued to criticize the *cajas* system for its inefficiency. However, Perón claimed, the government's objective for the immediate future was "to protect the *cajas*," making sure that the official bodies such as the INPS did not interfere with the provision of social welfare.[16] The Second Five-Year Plan made only vague references to the organization of a welfare system, while giving the unions a specific role to play in social welfare. According to the plan, social assistance would be "conducted by the state, and carried out by its organizations through the coordination of functions and jurisdictions, and by the concurrent action of social assistance services of the professional associations."[17] Finally, in 1953, the *cajas* recovered the autonomy they had had in the pre-1943 period.

The centralization of the health-care system suffered a similar fate. Although the military government had created some institutions in order to centralize medical services, Perón soon realized the political potential of the

issue for him, as he had in the *cajas* issue. Although the DNSP was supposed to centralize the administration of medical care, and the INPS was
required to perform preventive medical examinations on workers, the Secretariat of Labor and Welfare granted money to unions for building hospitals and providing health services under their control.

This ambiguous policy toward the health issue continued after Perón
came to power, when he named Dr. Ramón Carrillo as secretary of public
health. Carrillo was a fervent supporter of the creation of a centralized health
system and formulated policies toward that end. He proposed, among other
things, that the state absorb all provincial systems. He also drafted a proposal for a National Code of Health. It should therefore not be surprising
that one of Carrillo's first targets was the SBC, which was also being criticized by the regime because of its "oligarchic" nature, and the state's lack of
control over its funds. The SBC was taken over by the government in September 1946.

Carrillo's plan, however, failed because of lack of funds. Moreover, by
the time the Second Five-Year Plan was put into effect, the Secretariat of
Public Health (already the Ministry of Public Health) had to compete with
other official and semiofficial organizations. The most important of these
was the FEP, which already had a secure position in the plan.

In sum, the failure to establish a system of social security had several
causes. The first was lack of money. After 1949 the regime underwent an
economic crisis from which it started to recover only toward the end of
Perón's second presidency. Growing inflation and ballooning budget deficits were now problems to consider in the design of social policies.[18] The
Second Five-Year Plan did not earmark funds for social assistance and limited the role of the state in this regard to mere "coordination."[19]

The second cause was the very structure of the Peronist state. Perón was
essentially a pragmatist. Although as secretary of labor and welfare he had
painstakingly sought the support of the unions, he nevertheless realized the
political importance of having discretionary power in the handling of social
services, a power that could be used later to generate electoral support. It
became clear to him that the establishment of a rational, centralized structure for providing those services would jeopardize his ability to attract support from the unions. Later, when his relationship with the unions was
more secure, he was unable to overcome their resistance to such a plan.

Although the loss of independence of the worker movement—especially of the CGT, which in 1950 officially became a "branch" of the Peronist
Party—is undeniable, the relationship between Perón and the trade unions
was more complex than was usually believed. The trade unions, one of the

pillars of Perón's support, retained their veto power over some of the policies of the regime and exercised significant pressure on it. Louise Doyon has shown that most of the benefits obtained by the workers during Perón's first presidency were more the result of union pressure than gracious concessions granted by the regime.[20] Even after 1949, when as a result of the economic crisis the government was forced to carry out a more restrictive policy in granting workers social benefits, workers were still able to keep the benefits obtained during the bonanza years. This was true both in terms of real wages and wages as a percentage of GNP.[21] The same union structure Perón had created, which was a powerful component in the structure of the regime, was, for this very reason, able in certain circumstances to impose its own conditions and veto policies.

Perón, then, was interested in broadening his social base of support in order to generate a counterweight to union power. This counterweight would be sought in the incorporation of those sectors outside the union structure.

The FEP and Its Role in the Peronist State

Although the unions grew quickly during the Perón regime as a result of government policies, there was still a significant proportion of workers who were not incorporated into the system. The percentage of workers who belonged to unions was high by the end of Perón's second presidency, but it was far from 100 percent. The rate of union membership of all urban and agricultural workers in 1954 was 42 percent. This means that more than half of the workers were outside the union system and its social services. In addition, half of all state employees were not members of any union.[22] It is possible, therefore, to speak of a division in the working class between those who were incorporated into the powerful union system and those who were not.[23]

In this context, the role assigned to an institution like the Fundación Eva Perón should be made clear. The Peronist regime needed a mechanism to balance the political power of the unions by obtaining a broader base of support and by incorporating within the system those sectors, workers or not, who had been left out. It is difficult to determine whether the creation of the FEP was a rational and conscious response to this problem. What is clear is that, once created, Perón molded it to fit his political needs. The FEP would work as the arm of the Peronist government, reaching those sectors outside the union system and incorporating them into the structure of the regime. In a sense, it can be argued that the FEP served as a substitute for the social security system Peronism was not able to create. Moreover, the supposedly private character of the FEP gave it an independence and a margin of discretion in its functioning and handling of funds that no official body could ever have. Furthermore, the existence of the FEP, included in the Second Five-Year Plan, allowed the state to cut spending on social policies in the budget. Although the state transferred some sources of funding to the FEP and provided, at the same time, important indirect subsidies not included in the national budget, the truth is that this was a relatively cheap institution for the state, since it had its own financing outside the national budget. The only cash donation for the FEP voted by Congress in 1949 was, in fact, vetoed by Perón.

The FEP worked as a link between the Peronist regime and the weakest and least structured elements of society: the poor, women, children, and young people (and through these to their families), and the under- and unemployed, incorporating them into the machinery of the regime.

The Takeover of the SBC and the Creation of the FEP

It has often been said that Eva Perón created her Fundación as an act of vengeance against the SBC, after the "ladies" of the Sociedad, breaking with tradition, refused to appoint her as its honorary president.[24] Peronist propaganda reinforced this version by contrasting the way in which the SBC granted its "humiliating alms" with the "social justice" delivered by the Fundación. In official propaganda, the SBC was presented as an oligarchic organization, which had been replaced for the good of society by the Fundación. As Eva herself said, "To me, giving alms was always a pleasure for the rich: the cruel pleasure in exciting the desire of the poor without ever satisfying it. And in order to make the giving of alms even more miserable and cruel, [the rich] invented beneficence. They thus added to the perverse pleasure of the alms the pleasure of having fun by using the pretext of poor people's hunger. Alms and beneficence are, to me, the use of ostentatious wealth and power to humiliate the poor."[25]

Although it has not been possible to establish whether or not Eva was, in fact, rejected by the "ladies," we do know that the two events—the takeover of the SBC in 1946 and the creation of the FEP in 1948—were not directly related. There had been complaints against the working conditions in the institutions dependent on the SBC long before Perón came onto the public scene. In 1939 a member of Congress estimated that the nurses at the hospitals of the SBC worked twelve and fourteen hours per day.[26] Many of the institutions under the SBC, including the orphanages and the asylums, had been closed down at various times because of serious deficiencies in sanitation. Shortly after Perón came to power, the Peronist press began a campaign against the SBC, denouncing its oligarchic character and calling attention to the poor working conditions to which its employees were subjected. Just before the government took control of the SBC, the attacks became more open, and personnel of the SBC were accused of antipatriotic activities.[27] The fact is that when the SBC was finally placed under the control of the state, a measure consistent with the tendency toward the centralization of the social services under Perón, nobody seemed particularly offended. Neither *La Prensa* nor *La Nación* considered the issue important enough to devote an editorial to it. Not even the Radical Party opposition in Congress defended the institution.[28] The Catholic Church, apparently more interested in securing its foothold in the area of public education than in irritating the government by defending the SBC, did not react.[29]

The new administrator, Armando Méndez de San Martín (later administrator of the FEP and minister of education), modernized the bureaucratic structure of the SBC and improved the working conditions in the hospitals. In March 1947 the government granted new salary scales to the SBC's employees.[30] In addition, the uniforms and identification numbers used for patients were abolished. Under the new administration, the SBC created new agencies such as the *refugios maternales* for pregnant minors and single mothers.[31]

The takeover of the SBC was consistent with the Peronist policy of centralizing the welfare system. The SBC was too powerful, and its autonomy was not feasible within Perón's plan. The takeover was also made easier because the institution was perceived as a stronghold of the oligarchy and because most of the accusations against it seemed to have had some basis in reality. Finally, toward the end of 1948, the SBC was absorbed by the new Dirección Nacional de Asistencia Social (DNAS), which was also placed under the supervision of Méndez de San Martín. It is therefore not easy to establish a direct link between the elimination and absorption of the SBC and the creation of the FEP in 1948, except for Méndez de San Martín's accumulation of posts. Actually, the two events seem contradictory, because the FEP remained outside the jurisdiction of the DNAS, which was supposed to centralize the social welfare system. The goals of the FEP and the DNAS overlapped. The FEP was intentionally not included in the DNAS, since it was supposed to act as a substitute for the centralized social security system that Perón was ultimately unable to set up. In this way, it would also keep an even greater degree of discretionary power.

The FEP and the Role of Eva in the Peronist Regime

The process that brought Perón to power was unique in many respects. He won the election in 1946 against a coalition of all the traditional political parties (except the conservatives) without himself heading a real party. From the beginning, Perón tried to base his legitimacy on "direct contact" with the people and on the memory of the policies he carried out as secretary of labor and welfare. Since the opposition from the start questioned the legitimacy of the regime,[32] Perón constantly needed to recreate the sources of his legitimacy (real or imagined), stressing the existing continuities between Colonel Perón, secretary of labor and welfare, and General Perón, President of the Nation. However, his functions as president did not allow him to keep day-to-day contact with his constituency, except at very necessary times. It was Eva Perón who would have to act as the symbolic link in this continuity. In this way, she became the only First Lady, since Rosas's wife, Doña Encarnación Ezcurra, to play a crucial role in her husband's government.

Eva's political activities began to develop even before Perón was elected. In 1944 she had participated in a radio program called *Hacia un Futuro Mejor* (Toward a better future). The program was more or less openly propaganda for the policies carried out by the secretary of labor and welfare. Immediately after Perón came to power, it was obvious that Eva would not be a traditional First Lady. She was seen with Perón in all his official activities, including his visits to the unions. She was soon replacing him when he could not attend such functions. Her role went far beyond the merely ceremonial. Although officially she did not hold any position, Eva became a very powerful figure within the regime, able to attract personal loyalty even from government administrators.

Shortly after Perón came to power, he gave Eva an office at the Central Post Office Building where she started to receive representatives from the unions. Gradually, she became a necessary bridge between the unions and Perón. Through her, the unions could avoid the Secretariat of Labor and Welfare's bureaucracy and get to Perón directly. In September 1946, Eva took an important step and moved her office to the building of the Concejo Deliberante, where the old Secretariat had had its offices.

In the speeches Eva soon began to deliver, she stressed her role as the bridge between Perón and the people, talking to them in the name of Perón, and to Perón in the name of the people. She also emphasized her role as a link of continuity between Perón the secretary of labor and Perón the president:

In the same way that fate made me the wife of General Perón, your president, it also made me acquire the parallel notion of what it means to be the wife of Colonel Perón, the fighter for social justice. It is not possible to be the wife of the president of the Argentine people without being at the same time the wife of the first Argentine worker. It is not possible to come to the high and useless position of wife of General Perón, and at the same time forget the tenacity and struggle involved in being the wife of the old Colonel Perón, the defender of the *descamisados*.[33]

Eva, therefore, became a crucial element in the relationship between the regime and the unions.[34] This role was particularly clear when, during the wildcat strike of the railroad workers of early 1951, Eva personally visited all the union locals on strike, urging them to go back to work. Her relationship with the unions would be crucial for the financing of the FEP.

The Fundación de Ayuda Social María Eva Duarte de Perón was legally born on June 19, 1948, almost two years after the takeover of the SBC. Eva, however, had already begun her social work shortly after Perón was inaugurated. She gradually became not only the bridge between the state and the unions but also the bridge between the center of power and the most marginal sectors of society, such as the urban and rural poor, the aged, and the unemployed. During 1946 she distributed gifts and conducted charity drives. In December 1946, cider and fruitcake were distributed for the first time among the needy using the official postal service. As early as August the Asociación del Personal de Hospitales y Sanatorios Privados (Hospital and Private Clinic Workers' Association), in a meeting in her honor, gave Eva the title "First Samaritan."[35] In 1947 the work of what by then was known as Obra de Ayuda Social Doña María Eva Duarte de Perón had become better organized and more ambitious in its outreach. By June, the Obra de Ayuda Social had a semi-institutional organizational structure which allowed it to distribute clothing to 110,000 public school pupils and 500 sewing machines to the needy. In addition, it advertised in *Democracia*, which had already become the semiofficial organ of the organization, that it would distribute gifts to those who could demonstrate, by filling out income disclosure forms, that they were living in poverty.[36] Six months later, more than 5 million toys were handed out to poor children around the country.[37] By then the Obra de Ayuda Social had established a system of *células mínimas*, which would later be used by the FEP and by the Feminine Peronist Party.

Each *célula mínima* was made up of four social workers, a cell leader, and a secretary who would travel to the poorest areas of the country to gather information about the needs of the people. This information was later relayed to the appropriate institutions, which would search for solutions. According to *Democracia*, the *células mínimas* collected information on the needs of 25,000 families in six months.[38] The concrete work of social assistance was soon matched by well-orchestrated symbolic gestures, such as the declaration of the rights of the aged, among others.

At the beginning of 1948 the Obra de Ayuda Social began to acquire real estate. In January, *Democracia* advertised a bidding for the acquisition of twenty blocks in the province of Entre Ríos in order to build public housing.[39] In the same year, the Obra and the Ministry of Public Works began what would later be called Ciudad Evita (Evita City).

Since early 1947, *Democracia* had been publicizing donations received by Eva for her Obra de Ayuda Social. The unions started to approach Eva not only to request social benefits from the government, but also to offer donations. In December 1947, for instance, the Liga Argentina de Empleados Públicos (the Argentine League of Civil Servants) donated $30,000. Unions became a major source of funding (although not the most important, as we will see) for the FEP. In addition, when a particular union received a benefit through Eva's intervention, it usually donated part of it to the Obra. Thus, it could be said that by the time the Fundación was officially created and granted *personería jurídical* (legal corporate status) in 1948, it already had a functioning structure and its own sources of funding.

Organization and Sources of Financing

According to *Democracia*, the new Fundación would complete the state's tutelary activities toward the less favored sectors of the population.[40] Its objectives, as stated in its by-laws, were the usual ones for an institution devoted to social aid.[41] The only difference was that the administration was placed solely in the hands of Eva, who was not accountable to anyone. She had absolute power to appoint or dismiss employees, to dictate regulations, and to change the by-laws. From the moment of its creation, the Fundación was allowed to function without any kind of external interference. The Peronist majority blocked attempts made by the Radical Party in Congress to obtain information on the financial standing of the FEP. A good example of the sort of treatment these matters received is the following exchange between two lawmakers—Radical López Serrot and Peronist José Visca:

> *López Serrot*: I would like to know if the Fundación really needs funding now. I would ask if the congressmen . . . could tell me if they have any concrete knowledge of its resources, how much capital the Fundación Eva

Perón has, and if it is absolutely indispensable that the yields of the tax on gambling be given to the Fundación.

Visca: The question asked by the congressman is completely materialistic . . . and shows a preoccupation which tends to underestimate a problem that is purely spiritual. We cannot accept, given the Fundación's achievements, both in and out of the country, our being asked such a question whose character is merely political, sensationalist, and, if you will, a bit demagogic.[42]

During Eva's lifetime, the Fundación lacked any organizational structure. In fact, Eva made all the decisions without consultation. After her death the administration of the FEP was taken over by a board, presided over by Perón, made up of representatives of the CGT and the Ministry of Labor and Welfare. The FEP suffered a process of bureaucratization, and its structures became more rigid. Perón also imposed a stricter control on its expenditures.

Although legally the FEP was a private institution and theoretically completely independent of the state, its semiofficial character was difficult to hide. Most of its technical personnel belonged to the Ministry of Finance. In fact, the minister of finance, Ramón Cereijo, served simultaneously as the general manager of the FEP. All of the Fundación's buying and selling were done though the ministry, and the workers of the Fundación belonged to the Asociación de Trabajadores del Estado (Civil Servants' Association).

At the same time, the state progressively delegated some of its own functions to the FEP. With the conscious intention of turning the FEP into the substitute for a universal social security system, an Executive decree transferred the administration of the system of pensions established by Law 13,478 to the FEP. By 1949, *Democracia* was already advertising the pensions "given by the Fundación."[43] In 1950, Law 13,992 transferred responsibilities previously held by the Instituto Nacional de Remuneraciones (INR) to the FEP, as well as the Instituto's income derived from a tax of 3 percent on all salaries paid.[44]

Although a substantial part of the financial resources of the Fundación came from donations made by unions and the CGT, it is also true that the state provided—in general, through indirect means—major financial support. In some cases, the support came through laws passed by Congress. Law 13,941, for example, created a 3 percent tax on horse races, which would go entirely to the FEP.[45] Law 14,028, in 1951, diverted to the Fundación $97 million in fines imposed on the Bemberg Group (an industrialist family, allegedly being punished for their anti-Peronism), while Law 14,044 gave the Fundación the yield of fines on illegal gambling. But the state also made direct contributions to the FEP. A decree passed in 1948 authorized all official organizations to give donations to the FEP, while another decree of the same year ordered that all the surpluses in the funds assigned to the ministries be transferred to the Fundación.[46] Moreover, from 1948 onward, Congress each year passed laws providing small cash contributions to the Fundación for the organization of sporting competitions, such as the Eva Perón Children's Soccer Championships (see Chapter 8). Periodically, Congress passed laws making specific contributions, most of which were in the form of public buildings.[47] In turn, provincial and municipal governments also made donations in cash or in land. Various ministries also provided the FEP with technical personnel and infrastructure. Thus, the Ministry of Public Health, for example, provided technical support for the children's sports competitions, while the Ministry of Public Works provided such support for construction plans. Unlike the contributions the state formerly made to the SBC, most of the donations to the FEP were made outside the national budget.

Coerced Donations: The Case of the Convenio Cinematográfico

It has been repeatedly argued, mostly in anti-Peronist literature, that a major source of financial resources for the FEP came from coerced donations from businesses and industries. The two most-cited cases are those of the Mu-Mu Candy Co. and Massone Pharmaceuticals, [48] both closed down by the government for alleged unsatisfactory sanitary conditions. However, it was rumored among the anti-Peronists that the real reason behind the closings had been that both companies had refused to make "donations" to the FEP.[49] Although I was not able to find any evidence of the veracity of these claims, the truth is, as Nicholas Fraser and Marysa Navarro Gerassi point out in their book on Eva Perón, that after Perón's fall, a commission was set up to investigate the alleged extraction of forced contributions by the FEP. Only *one person*, a furniture manufacturer, lodged a complaint, and the case was not decided in his favor. Given the level of anti-Peronist feeling after the so-called Liberating Revolution, it is hard to believe that anyone who had the slightest evidence of having been forced to make donations would not have come forward to lodge a complaint, especially to an organization predisposed to believe such complaints were true.

It is probable, however, that the FEP exercised some kind of "informal coercion," or that some businessmen were simply afraid to refuse making "voluntary" donations. It is clear that the FEP was able to obtain donations from businessmen that it would be difficult to believe were voluntarily granted. But in some cases, these donations were part of agreements (sometimes irregular) between businessmen and the FEP from which both parties benefited. Eva, for example, could make it easy for a particularly generous businessman to obtain a credit from official banks.[50] A specific case in which important contributions to the FEP resulted in mutual benefits for the FEP and the business involved was the agreement between the FEP and the film exhibitors, known as the Convenio Cinematográfico.[51]

In 1948 a ticket seller from an important theater in Buenos Aires accused the owners of movie theaters of evading municipal taxes. A city official suggested to the owners that they could simply make a cash donation to the FEP in order to avoid further investigation. The owners of the theater made a "voluntary" contribution of $5 million to the Fundación. Shortly thereafter, however, in order to prevent future fines (and presumably—although there is no evidence of this—to avoid paying future taxes), they signed an agreement with the state in which the theater would provide a percentage of the sale price of each ticket to the FEP. In principle this agreement, which established a surcharge of ten cents on the price of each ticket, would benefit both parties. The surcharge was to be divided as follows: 50 percent would go to the FEP, 40 percent to improve the quality of the national film industry, and 10 percent to the Obra Social de Empresarios Cinematográficos. In order to supervise the agreement, an administrative committee was set up, composed of representatives of the owners and a president appointed by the government, with veto power.

The agreement was renewed in 1950, but by this time the balance of power had decisively shifted. The president, treasurer, and two members of the administrative commission would be appointed by the FEP, although the FEP was not formally part of the agreement. The agreement was reformed again in 1953. This time, 59 percent of a forty-cent surcharge on the ticket price would be transferred to the FEP. The part which in the past had been assigned to improvements in the cinema industry was now to be transferred to the Sindicato de la Industria Cinematográfica Argentina (Union of the Argentine Cinema Industry). This, however, was to be done only under the explicit condition that "in the judgment of the president of the administrative committee (who was appointed by the FEP), there is not in the union any situation which might be opposed to the national or collective interest, or which might oppose in any way the high and patriotic principles upon which the labor, social, and political orientations of the current government of the nation are based." Otherwise, the total amount of the funds would be turned over to the FEP.

The Convenio Cinematográfico is an example of a group of business-men giving a large contribution to the FEP and trying to use it for their own benefit (here, to avoid an investigation into their tax records and, perhaps, to avoid paying taxes in the future). The FEP, on the other hand, was in a stronger position each time the agreement was renewed, and obtained big-ger and bigger concessions. By the end of the period, it was obvious who was profiting more from the agreement.

Workers and the Fundación: A Complex Relationship

Although the unions were major contributors to the FEP, their relation-ship with the Fundación was not always smooth, particularly after Eva's death. In 1950, for example, the CGT passed a resolution donating the wages of May Day and the Seventeenth of October to the FEP. Soon after, several unions expressed their disagreement with the resolution, which had been enacted without consulting union members, and asked for their sala-ries back. Although Eva publicly announced that she would return the do-nations, the money was retained after the CGT and the most "loyal" unions insisted that she do so.[52] Although the donations made by the workers were supposedly voluntary, incidents such as this suggest the existence of an un-dercurrent of tension between the FEP and certain unions that were not particularly happy about making the donations.

In general, the donations from the unions took the form of a percent-age of the salary increases obtained through Eva's intervention. The dona-tion made by each member of the union was voluntary, at least in theory, and the worker could object and therefore avoid making a donation even after the union had agreed to it. In practice, however, this was hard to do, as the money generally was withheld directly from the salary. Those who did not want to contribute had to fill out a special form indicating to the union leaders and the employers that they did not want to have the contribution deducted. This procedure, of course, made the reluctant workers easy tar-gets for reprisals. Nonetheless, it is difficult to know to what extent those who did not contribute were actually punished. For example, in the Instituto Bernasconi, a model public school located in the Parque Patricios neighbor-hood in Buenos Aires, there were three teachers who refused to make dona-tions to the FEP throughout Perón's presidencies. They had their names placed on a special list, but they still had their jobs at the time of the Liber-ating Revolution. Similar situations can be found in other schools.[53]

There are other cases that illustrate that the relationship between the FEP and the unions was less than smooth. In 1952 the CGT had an outstanding debt to the Fundación totaling $125,400,021. The interesting thing is that the 1952 minutes of the FEP mention several times that letters had been sent to the secretary general of the CGT (who, incidentally, sat on the Executive Committee of the Fundación), requesting information about the funds. The letters went unanswered. In November 1952 the Executive Committee requested of the national treasury that all the money withheld from the workers as donations for the FEP not be deposited in the account of the CGT but deposited directly to the FEP account, since the CGT had failed to transfer the funding.[54]

By the time of Eva's death, the FEP had become an extremely powerful institution, handling enormous amounts of money without any form of outside control. It had also absorbed and centralized most activities that had previously been carried out by both public and private charitable organizations. The state promoted this absorption by drastically cutting the subsidies it had traditionally provided to many private charitable organizations and by taking over the most powerful of them.[55]

The state also limited the ability of private charitable institutions to secure funding. A resolution by the Ministry of Education in June of 1949, for instance, prohibited the traditional collection of donations by charitable institutions in the public schools, on the grounds that social assistance was inherently a function of the state. In July of that year, the ministry also ordered the suspension of all prizes and donations granted by private institutions to pupils of public educational institutions.[56] At the same time, the donations made by the FEP to needy students in public schools increased enormously. In one public school, for instance, the FEP by 1952 was the only institution providing social assistance for the pupils, donating $23,217 to one school and completely replacing the assistance historically given by traditional charitable institutions.[57]

The Fundación and Its Works as a Source of Political Mythology

The Politicization of Social Services

Even before the FEP was officially created, the Obra de Ayuda Social had started to build new institutions, and in 1947 it had opened the first Hogar de Tránsito (halfway house).[58] In the following years, two more would be created. The Hogares de Tránsito had originally been created to give shelter to single mothers, wives abandoned by their husbands, and women coming from the provinces to look for a job. As *Democracia* said, "The homes give aid without regard to age, nationality, religion, opinion, or sentiment, their only concern being that the streets do not witness the rebellion that comes from a troubled heart."[59] In the following years, the homes expanded their objectives. In 1954, out of the 1,615 "guests" residing in the three existing homes, only 477 were single or abandoned mothers. The rest of the cases involved families with numerous children, the unemployed, the needy sick, the aged, and handicapped children.[60]

In 1949 the FEP opened other institutions for working women, such as the Hogar de la Empleada. The very name, Home of the Employed, is interesting, because female employees had long been the special concern of Catholic associations. In 1922, Msgr. Miguel de Andrea, one of the few members of the Catholic hierarchy who would become openly anti-Peronist, had organized the Federación de Asociaciones Católicas de Empleadas,[61] and in 1954 established his own Hogar de la Empleada Santa Teresita. Until the eruption of the open conflict between the Church and the state in 1955, however, the Church did not publicly object to the expansion of the activities of the FEP, which now operated in areas that had traditionally fallen within the Church's sphere of influence.[62] In any case, it is important to remember that social work was one of the areas of potential conflict between the Church and the state, and it is thus not surprising that the FEP became the favorite target for attacks by Catholic groups once the conflict erupted. Nor should it come as any surprise that, in 1955, Catholic education in the schools was replaced by "spiritual counseling" provided by the FEP.[63]

Concerning health services, the FEP created a network of modern and efficient hospitals and first-aid facilities. In 1948 the FEP announced a plan to build the first in a series of hospitals in the working-class suburbs of Buenos Aires.[64] By 1951, the FEP had eighteen health centers in various stages of construction all around the country,[65] and two years later, there were four finished clinics: three in the suburbs of Buenos Aires and one in Catamarca, with twenty-three under construction in the interior.[66] At the same time, the Fundación organized a nursing school, which absorbed all the pre-existing nursing schools. The success of the FEP's health programs was, however, not so spectacular as these statistics seem to suggest, or as was claimed in Peronist propaganda. By 1954 the FEP's health centers had a capacity of only 1,251 beds.[67] But it is true that its hospitals were equipped with modern technology and provided health services to people who otherwise would have had difficulty getting access to them.

That the FEP was a highly politicized institution so intimately associated with the regime made the mere use of its services an implicit statement of political support for, or at least of neutrality to, the regime. Moreover, as the FEP was nominally an institution independent of the state, the services it provided could not be seen as "rights," as would have been the case had there been a universal system of health insurance. Rather, through its work, the FEP created a relation of personal loyalty between it and the person receiving benefits. Applications for admission to FEP's boarding schools, for example, had to be sent as personal letters to Eva (even after her death), who would supposedly decide on admission on a case-by-case basis.[68] In this sense, it can be argued that the FEP recreated the worst characteristics of the social paternalism of the SBC that had been so criticized by the Peronists. The difference was that the FEP used the loyalties and feelings of gratitude for political purposes, as Eva herself acknowledged.[69]

The provision of social services by the FEP was used by the regime in the construction of a political imagery. In 1949, for example, the FEP imported from the United States more than 30,000 units of X-ray film, which were costly and scarce in Argentina, and sold them to the people who needed them at no profit. People interested in the film had to go to the Secretariat of Labor and Welfare with a medical order. There, Eva "personally" would deliver the material. A record of this, of course, would be immediately published in *Democracia*.[70] Similarly, in November 1949, the FEP sent $6 million worth of medical equipment to different hospitals in the provinces. According to official propaganda, the medical material would bring "health and relief, and what is even more important, the confidence of knowing that one is taken care by the woman who has become the guardian angel of all the dispossessed."[71]

In 1951 the FEP sent a hospital train through the interior of the country. It would stop in areas where medical facilities were scarce. The train boasted surgery facilities in a specially built car, a laboratory, and medical personnel. For many residents in the regions along its itinerary, the train was their only access to modern medical care. Small wonder that among the features of the train was a "theater car," which showed documentary films glorifying "the extraordinary work accomplished by the government of General Perón and the different aspects of the work carried out by the Fundación Eva Perón."[72] As we have seen, school textbooks made reference to the "medical train" as evidence of Eva's direct communication with God.

The areas of FEP activity went beyond the provision of medical services. The Fundación owned a home for the aged in Burzaco and organized a system of boarding schools to provide education to poor children in remote areas. If possible, children who were lodged in boarding schools were taught in public schools, but their moral, religious, and political education (indoctrination, in the regime's discourse) took place in the boarding schools. The FEP had planned the construction of twenty such boarding schools, and by 1954 there were fifteen in use, housing a total of 8,516 children.

In addition to the boarding schools, the FEP also built other education-al facilities more openly dedicated to the political socialization of children and youth. Two institutions of this kind were the Ciudad Infantil (not to be confused with the Ciudad de los Niños located near La Plata) and the Ciudad Estudiantil, both in the neighborhood of Belgrano.

The Ciudad Infantil, called "Amanda Allen" after an FEP nurse who had suffered severe injuries in a plane accident, was opened in July 1949. According to official sources, it had been built in a mere five months at a total cost of only $1,200,000. It had a capacity of 110 beds and a dining hall for 450 preschool children.[73] It was a scale replica of a city, featuring small shops, a bank, a post office, streets with traffic lights, and a church. Children's activities included games, physical education, a theater, movies, and, of course, political indoctrination.[74]

It is interesting to note that, like other aspects of the Peronist discourse, the message transmitted by the Ciudad Infantil tended to reinforce accepted social roles rather than subvert them. Girls, for example, were supposed to carry out "feminine" tasks in the small city, while boys took care of those considered "typically masculine." Similarly, other social inequalities were also reproduced in the children's games. A picture in a brochure touting the city shows a child parking a small car in front of the miniature bank. The caption read: "There are always children who come to the bank by car in order to check their accounts, while others come on foot, probably to check their savings in their savings accounts."[75] A visit to the city was obligatory for all distinguished foreign visitors to Buenos Aires.

The Ciudad Estudiantil, located close to the Ciudad Infantil, was fin-ished in 1951. Its function was not to provide formal education, but lodg-ing for poor children of school age. However, the education received in the "Student City" complemented that given in regular schools with "forma-tion in civic consciousness, framed in the respect for the fatherland, for Argentine history, and for the democratic and republican institutions of the country, sustained in the teachings of the Justicialist Doctrine."[76]

Among the educational activities offered by the Student City, there were different "academies" that children could join according to their personal preferences. There was one "academy," for example, of "political studies," with a section on Peronist doctrine. During the year, this section "devoted itself to reading doctrinal works and to studying the most outstanding aspects of Peronist thought."[77] These educational institutions, beyond their political component, provided services to needy families. In addition to those institutions under its direct administration, the FEP also built a large number of schools, most of which were located in remote areas. The schools, upon completion, were sold to the state under the "Plan of the 1,000 Schools." I have not been able to establish how many of those 1,000 schools were, in fact, built.[78]

The FEP also provided other services. In 1952, for example, it carried out the Plan Agrario Eva Perón, presenting it as "an important contribution to the economic plan." The agrarian plan consisted in the organization of teams of agricultural workers—the "Justicialist Agrarian Teams"—who, equipped with modern machinery, hired themselves out to farmers at market prices. On April 13, 1952, *Democracia* announced with the usual pomp that the first team had begun work. The plan, however, was shortlived. The teams proved to be much less efficient than expected, and it was soon clear that the plan was running at a deficit and did not interest the farmers. In October 1952 the government announced that it would sell the equipment to cooperatives.

The final area of FEP activity, besides the hotels and holiday camps for children run in various parts of the country, was a network of grocery stores opened in 1950 called *proveedurías*, which sold scarce or expensive products almost at cost. These stores (there were close to a hundred functioning by 1951) were part of a government plan to fight the alarming rate of inflation. The stores were bought from their original owners, many of whom were forced to sell them.[79]

By providing essential and useful services in a climate of aggressive political propaganda, the FEP contributed to the process of the politicization of everyday life. Those who had to or wished to use these services, sometimes only available through the FEP, were forced to make an implicit political statement of support for the regime. However, there was another aspect of the work of the FEP that contributed in a even more direct way to the creation of the Peronist political imagery and, in particular, of the charismatic image of Eva: the provision of direct social aid.

Direct Assistance and the Construction of Eva's Image

Eva spent most of her afternoons in the Secretariat (after 1949, the Ministry) of Labor and Welfare receiving needy people who came to ask for jobs, housing, sewing machines, and a hospital bed. She did not have a regular schedule and saw the visitors whenever she was available, sometimes making high-ranking officials wait for hours. The sight of a long line of poor people alongside official dignitaries, all waiting to see "la señora," amazed more than one foreigner. In 1949 the American writer John Dos Passos visited Argentina. This is the description of what he saw one afternoon:

> In a small office with red-damasked walls were rows of benches packed with ragged-looking women and children facing her [Eva's] desk. Babies squawked. Everybody talked at once. . . . The corridor outside was full of people waiting to get a glimpse of the Señora. . . . Distinguished visitors were posed in an admiring group behind the Señora's handsome blonde head as she leaned over her desk to listen to the troubles of the poor women with their tear-grimed children.
> "She is too thin," one of the women was muttering aloud. . . .
> At the end of each hard-luck story the Señora reached with jeweled fingers under the blotter on the desk and took out two fifty-peso notes. Then she made out with a rapid scratch on a pink slip an order for a doctor or a doll for the baby girl.[80]

Gaining access to Eva was a relatively simple task. Any needy person interested in receiving "direct assistance" could send a letter addressed specifically to Eva, either to the ministry or the presidential residence. After some time, he or she would receive an answer with the date and the time for an appointment with Eva. Eva herself would make sure that the assistance was delivered.

The image of an easily accessible center of power personally treating the problems of its citizens is essential for the generation of "passive consensus." Teresa Mazzatosta and Claudio Volpi have described, in their book on the letters sent to the Segreteria Particolare del Duce during the Mussolini regime, how this institution (which was somewhat similar to the FEP) was instrumental in manufacturing a certain image of Il Duce and his family. Not only did this institution make Il Duce seem accessible, but it also created the image that he and his family were personally in charge of attending to the needs of the poor and delivering favors.[81] In the case of the FEP, this image of accessibility to power was more obvious because, unlike Donna Rachele or Edda Ciano in Italy, who communicated with the people through letters, Eva established direct physical contact with the people.

The image of Eva working beyond her physical capacity—"burning up her life"—for the needy was one of the essential components the official propaganda machine used to create a mystique around Eva's person.[82] Well before her death, she was being portrayed as a saint.[83] She was the First Samaritan, the Lady of Hope, and just before her death, she became the Spiritual Leader of the Nation. Unexpected events, such as those generated by her public renunciation of the vice presidency in 1951, were used by the regime to stress Eva's "martyrdom."[84] After her death, the representations of her image, now completely controlled by the government—all graphic representations of Eva had to be approved by the Secretaría de Informacion Publica before publication—were in general associated with religious imagery.

Eva's image as saint or redeemer endured in anecdotes told by people who had been close to her. Eva's work at the FEP was essential in the creation of myths about her. One of these stories, interesting because of the obvious religious connotations, was the kiss on the mouth she gave a leper (or a person suffering from syphilis, in another version of the anecdote). Apparently, the event was witnessed by José María Castiñeira de Dios:

> There were human beings in that room with dirty clothes, and they smelled very bad. Evita would place her fingers on their open wounds, for she was able to see the pain of all these people and feel it herself. She could touch the most terrible things with a Christian attitude that amazed me, kissing and letting herself be kissed. There was a girl whose lip was half eaten away with syphilis, and when I saw that Evita was about to kiss her, I tried to stop her. She said to me, "Do you know what it will mean that I kiss her?"[85]

Although Castiñeira stops short of suggesting that Eva could heal the sick just by touching them, the analogy between this story and Christian imagery speaks for itself. Eva's kissing a syphilitic is particularly interesting. Syphilis is a sickness associated in popular culture with lack of morality. The syphilitic girl was not only sick, but damned. By kissing her, Eva not only showed her Christian love, but also redeemed her. This story was repeated many times with variations and different degrees of detail. According to Arturo Jauretche, for instance, Eva was more cynical, saying to Castiñeira when he tried to stop her: "Castiñeira, never do that again, because this is the price I pay."[86] Eva would not say for *what* she was paying the price.

A similar story was told by Irma Cabrera de Ferrari, a nurse from the FEP, who was present when Eva kissed a leper. Commenting on Eva's reaction when she tried to disinfect Eva with alcohol, Cabrera said, "She wanted to kill me! That was the only time she really got mad at me. She threw the bottle against the wall."[87] In all these stories Eva appears in a semireligious aura. She touches and kisses people with contagious diseases, refusing to take even the most obvious hygienic precautions. This attitude was consistent with her image as a saint. After all, she was never infected with any of those contagious diseases. Her charisma was in part based on these almost supernatural qualities with which she was endowed.

How the Fundación Shared Eva's Charisma

Official propaganda not only presented Eva as a saint but also the FEP as a semimagical organization that could solve the problems of the poor immediately. A publication of the Fundación de Ayuda Social María Eva Duarte de Perón (the name of the FEP until 1950) shows the process of change undergone by a group of children from the province of Santiago del Estero. The children are described in this way: "A scattered childhood in run-down huts, dirty, their present diluted in an insipid horizon of maté cocido and hard bread, their future limited for the males by the sure-to-arrive form which will read 'Unable to serve in the military forces,' and for the women by a lifetime of social inferiority."[88]

The children were brought by train to Buenos Aires, where Eva, "a blonde fairy with a maternal smile, would take them by the hand to Aladdin's lamp and the talking bird."[89] The children were taken to FEP facilities where they went through a process of physical transformation, chronicled in a series of "Before" and "After" photographs. After visiting Juan Perón and enjoying the use of all the facilities of the Fundación, the children were sent back to their home province where they could tell their relatives about the magical things that happened to them. Finally, Eva's "magic wand" is compared with the "previous rusty norms, when beneficence equaled an old, severe-looking matron, wearing gray clothes smelling of mothballs, who lavished her gifts on destitute children, marking them with a uniform and throwing them out on the streets with a piggy bank under their arms to make them beg for their own coins."[90]

The semimagical character of the FEP also extended to its employees. In 1949, the FEP sent an aid mission to Ecuador with seventy tons of food, medicine, and clothes for the victims of an earthquake. This would not be the last time the FEP would send help to countries in America and Europe. This time, however, an accident provided material for another myth. When the plane bringing the FEP delegation back was approaching the runway to land, an explosion brought the plane down in flames. Many members of the delegation died and the rest were severely injured. The survivors were treated like national heroes, the dead like national martyrs. The government officially declared a day of national mourning to honor the memory of the dead.

But the story did not end there. One of the survivors said to *Democracia* that minutes before the accident the passengers on the plane had been practicing the march "Los Muchachos Peronistas," which they planned to sing to Perón and Eva upon their arrival. When the fire began, the passengers (all FEP members) hugged each other and cried the names of Perón and Eva. Only a miracle could save them, and the miracle happened. Although some died, many survived.[91] *Democracia*, in its own version of events, added a new element to the myth by subtly associating the singing of the march to the miracle that saved the lives of some passengers: "The passengers of the Douglas understood that only a miracle could save them . . . and, already face to face with death, they embraced each other in a great hug . . . and the memory of Perón and Evita made the song flourish upon their lips. . . . Then, the miracle happened."[92]

Perón, Evita, and the Peronist symbols were thus endowed with a semireligious character in two senses. First, these were the images the "believers" invoked in moments of extreme anguish or moments close to death. Second, as *Democracia* suggested, there is the subsequent judgment that the invocation of the Peronist icons might have had something to do with the "miracle" that saved some of the passengers' lives.

The story of the accident quickly became part of the Peronist mythology. In 1950, Perón awarded the Peronist Medal to the survivors because of their heroic behavior, and in particular because, "in such a tragic moment, when powerlessness left them at the mercy of destiny, in a brotherly hug they faced death singing the song that unites us: 'Los Muchachos Peronistas.' "[93] The story was later repeated on numerous occasions,[94] and in 1986 a former member of the Partido Peronista Femenino even suggested that, as she waited at the airport for the delegation, she heard the passengers singing the march as the plane crashed.

In his classic study on the healing powers of medieval English and French kings, Marc Bloch noted that a belief in the supernatural power of those kings was crucial for the establishment of their charisma and, indirectly, their legitimacy. The Peronist regime tried to create Eva's charisma by using a similar image, and her role in the FEP provided material for the generation of myths. The FEP, therefore, was not only instrumental in providing assistance to marginal or semimarginal sectors of society, but was also used as a source for the modeling of Eva's image. Even if, in moments of austerity, Perón was forced to cut back on social benefits, there seemed to have been no limits to Eva's ability to distribute social justice.

It is difficult to determine to what degree the Peronist regime was successful in generating the kind of feelings they were aiming for. Unfortunately, all letters sent to the Fundación have disappeared. After Eva's death, however, *Mundo Peronista* published some of the letters sent to the FEP.[95] Although it is difficult to establish their authenticity, there are indications that suggest they are genuine. They were reproduced as handwritten facsimiles, many times filled with misspellings and sometimes with so many grammatical errors that the editors felt it necessary to provide a "translation" in correct Spanish. Although we cannot know how representative these letters were, there are some points worth noting. One is the idea of Eva's immortality, or, if not, the idea that even after her death, she could deliver social aid. These images of an almost-eternally present Eva were stimulated by official propaganda. In its section entitled "Doctrinal Activity," for example, *Mundo Peronista* reminded its readers that "the party cells and trade unions must remember that Eva has not died; she has been glorified."[96] Moreover, remember that Eva herself, just before her death, had asked her people to continue writing to her even after she was gone. This wish was apparently respected by some. A woman finished her letter addressed to Eva on August 1, 1952, saying: "Hoping to receive your help, which I need so much, I say good-bye to our immortal Sra. María Eva Duarte de Perón as a citizen who, no matter what, will never stop thinking that she is immortal and eternal in our hearts."[97] Another woman wrote that she could feel the presence of Eva in her dreams. The woman also begged Eva to send her a black dress so she would have mourning clothes to wear for her.

However, there is more concrete evidence, although still indirect, that this type of semireligious feeling, as well as the homages to Eva, were not so widespread as the regime claimed. After Eva's death, the Ministry of Education received a flood of petitions to name schools and classrooms after her.[98] The ministry published those petitions in the *Boletín de Comunicaciones* to show the depth of the nation's mourning. But a closer look reveals that those petitions were signed by teachers and headmasters of the schools in question, rather than by parents or students. This might suggest that the petitions reflected more the teachers' interest in showing off their loyalty than demonstrating authentic popular mourning. This seems to be consistent with Julie Taylor's hypothesis that the semireligious image of Eva was more the result of Peronist propaganda than of the spontaneous feeling of the people.[99]

The FEP was used by the Peronist regime as a tool for the co-optation of traditionally marginal groups. In this sense, the FEP was meant to act as a counterweight to the organized sectors of the Peronist constituency. Perón needed to broaden his base of support, and the FEP served in part to meet this need. The FEP was also used as a source for the creation of myths that would come to form part of the Peronist political imagery. In this sense, it was one of the elements used by the regime to create a political religion.

In the functioning of the FEP and in the discourse around it, one can see the tension between a modernizing and a "traditional" pole that permeated the whole structure of the regime, and that seems to have been a defining characteristic of all regimes usually defined as "populist."[100] The FEP was presented in Peronist rhetoric as one more piece of evidence of the rupture with the past that Peronism represented. The work of the Fundación had substituted Peronist social justice for the old charity of the ancien régime. Although beneficence was portrayed as an entirely oligarchic enterprise, social justice was carried out by the people and for the people. In addition, unlike the old beneficence, social justice had scientific foundations.[101] It is true that some of the more offensive features of the old charitable organizations, such as the use of uniforms, were eliminated during the Peronist regime. In addition, the FEP created a network of modern health-care centers and other institutions, such as the Hogares de Tránsito for the protection of unwed mothers, which did not exist before.

The FEP, however, combined those modern tendencies—some real, others merely rhetorical—with a method of working that resembled the despised traditional charity. The FEP gave without asking questions. It delivered houses, sewing machines, and dolls without taking into account the actual social and economic conditions of the recipients. Moreover, and in contradiction with the regime's rhetoric, it established a personal link between the donor and the beneficiary that turned the benefits and services it provided into gracious gifts rather than social rights.[102]

How successful was the FEP in achieving its principal goal of expanding Perón's social base of support? It is difficult to answer this question with the evidence available. There is, however, some evidence suggesting that the regime did succeed in attracting formerly marginal sectors of society. Ignacio Llorente, for instance, has compared a series of correlations between the Peronist vote and several variables for the election of 1946 and that of 1954:

**Comparison of Correlations between the Peronist Vote and
Some Variables of Development for the Elections of 1946 and 1954**

	1946	*1954*
GNP per capita	.07	-.39
Illiteracy	-.08	.63
Immigrants	.18	-.29
Industrialization	.32	-.16
Urbanization	.20	-.48
Primary sector	-.24	.28
Secondary sector	.32	-.18
Tertiary sector	.30	-.14

Source: Ignacio Llorente, "La composición social del movimiento peronista hacia 1954," in Manuel Mora y Araujo and Ignacio Llorente, eds., *El voto peronista: Ensayos de sociología electoral argentina* (Buenos Aires: Sudamericana, 1980).

These figures suggest that in 1954 there was a higher correlation between the Peronist vote and those variables that could be considered an indicator of marginality than in 1946. Similarly, in 1954 there was a lower correlation between the Peronist vote and those variables that could be considered indicators of "modernity." Illiteracy, for instance, which was negatively correlated to the Peronist vote in 1946, was positively correlated in 1954. The opposite effect can be seen with urbanization. The data presented in the table suggest that by 1954 the social composition of the Peronist vote was changing and, we can presume, broadening. It was incorporating "backward" and marginal sectors. Extending the argument, it is possible that the FEP might have played some role in attracting members of those sectors.

8

THE "PERONIZATION" OF WOMEN AND YOUTH

In the previous chapter we analyzed how the Peronist regime, in its efforts to broaden its social base and generate "spiritual unity," sought to incorporate social sectors traditionally excluded from political participation. Two important sectors that the regime tried to bring into its machinery were women and children. Women were quickly and successfully turned into voters. In 1951, the first time they participated in a national election, a record 90 percent of the women who were registered to vote showed up at the polls, compared to 86 percent of men in the same election. But Perón had other more important reasons to consider the enfranchisement of women a success. Sixty-four percent of the women who cast ballots in 1951 voted for the Peronist Party.[1]

The integration of women into political life was important to the regime for two reasons. First, Perón needed to broaden his political base, and the recently enfranchised women were "fertile ground" for the garnering of new votes. Second, Perón perceived women as potential domestic missionaries who would spread the Peronist creed within families and thus further the creation of "spiritual unity." To the regime, women were not only important as voters but also as mothers and wives. Eva Perón stated this openly in 1950: "Women have an important role to play in this movement, because we will try to bring Peronism to the soul of the Argentine child, and because we reserve the right to see that Argentine children learn to love the fatherland and Perón from the cradle. Because now, . . . all Argentine children, I believe, even before they learn how to say 'Papa,' should say 'Perón.' "[2]

As I establish here, the Partido Peronista Femenino (PPF), which was closely linked to the FEP, would become an instrument for incorporating women into the political system. Although the PPF was a branch of the

Partido Peronista, Perón and Eva stressed its nonpolitical character. Women, according to the official discourse, did not join the PPF for political reasons, but to provide and receive social assistance. The *unidades básicas* of the PPF were supposed to provide alternative spaces for women's social gatherings in the neighborhoods.

The regime's interest in children was based on the same ideas. Children were seen as the other means of introducing Peronism into Argentine homes, a high priority for the regime. The Peronist regime spent large amounts of money on propaganda aimed at attracting children and youth. The semiofficial magazine *Mundo Peronista* featured a section called "Tu pagina de pibe peronista" (Your page as a Peronist kid), where children were encouraged to "convert" other children to Peronism.

In Part III, I have discussed how the official educational system was turned into a tool for the formal indoctrination of children. This chapter approaches the subject from a different perspective. Although the educational system was used as a tool for the compulsory indoctrination of children—all children had to go to school—the regime also had other more informal mechanisms, such as the organization of sports competitions or the publication of children's magazines, with which to attract children and adolescents. The sports competitions were an attempt to give political (that is, Peronist) meaning to existing and accepted forms of social interaction, in order to generate passive consensus. Parents who allowed their children to participate in the competitions, or members of clubs who organized teams, were tacitly accepting integration into the regime's machinery, although they were not necessarily making an explicit statement of Peronist faith. The same can be said about parents who allowed their children to read the Peronist children's magazine.

First we deal with the integration of women into the structures of the regime through the PPF and discuss Perón and Eva's ideas about the role of women in political life. Then we discuss two of the regime's ways of attracting youth: the Campeonatos Infantiles Evita, organized by the FEP, and the magazine *Mundo Infantil*.

How Perón and Eva Reformulated Old Patterns of Women's Role in Society

From the beginning of Perón's regime, women had been seen and treated as potential targets for political mobilization.[3] Although women could not yet vote, during the electoral campaign of 1946, Perón encouraged the creation of Centros de Mujeres Peronistas. From his post as secretary of labor and welfare, he had granted some benefits to working women. In October 1944 the military government created the División (later Dirección) de Trabajo y Asistencia a la Mujer headed by Lucila Gregorio Lavié, María Tizón (Perón's sister-in-law from his first marriage), and Haydeé Longoni. The new organization began studying the economic and social problems of the female workforce in order to make recommendations for improvements in their working conditions.

The Situation of Working Women before Perón

Women in Argentina, as in other countries, had always been an important component of the labor force. Although concentrated mostly in domestic services, women also worked in such industries as textiles, tobacco, and, above all, in the service sector. In 1914 women constituted 30 percent of all industrial workers, 52 percent of all instructors and educators, and 84 percent of those providing personal and domestic services.[4]

Although more women than men were laid off during the economic crisis of the early 1930s, the availability of cheap female labor—cheaper than male labor—played an important role in the economic recovery and the process of industrialization that took place later in that decade. Between 1937 and 1939, the number of women working in industries increased by 8.2 percent while the number of men working in the sector increased by 6.4 percent.[5] This increase in the number of women working in the industrial sector was a response to a broader trend. Between 1935 and 1939, the number of women working in all sectors of the economy grew by 27.4 percent.[6] By 1949, women accounted for 45 percent of the industrial workers in Buenos Aires.[7] In 1947, however, 60.2 percent of all women did not work outside their homes.[8]

Historically, women's salaries had been much lower than men's, and female workers had been subjected to abuses and exploitation by employers and foremen. Juan Bialet Masse, who had been commissioned in 1904 by the Ministry of Domestic Affairs to write a report on working conditions in the interior of the country, interviewed employers who candidly admitted that they hired women for certain jobs because female workers were paid a lower salary and were more submissive.[9]

Marysa Navarro Gerassi and Catalina Wainerman have shown that, until relatively recently, there was a consensus in many sectors of Argentine society that the proper place for women was at home raising children. Working women were seen as a "necessary evil."[10] A popular magazine of the twenties, for example, advertised courses for women who needed to work "either because they were widowed, or had a husband who was crippled, had tuberculosis, or was unable to perform his role as the breadwinner."[11] Women worked, according to the magazine, only when circumstances forced them to. This perception was even shared by some feminist groups.[12] This image of the role of women permeated and was also reinforced in primary school textbooks. The only activities outside the home perceived as proper for women were those related to education and charity.

During the first decades of the twentieth century, Congress passed several laws, most of them proposed by the Socialists, providing some protection for working women. One law passed in 1907, for example, originally introduced by feminist leader Gabriela Coni, established a six-hour workday for women, and provided up to sixty days for maternity leave. This law, however, was often ignored. A report of the Departamento Nacional de Higiene of 1912 found that over 50 percent of the factories inspected did not follow the provisions of the law.[13] In 1924 the law of 1907 was replaced with one that prohibited women from working night shifts and from doing dangerous jobs. It also prohibited employers from firing women because of their pregnancy and extended their maternity leave. In 1934 the government established a maternity fund in order to provide income for working women on maternity leave. Agricultural workers, domestic workers, and housewives, however, were ineligible for such benefits.

In spite of these advances for women, the situation of working women was not much better in 1943 than it had been in 1910. The few laws that protected them were difficult to enforce. Women tended to be laid off more frequently than men, and their salaries were about 50 percent lower than those of their male counterparts.[14] Furthermore, inequality between the sexes was legally sanctioned. Until 1926 the Civil Code regarded women as legally equivalent to minors or the handicapped. In that year Congress, under pressure from some feminist groups and the Socialist Party, granted civil rights to women. They could now choose the job and make free use of their income. However, it is worth remembering that, until recently, the legal guardianship of children remained a male right.

Feminism before Perón

If working conditions for women were bad, their civic situation was even worse. Except for the province of San Juan, which had granted limited political rights to women in the 1920s, women were, until 1947, excluded from political participation.

The suffragist movement in Argentina had never been very strong.[15] Since the last decades of the nineteenth century, there had been groups of women who had fought for women's civil and political rights. These were usually allied either with the Socialist Party (the only party to include the enfranchisement of women in its platform), with Anarchist organizations, or, until 1910, with the Consejo Nacional de Mujeres (CNM).[16] In that year, there was a major division in the CNM. Since the more conservative faction that had taken over the organization opposed the enfranchisement of women, a radical faction led by Cecilia Grierson left the CNM.[17] The difference between the kind of "feminism" advocated by the conservative CNM and the "other" feminism was clear for the *Boletín del Museo Social Argentino*, which noted in 1912 that "the CNM has a feminist flavor, but not like that of the sectarian or combative feminism; no, it has the flavor of the tender and tutelary feminism that serves as a shelter to those who suffer from hunger for bread, love, or wisdom."[18]

Although women workers had played an important and active role in some demonstrations, such as the Tenant Strike of 1907, feminist groups failed to attract their broad, active support. This was due, in part, to the predominantly upper- and middle-class composition of the feminist leadership. It was also due to the fact that many feminist organizations had close ties with political parties, particularly with the Socialist Party, which had a predominantly middle-class constituency.[19] Supporting the feminist organizations meant implicitly supporting the Socialist Party, something that not all women were inclined to do. The lack of interest in feminist struggles became evident when, in 1920, feminists led by Dr. Julieta Lanteri organized a mock election. Fewer than 4,000 women bothered to participate.[20]

In 1930 a new suffragist group, the Asociación Feminina por el Sufragio Feminino (Female Association for Women's Suffrage), was organized by Carmela Horne de Burmeister. This group, which claimed 10,000 members in 1934, owed its success in part to the fact that it declared itself apolitical, stressing instead purely patriotic concerns.[21] Participation in politics was seen as an essentially male sphere of action, while patriotic activities were seen as appropriate for women as well as men.[22]

Although the majority of feminist groups were ideologically liberal or Socialist, there were also attempts on the part of right-wing and Catholic organizations to mobilize women, although not for the purpose of securing political rights. Instead, those groups sought to reach families through women. Fearful of the anarchist influence among the working class, socially active Catholic clergy such as Msgrs. Gustavo Franceschi and Miguel de Andrea sought to attract working-class women so they could spread "healthy" ideas, rather than "dissolvent" ones, among their coworkers and within their families.[23] De Andrea encouraged the organization of confessional unions for women (and also for men), which in 1922 were absorbed by the Federation of Catholic Associations of Women Workers.

The ultraright-wing Liga Patriótica Argentina, created in 1919 by Manuel Carlés in response to the Tragic Week, also attempted to mobilize women. For the members of the league, strengthening the family and introducing Catholic education into the schools were essential steps toward the restoration of social order. Those tasks required, naturally, the participation of women, who would play an essential role in generating patriotic consciousness.[24] The league founded female brigades of "Señoras" and "Señoritas," and tried to mobilize schoolteachers. The right-wing groups attempted to recruit women by emphasizing their natural role as mothers, teachers, and charity workers.

These antiliberal organizations seemed to have had some success in attracting the attention of women, at least that of women from the upper classes. The Anarchist paper *La Protesta* observed in 1919 that hardly a day passed without the announcement of a new female brigade of the Liga Patriótica.[25] A few days after the 1930 coup, several thousand women paraded down the Avenida de Mayo to show their support for the new government.

During the 1920s and 1930s there were many attempts by Socialist lawmakers to introduce a law giving women the vote in Congress. None of those attempts succeeded, although female suffrage had been a plank in the Radical Party platform since the 1930s. The conservative coalition that governed the country in the 1930s was not sympathetic to the enfranchisement of women. In fact, President Agustín Justo made unsuccessful attempts to redraft the Civil Code in order to annul the reform of 1926. In order to oppose such attempts, liberal writer Victoria Ocampo created the Unión Argentina de Mujeres in 1936.

Peronism and Women

The revolutionary government that took power in 1943 was even less interested in the enfranchisement of women than the conservatives of the previous decade. This is evident in the stark choice offered to women by one high official of the regime: maternity or the convent.[26] President Pedro

Ramírez explicitly encouraged industries and public organizations to hire only men, since the only proper place for women was at home.

Perón, however, did not share these ideas. He was certainly less of a misogynist than his fellow officers, as the prominent role that Eva would play during his government would show. Moreover, from the beginning, he saw women as a potential source of support for his political ambitions. Women accounted for a large portion of the workforce, and, as we have seen, their working conditions were even worse than those of men. In addition, since women were a sector of society entirely excluded from political life, Perón had more freedom in creating the conditions for their incorporation.

Within the Dirección de Trabajo y Asistencia a la Mujer, Perón created the Comisión pro-Sufragio Femenino, headed by Haydeé Longoni.[27] It was the first time in Argentine history that the state itself encouraged the political organization of women. The enfranchisement of women became part of the First Five-Year Plan, and it became law in 1947. Apparently, Perón had considered the possibility of granting women the right to vote by decree even before October 1945.[28] This alternative enraged feminist leaders from the Socialist tradition who thought, like Alicia Moreau de Justo, it would be humiliating to receive the long-sought-after franchise through a decree issued by an authoritarian government that they opposed and whose legitimacy they questioned. This led to a paradoxical situation: well-known feminists, who had fought long and hard for the right to vote, now rejected it when it was offered to them. Some less politically committed leaders, such as Horne de Burmeister, however, supported the policy of the secretary of labor and welfare.

Simultaneously, groups of Peronist women were organized. On February 8, 1946, the Secretaría Femenina del Centro Universitario Argentino, led by Haydeé Longoni, organized an all-female demonstration in Luna Park to show support for the Perón–Quijano ticket. Several thousand Peronist women attended, and Eva Perón came in place of her husband, who had been specially invited. The women, however, wanted to hear Juan Perón in person, and their angry shouts prevented Eva from delivering her speech.

After the elections of 1946, Eva Perón took it upon herself to mobilize women for the Peronist cause. In her first official speech, delivered to express her gratitude to those women who had organized to support Perón, she said: "The Argentine woman has overcome this period of civil tutelage. The woman who went to the Plaza de Mayo on October 17; the one who made her voice heard at the factory, office, and school; the one who works day after day with men in all kinds of activities in a dynamic community, cannot be merely a passive witness to political developments. Women must vote."[29]

Eva's perception of the role of women in society, however, was full of the ambiguities that also permeated other areas of Peronist discourse, such as the image of women presented in school textbooks.[30] Although it was agreed that women should be able to vote and deserved political rights, for Eva their natural place was still at home, where they could exercise their influence: "the home, that cell of society where people are incubated, is the most noble and zealous mortar of our task."[31] In this respect, Eva's discourse was similar to such Catholic and right-wing organizations as the Liga Patriótica. However, there were two important differences between them. First, while the Catholics and right-wingers tried to mobilize women for more "patriotic" and apolitical purposes, Eva's discourse focused on the need for mobilizing women in support of a specific political movement: Peronism. Second, Eva emphasized the importance of women's suffrage, which had not been part of the program of the Catholic or right-wing organizations.

By the time Perón took power, there was broad consensus that women should be given the right to vote. The opposition in the Chamber of Deputies (Perón had won 100 percent of the Senate seats) was mostly composed of Radicals, who were in favor of granting women the franchise. No opposition was expected.[32] A law providing the granting of political rights to women had been passed by the Chamber of Deputies in mid-1946. The Catholic Church, one of the most important allies Perón had had from the beginning, was, by then, also in favor of women's suffrage.[33] In fact, since 1945, *Criterio* had carried out a campaign in support of political rights for women.[34]

In the early months of 1947, Eva began a radio campaign to promote the enfranchisement of women. She and the official propaganda presented the granting of political rights to women as if it were a new idea, and stressed that the idea had started with Eva. In the tone of her speeches it is possible to detect the fundamentals of the Peronist discourse concerning women. Since most of the feminist groups were in the opposition, and since suffrage was not a cause powerful enough to generate enthusiasm among the vast majority of women, Eva and the regime had to generate a myth around the issue and incorporate it into the Peronist imagery. In order to do that, Eva had first to define her audience. She was talking to women, but who were those women?

For Eva, they were primarily defined as "women of the people," that is to say, *descamisadas*. According to Eva, women had shown that they had overcome the political tutelage of men when they went to the Plaza de Mayo on October 17.[35] Women would gain political rights because Perón needed women to bring his doctrine into the home.[36] It was women's task to educate great men, and, by being given the vote, they would have more incentives to educate men in the Peronist doctrine.

There are two particularly important elements in Eva's characterization of women. First, according to Eva, women won the vote because they were Peronists and had participated in the events that brought Perón to power. Therefore, the earning of their political rights was closely linked to the birth of Peronism. Second, although women had overcome the stage of political "tutelage," their primary role was still motherhood. Enfranchisement was a way for women to have more influence over important political decisions, but this influence was, for Eva, to be exercised from within women's "natural" sphere, the home. In the Peronist discourse, the political participation of women was seen as an extension of their domestic role.

The other discursive tool that Eva used in order to generate enthusiasm for women's enfranchisement was presenting it as the product of a struggle between Peronism and the obscure forces of the opposition: "Our eternal enemies, the enemies of the people and their recovery, use all the resources of the oligarchy in order to prevent our victory. A sector of the press at the service of anti-Argentine interests ignored this legion of women who are with me. A minuscule sector of Congress tried to delay the passing of this law."[37] Those enemies were entirely imaginary since the movement to enfranchise women, as we have seen, had virtually no opposition.

Although Peronist women were the main target of Eva's discourse, focusing only on them was risky. Eva tried to broaden the base of her audience by interpolating two groups: one discourse was aimed at Peronist women, and another was aimed at a broader category, Catholic women: "When we talk about the Argentine home, and about woman as the symbol of that home, we are talking about the Christian woman, and about the home based on a solid traditional morality. Actually, in order to legitimize our desire that all women vote, we should add that every woman should vote according to her religious feelings."[38]

Paradoxically, Eva presented the granting of the female vote as both a revolutionary measure and as one that would preserve traditional values: "By voting, the woman will defend not only the eventual candidate, but a permanent principle; in choosing a candidate, the woman will define herself in all matters relating to the preservation of her home, her family, and the Catholic faith, leaving behind all that could lead to a dangerous push toward what is unscrupulous or anti-Argentine."[39]

Following in this respect the traditional right-wing discourse, Eva from the beginning distanced herself and Peronism from the "old" suffragist and feminist movements. The goal of the feminists had been—according to Eva— to fight against men. Peronist women, on the other hand, sought their incorporation into political life through collaboration with men. While the "old" feminists wanted to turn women into men, Eva wanted women to fulfill their role as women.

In September 1947, after Eva's highly visible campaign, Congress unanimously passed Law 13,100, granting the franchise to women. As with all important events of the regime, the law was celebrated by an official meeting at the Plaza de Mayo, where Perón handed Eva a copy of the law he had just signed.

The Partido Peronista Femenino

Although women were legally enfranchised in 1947, the feminine branch of the Peronist Party was not organized until 1949. On July 20, 1949, a thousand Peronist women gathered for the First National Congress of the Partido Peronista Femenino (PPF). The PPF was an impressive success. By 1952 it boasted 500,000 members and 3,600 Unidades Básicas.[40] It soon developed strong ties with the state and with the Fundación Eva Perón.

In the first conference, Evita made clear the objectives and goals of the PPF: "To be a Peronist for a woman means, above all, fidelity to Perón, subordination to Perón, and blind confidence in Perón."[41] From then on, all their political activity would be presented as complete subordination to Perón: "All of us [women], with no exception, from the one who considers herself to be the humblest, to the one who is considered by her companions to be the most efficient and the smartest, are not, nor expect to be, anything else but General Perón's helpers."[42] Later on, before the election of 1951, Eva would be even more explicit: "For us, Perón is everything. He is the light, he is the air, he is life. . . . He is beyond discussion, because he has given us a free, just, and sovereign fatherland, and has given us back our dignity."[43]

The PPF was created as an independent branch of the Partido Peronista (PP), linked to it through its complete loyalty to Perón. However, the PPF, for all practical purposes, much like the FEP, was under the absolute command of Eva. Susana Bianchi and Norma Sanchís argue in their perceptive study of the PPF that although in the male branch of the party there existed at least the appearance of democratic procedures, this was not the case in the Partido Peronista Femenino. There, Eva reigned as a veritable monarch. Under her direction, the PPF absorbed all preexisting Peronist organizations for women, such as the Centro Femenino María Eva Duarte de Perón, the Unión Argentina Peronista, the Asociación Peronista Pro-Derechos Políticos de la Mujer, and others.[44] Eva handpicked both party officials and candidates for elections. She would not tolerate the presence of independent-minded women in the party who might overshadow her.[45]

After the first congress, Eva picked twenty-three women, who, with the title "census delegates," were placed in charge of the organization of the PPF. For Buenos Aires, Eva appointed Teresa Fiora, head of the nursing school of the Fundación and the Ciudad Infantil. These twenty-three women's first task was to take a "census" of Peronist women throughout the country. At the same time, they were supposed to organize the Unidades Básicas (UB) of the PPF. The first UB opened in January 1951, in the Presidente Perón neighborhood.

From the beginning, Eva stressed the apolitical character of the PPF, which was twofold. On the one hand, Eva, like Perón, emphasized that Peronist politics had nothing in common with the politics of the ancien régime. Peronist propaganda claimed that while the old *comités* (neighborhood political committees) had been the centers of vice and corruption, where votes were bought, the Peronist UBs were centers of virtue and morality. But, on the other hand, the PPF was even further removed from traditional politics, because politics was not seen as a proper sphere of activity for women. Peronist women were not involved in politics, but in "social assistance." The FEP and the PPF were the regime's primary means of providing social assistance. In February 1951, Perón described the UBs of the PPF as follows:

> One simply has to visit a Unidad Básica of the PPF to see that from the threshold of that house one starts to breathe cleanliness and honor. It is enough to lean out of one of those unidades to realize that there everything is moral, everything is virtuous. . . . When I see that each of those Unidades Básicas is a center of political aid, a center of social assistance, and a refuge for all those who are in need of advice or help; that it is at the same time a center of cultural elevation, where women can gather together to talk, . . . to sew on a machine, or to give training to those who were not lucky enough to learn the things needed to earn a living, I remember that [the UBs] represent the fulfillment of my dream as far as political organization goes: to change the old *comités* from centers of vice to centers of virtue like the new Unidades Básicas.[46]

The UBs of the PPF were, in fact, extensions of the FEP, with personnel being exchanged between the two organizations. The UBs were centers of social activity where women could learn a craft, take their children for child care while they worked, or borrow sewing machines. The UB provided health services such as first aid or vaccinations. In 1952 the UB located at Rivadavia 5161, Buenos Aires, offered courses on dressmaking, sewing, toymaking, hatmaking, home economics, typing, English, French, public speaking, drawing, dancing, guitar, violin, and sports to more than 900 women. Not surprisingly, the most popular courses were those that taught a potentially profitable activity, such as sewing (210 women), or hatmaking (110 women).[47]

The delegates to PPF were sent to the provinces for the purpose of getting women to affiliate with the Peronist Party. However, they were to introduce themselves as census-takers. One of them remembers:

> [Eva] told us: first, say the word census-taker. We came to take a census. . . . Do not say: We came to persuade you to join the party. Because there are people from other political parties who will not want to join us. You have to disguise the word. . . .
>
> We went house by house. . . . We made them sign the book and sign the application, and we gave them the membership card on the spot. We told them that we had done so, so they did not have to bother going to the UB. However, if they needed anything, if they had any request, we told them to go to the UB.[48]

Most of the delegates and "subdelegates"[49] were also nurses of the FEP. As Bianchi and Sanchís point out, there was a complete lack of differentiation among the personnel of the two organizations. One delegate remembers that on the occasion of the visit of Prince Bernhard of Holland to Buenos Aires, Eva ordered the most beautiful members of the PPF to wear the nurse uniforms of the Fundación to parade for the prince, whether they were nurses or not. Teachers of the Ciudad Infantil were used as subdelegates on various occasions.

Although Catholic and right-wing organizations wanted to keep women away from politics, Peronism wanted to incorporate them into politics, while still stressing their traditional role in society. In order to attract women, Peronism reformulated the meaning of their "natural" activities. If the nursing profession, for example, had traditionally had a bad reputation, the nurses of the FEP, in contrast, proudly paraded in their uniforms for foreign visitors and were guaranteed a place in patriotic celebrations.

The state, the Fundación, and the PPF were three elements closely joined in the task of attracting women to Peronism. A woman in need could go to a UB of the PPF, where her problem would be reviewed. Afterward the UB would either solve the problem or send the petitioner to the FEP or to the appropriate state agency. The same lack of differentiation among the state, the FEP, and the PPF was also evident in the handling of personnel and property. Some women were on the state payroll, but were temporarily "lent" to the FEP or the PPF. A census delegate, who also held an important position in the Ciudad Infantil and in other FEP institutions, remembers that once she needed some kindergarten teachers for the Ciudad Infantil. She went to the state kindergarten close by, and since she could not locate the headmaster of the school or any other director, she simply "borrowed" the teachers without informing anybody else.[50] On another occasion, female employees of the Ciudad Infantil asked the city government to chop down pine trees in Palermo Park so that the children in the Ciudad could have real Christmas trees.[51]

It is difficult to find out what the rank and file of the PPF thought about their political activity. We do have, however, some testimony from midlevel leaders collected by Susana Bianchi and Norma Sanchís. As is often the case with oral history, it is sometimes difficult to separate memory of events that actually occurred from what might be a later reconstruction of the past. There are, however, some similarities in the testimonies that are worth noting.

Most of the women interviewed did not distinguish between the party and the FEP: "The UB were branches of the Fundación."[52] Almost all women interviewed remember their participation in the PPF as semireligious and totally detached from politics, and closer to social work. One delegate, for instance, said that she was not at all interested in politics, and that she saw her participation in the PPF as a "divine mandate."[53] Another census delegate referred to enlisting people in the party as a matter of faith. According to her, registering people in a certain province was more difficult because there, people were not "believers."

Many women saw their contact with Peronism as a moment of personal redemption. A former nurse of the FEP, for example, presented herself as a frivolous woman who liked to dance and wear fashionable clothes. Eva taught her to "love the other."[54] The delegate referred to above also went through a similar process of transformation. She had also been frivolous until "Eva taught us how to give." As we have seen, this image of Eva as a redeemer was one of the central motifs in Peronist propaganda, and lingered in the memory of those who met her.

A Different Feminism

Eva always stressed the "feminine" character of "her" women as opposed to the "old" feminists. She did not allow men in the UBs of the PPF, and wanted her women always to be well dressed and ladylike in their appearance. Eva did not allow married women to use their maiden names.[55] However, at the same time, she demanded a level of commitment from the PPF members that was sometimes incompatible with the type of family life they were supposed to lead. A member of the PPF recalled, for example, that from 7:00 A.M. to 2:00 P.M. she worked in the Ciudad Infantil, after which she went to the primary school from 6:00 to 8:00 P.M.. She would then go home to be with her husband until 10:00 P.M., and would go out to work again at the Women Workers' House until 2:00 A.M. The nurses of the FEP and the delegates and subdelegates of the PPF were required to be on call twenty-four hours per day, seven days per week. Eva could call them at any time for a sudden meeting, or could send them to the provinces with only a few hours' notice. Women were supposed to behave like missionaries of the doctrine: "At home, in the street, in family meetings, in the shop, in the market, at work in the office or in the factory, [she] has to find the means to make known the truth about Perón and all that he is doing for the happiness of the people."[56]

Why, we should ask at this point, did Peronism succeed where feminist groups had failed? Peronism combined two elements that made it attractive: on the one hand, a traditional discourse, and on the other, concrete improvements in women's conditions. In her book on the feminist movement in Cuba, Lynn Stoner points out the cultural relativity of feminism: "All feminist movements by definition rejected conditions of gender bias. The means and the definition of the struggle, however, differed from society to society."[57] The success of a particular feminist discourse, therefore, is related to the distinctive conditions of each society. In a country such as Argentina, with a strong Catholic tradition, it was generally agreed that the proper place for women was at home, while men held the monopoly on public space.[58] In that context, radical feminist discourse could have had only limited appeal. Moreover, the working-class women who followed Eva did not share the values of the middle- and upper-class feminist leaders of the pre-Perón era. By reinforcing values already internalized, Peronism could attract broad sectors of women. What the regime did was to redefine already socially accepted values.

At the same time, Peronism could offer something that other groups interested in attracting women could not: the power of the state to grant women tangible improvements in their conditions. It took only one year for the Peronist government to enfranchise women and put the liberal feminist groups in the embarrassing situation of being forced to accept the franchise from "that government."

How much did women's situation really change during Perón's regime? This question does not have a simple answer either. In strictly legal terms, Perón's government did not greatly change the situation of working women. But although the regime did not pass any laws providing women equal pay for equal work, their salaries did rise and the disparity between men's and women's salaries decreased considerably. In 1949 the salary of female textile workers, for example, was the same as those of men. By the end of Perón's governance, women workers received on average from 7 percent to 15 percent less in wages than their male counterparts, which was not bad considering the world standards at that time.

However, if women made gains, it was not so much because women in particular were receiving better benefits, but because of the general improvement in the living and working conditions of the working class under Perón's government. Better salaries and working conditions led to a general improvement in the standards of living for women as well as for men. In addition, the extension of services such as state-owned preschools and kindergartens provided working mothers with a cheap alternative for child care. While in 1940 there had been only 3,135 children enrolled in public kindergartens, by 1950 the number had grown to 32,745. The FEP, as we have seen, provided other services to women, such as the halfway houses that, by providing assistance to single mothers, helped to erase the social stigma traditionally attached to single motherhood.

In the area of education, there were clear improvements in the situation of women. The illiteracy rate among adult females was reduced drastically between 1947 and 1958, dropping from 15 percent to 9.38 percent.[59] In higher education, the situation for men was still better than for women, but the disparity was lower than in the pre-Peronist period. Comparing the period from 1941 to 1945 with 1955 to 1960, we find that women as a percentage of all university graduates rose from 15.67 percent to 24.15 percent.[60]

The most important benefit obtained by women during the government of Perón was, however, their right to vote. After the law was passed in 1947, women could vote and be elected to office. As a result of the elections of 1951, seven women became senators, and twenty-four women representatives were elected to Congress. A woman, Delia Parodi, was elected vice president of the Chamber of Deputies.

The incorporation of women into the Peronist Party, however, was not so smooth as expected. Although the PPF was theoretically one of the three branches of the Peronist Party, and therefore had the right to nominate one-third of the candidates in elections, their representation in 1951 was less than proportional. Using her familiar rhetoric, Eva tried to transform what had evidently happened as the result of pressures exerted by the other two branches of the movement into a voluntary sacrifice: "We do not fight for ourselves, or to get a job. We are used to sacrifice, which for us women is the most natural thing in the world; but our sacrifices always have a higher reason which, in this case, is the well-being of the people of the fatherland. . . . This is why at this moment of ambition and egoistic disputes, we do not demand nor want anything but a position from which to fight. Perhaps this is why the Partido Femenino is nominating very few candidates for [the election] of November 11."[61]

It is evident that the political condition of women during Perón's government improved. Although enfranchisement had been long overdue and was approved by almost all sectors of society, it was the Peronist government that took the decisive action to make it a reality and therefore deserved the credit. Nevertheless, in the Peronist discourse the role of woman in society did not change much. Her "natural" place was still the home, and her political activities were seen as an extension of her "natural activities": social aid and education. But by promoting women's mobilization, Peronism encouraged a change in their perception in society that went far beyond the limits of political discourse.

Children and Youth: Creating Future Peronists

If the Peronist regime was interested in attracting women as mothers who would instill the "doctrine" into the minds of their children, it also attempted to make itself directly attractive to the young.[62] This section deals with two interrelated mechanisms for attracting youth to Peronism: the sports tournaments called the Campeonatos Evita (CE), organized by the FEP, and the children's magazine *Mundo Infantil*, published by the government-owned publisher Haynes. *Mundo Infantil* was also the official magazine of the Campeonatos Evita. Its director, Oscar Rubio, was a member of the organizing committee of the competitions. Although *Mundo Infantil* was the only magazine published by the regime specifically for children, the regime made an enormous propaganda effort to attract youth. For example, the government also published a collection of openly propagandistic children's stories that were known as the *Biblioteca Infantil General Perón*.[63] The books in this collection were distributed free of charge in public schools.

In the same vein, the semiofficial *Mundo Peronista* had a section called "Your Page as a Peronist Kid," in which children were encouraged to "convert" their friends.[64] But while *Mundo Peronista* was only read by those who were already "converted"—it had no useful information for a non-Peronist—*Mundo Infantil*, on the contrary, was part of a broader project aimed at attracting not only "Peronist" children but also those from non- or even anti-Peronist families. Although during the Peronist regime there were other children's magazines, *Mundo Infantil* became the most popular.

The Campeonatos Evita and the Political Use of Sports

The Campeonatos Evita (CE) were one of the most visible events organized by the FEP. The tournaments were organized for the first time in 1948 as the Campeonato Infantil de Fútbol Doña María Eva Duarte de Perón, and 11,483 children from the city of Buenos Aires and 3,722 from the province of Buenos Aires took part. In the following years, the competitions were extended to the whole country, and in 1950 more than 100,000 children participated.[65] After 1951 other sports besides soccer were added, and from 1952 on, girls were admitted in some sports. In 1954 close to 216,000 children competed in ten sporting events. In 1953 the Campeonatos Juveniles Deportivos Juan Perón, aimed at teenagers, were created.

Although the FEP was in charge of organizing the tournaments, the state provided help in various ways. Dr. Ramón Cereijo, minister of finance and general manager of the FEP, was also the president of the organizing committee of the CE. Children from other provinces were brought by train to Buenos Aires for free. The children who were interested in participating in the competitions had to undergo a comprehensive medical examination administered by the Ministry of Public Health. Those found unfit were referred to an appropriate institution for treatment. The police also were involved, since the applications had to be filed at the local police station.

Every year Congress voted to provide cash contributions for the competitions, starting at $950,000 in 1949, and rising to $3 million by 1952.[66] The Radicals in Congress opposed the granting of subsidies on the grounds that, on the one hand, the FEP used the competitions for political purposes, and, on the other, no one knew exactly the state of the finances of the FEP.

It was therefore unclear, the Radicals claimed, whether the contribution was really necessary. Radical congressmen proposed instead (unsuccessfully) to give money to the Ministry of Education.

The CE were one of the most successful of the Peronist regime's attempts to organize informally the leisure time and spaces of social interaction of youth. Until then, social life in the neighborhoods revolved around popular libraries and local social and sporting clubs. The number of popular libraries, most of which had been organized by groups close to the Socialist Party, grew from 90 from 1930 to 1936 to around 200 by 1945.[67]

Unlike Fascist governments, the Perón regime, with certain exceptions, neither repressed nor seriously attempted to take over these centers of social life. Peronism did not have a consistent policy of organizing people's leisure time. However, attempts were made to create alternative institutions that would eventually compete with traditional patterns of interaction. A study of Peronist policies in this area remains to be done, but it is interesting to mention some examples, such as the failed "student clubs" created by Dr. Oscar Ivanissevich during his ministry.

The student clubs were created to transform public schools into neighborhood centers of social life for children and their families. They were organized by a resolution of the secretary of education in 1948 which established that each club should have a popular library and a museum and should organize cultural and sporting events for after-school hours. Their purpose was to bring families closer to the schools, which would eventually replace other centers of social life. In the school clubs, people would engage in "moral activities" under the supervision of teachers.[68] But as with most state-sponsored activities, the regime tried to turn the clubs into centers of political propaganda. Evita inaugurated most of them with great pomp—she, in fact, presented the clubs as her own idea—and she took the opportunity to distribute gifts from the FEP. Activities organized by the clubs included cruises on the presidential yacht, visits to the presidential residence, and excursions to see the "achievements" of the regime.

The failure of the student clubs was due in part to the lack of adequate funds,[69] and in part to the lack of interest shown by potential participants and teachers.[70] The clubs could not compete with other well-established centers of sociability. In 1950 the new minister of education, Armando Méndez de San Martín, disbanded the clubs, to the relief of teachers who would no longer have to work unpaid after-school hours.

The organization of the CE may be seen as a much more successful attempt on the regime's part to create alternative centers of social life. The participating teams were for the most part organized in neighborhood clubs or were created especially for the competitions. The first prize was usually a full-size soccer field for the winning team and money for the improvement of the club's facilities. Therefore, the fate of many clubs was closely tied to the FEP and to the competitions. In addition, the FEP provided sportswear for the players and other prizes. Many teams that would later become professional, and many players who would later become top professionals, began their careers with the CE.[71]

Much has been written on the political uses that authoritarian regimes have made of mass sports. Sports provide a nonviolent, nonsubversive way to channel people's anxieties. In addition, authoritarian governments can generate support for their regimes around sports (especially international competitions) by associating them with patriotic symbols and with the regime itself.[72] Peronism made extensive use of sports in this way, and the CE provided an excellent opportunity for doing so. The Campeonatos Evita were one link in a chain of sporting events sponsored by the regime. Professional sports figures (both men and women) were sponsored by the regime and given large sums of money to participate in competitions. International figures such as the racing driver Juan Manuel Fangio were awarded the Peronist Medal and allowed to address the people from the balcony of the government palace. Eva herself was the godmother of the children of José María Gatica, the famous boxer. According to official propaganda, Argentine sportsmen and women were internationally renowned (which was not always true) because they now had the support of the state. The same message was delivered to the participants in the CE:

> One hundred and fifty thousand children like you are today experiencing this great festival of soccer. It is a competition without precedent in the country, but consistent with the New Argentina to which you belong and for which you will try to become a worthy man. Older boys did not know anyone who cared about training them for gentlemanly sporting meets. Before, they played in pastures, and when they participated in a competition it was very difficult to find a field, and in order to find a ball or a shirt they had to empty their piggy banks. The matches lasted ninety minutes, and, as a result, children became sick and tired. . . . In order to participate in the First Campeonato de Fútbol Evita you started by appearing before the authorities with proper documents. Those who lacked these papers . . . had to regularize their legal situation, as hundreds of boys did.[73]

This "Before" and "After" image was reinforced by the fact that the first team to win a competition was organized by the Hogar (formerly Asilo) de Niños "General San Martín." What had previously been an ominous example

184   Mañana es San Perón

of an oligarchic charitable institution where children were humiliated was now, as a result of Perón's policies of social justice, a home where healthy children could organize a winning team.

The participants in the CE were presented as warriors of the national cause. Children also took part in "patriotic" activities organized for them, such as homages to San Martín and other national heroes. The competitions themselves would serve to shape the national consciousness: "The Campeonato Evita will make the dream of teachers and governments come true: it will unite Argentine youth over and beyond local loyalties, and even beyond provincial limits, because the voice of sports is stentorian and powerful, and it invigorates the young like an electrical charge. Under its spell, all will feel equal, all will think the same way."[74]

The required medical examination was also presented as a patriotic issue: "How many soldiers in military doctors' offices, when answering the call of the nation, could have seen their problems solved if in the past there had existed competitions like that of the Fundación?"[75] Teams were encouraged to use patriotic names, and there were teams from Patagonia supposedly representing the Malvinas Islands. There were numerous teams with names such as "Antártida Argentina," "San Martín," "Malvinas Argentinas," and, of course, "Perón," "Eva," and the like. The team "Evita Morning Star" (with the team name actually spelled in English), which won the 1951 competition, immediately after winning changed its name to the Spanish "Evita estrella de la mañana" in order to stress the strong national feelings of its members. Once, the goalkeeper of one of the teams refused to start a game when he saw that some people had remained seated when the National Anthem was being sung before the match. *Mundo Infantil* showed a photograph of the patriotic goalkeeper, who is seen in the picture holding a portrait of Perón in his hands.[76] The official discourse generated around the competitions was tinted with patriotic and Peronist tones. Dr. Cereijo said to the participants: "Go now to the field, play fairly. . . . For them [your parents], for Evita, for the fatherland dressed in its finest clothes in honor of your dream of athletic glory."[77]

Peronist imagery was also present in each step of the organization of the competitions. Perón and Eva went to see the most important games, and Eva gave the ball the first kick. Children were supposed to wear badges with Eva's silhouette and sing the official anthem of the competition that thanked her for the club.[78]

It is difficult to identify the children who participated in the CE. It is easy to imagine, however, how attractive those competitions were for many children. For poor children coming from the provinces, participating in the

CE meant the possibility of spending some time in the city of Buenos Aires at the government's expense. They also were given the required equipment, had the opportunity to meet sports stars, and received services such as medical examinations that would otherwise have been out of their reach. But in addition to the material incentives, there were others of a more symbolic nature that surely attracted many other sectors of the population as well. The possibility of playing on professional fields or meeting the President of the Nation and his wife were important symbolic rewards. The CE were treated as matters of state. In 1950 the minister of education decided to postpone exams in the secondary schools so they would not interfere with the CE.[79]

All provinces and all districts of Buenos Aires were represented in the competitions. The names of the teams do not help much in establishing the social origins of the participants. Alongside "17th of October" of Barracas, a mostly working-class area, we find "Barrio Norte," a wealthy neighborhood. However, it is possible to detect a tendency toward acceptance of the CE as a legitimate sports competition not only among the amateur clubs of the neighborhoods. The teams that participated in the early soccer-only matches were either created especially for the competition or organized in already-existing small local clubs. Some teams were organized in institutions such as vocational schools or orphanages.[80] None of the larger clubs from major cities took part. Later on, when the CE began to include sports that required much more sophisticated training, such as fencing or water polo, one may find the participation of large, well-established clubs, which were the only ones that could adequately provide the needed training for these sports. In 1951, therefore, we find, together with clubs such as "Eva Perón" of Buenos Aires, other more established and wealthy clubs such as "Harrods Gath y Chaves," "Sociedad Hebraica Argentina," and upper-class teams such as the Jockey Club of La Plata or the Jockey Club of Córdoba.

It is also interesting to note the clubs that provided (whether voluntarily or not is unknown) lodging and facilities for the participants coming from the provinces. These ranged from official or semiofficial institutions such as the Colegio Militar or Pabellón Santa Teresita del Aeropuerto Ministro Pistarini, to elite clubs such as the Hindú Club, the Yacht Club Argentino, and the Buenos Aires Rowing Club. We can conclude that, given the evidence available (admittedly fragile), participation in the CE was not restricted to one social group in particular, but was quite wide ranging. By 1952 the CE had a legitimate place among important children's sporting events.

As with all other events and institutions organized by the Peronist regime, it is difficult to evaluate the CE objectively. Undoubtedly, as the official Peronist propaganda claimed, these competitions provided the chance to play organized sports to some children who would otherwise not have had such an opportunity. The CE also helped to regularize the situation of undocumented children. Those who had no official documents of identification could not participate, and the police were supposed to help them do the necessary paperwork to secure their documents. The medical examinations that participants were required to undergo were another positive aspect of the competitions.

The CE also served as a mechanism for the political socialization of youth. The official propaganda stressed the fact that the competitions were made possible as a result of Eva's personal will. The CE were a step forward in the process of assigning political significance to daily activities; those ranging from school festivities to the practice of sports were given a Peronist stamp. Opposing the CE implied being against the government and therefore constituted a political statement.

The CE were also an informal attempt (in this area, largely successful) to politicize the leisure time of the popular sectors. Through the CE the fate of amateur clubs, many of which had emerged spontaneously in the neighborhoods, became linked to the regime. As the official anthem of the competition phrased it: "We owe our club to Evita/ For this reason we sing our gratitude to her."

Mundo Infantil

While the CE contributed to the politicization—that is, Peronization —of leisure time, *Mundo Infantil* (*MI*) provided an additional means for Peronism to enter people's homes. The magazine was issued by the semiofficial publisher Haynes, under the direction of Carlos Aloé, governor of the province of Buenos Aires. The first issue of *MI* came out in October 1949; its cost, forty cents, was within the reach of working-class families. Nevertheless, children were encouraged to circulate each copy among those friends who could not afford to buy one.[81] *MI* was not the first children's magazine published in Argentina, but in some aspects it inaugurated a new era.

The study of children's literature, and in particular of magazines, is a broad and interesting field, since it provides insight into the social definition of childhood, gender differentiation, and other related topics. To my knowledge, a thorough study of children's literature in Argentina has yet to be written. Although I make marginal references to more general topics, I limit my discussion to the ways in which the magazine served as a vehicle for political socialization and as a means for the transmission of a political discourse.

Before the Peronist era, the most popular Argentine magazine for children was *Billiken*, published from 1919 onward by the publisher Atlántida.[82] Throughout the 1920s and 1930s, *Billiken* had two apparent purposes: entertaining and moralizing children. The message delivered by *Billiken* was similar to that of the textbooks of the pre-Peronist era discussed in Part III. In fact, the magazine was supposed to complement in some way the ideological pattern transmitted in schools. Poverty, for example, was presented as the result of a natural order of things, while (as in the school texts) the only possible contact between people of different social classes was through acts of charity. The themes of the stories were usually about rich children helping poor, dependent children.

However, and partly because it was a weekly publication, *Billiken* was more flexible than the textbooks in adapting its message to the concerns and current fears of the dominant sectors. In the 1920s, one of the concerns of the elite was the problem of maintaining social order in a context of poverty and marginalization. Poor, abandoned children were seen as the seeds of corruption and social disorder.[83] *Billiken* encouraged rich children to organize charitable societies to help children in the poorer neighborhoods— "Billiken Committees." The emphasis was placed on the problem of orphans and on the danger they represented to society: "How worthy of pity are those homeless children! I think that those children will be dragged into the streets, which are full of corruption. Afterwards, they will fill the jails and houses of correction."[84] Children who had to work, usually portrayed as newspaper boys, were presented as very poor or as orphans exposed to the moral threats of the streets who were also seeds of corruption of the social order.

Following the ideological patterns of the time, the school and the family (both well constituted around middle-class values) were seen as the only environments that could make children moral and protect them from the dangers of the outside world. The streets were seen as a source of vice and immorality. Although an off-the-street job was more acceptable for children, ideally they should not work at all. In a story published by *Billiken* and presented as true, a newspaper boy who had found and returned a wallet full of money was rewarded with a job in the Jockey Club, a position which was, of course, more moral than selling newspapers in the street.[85] (It is interesting to note that an almost identical story was included in one of the texts analyzed in Chapter 6.) Children were seen as totally dependent beings who should be completely subject to the disciplining environments of the home and school.

MI started a new pattern in children's magazines. Unlike *Billiken*, the focus of *MI* was the child, and most of the stories dealt with things that interested both children and young boys and girls. *MI* featured fixed sections on model planes, sports, and a female adviser to whom girls wrote to seek advice for their personal problems. Moreover, and quite unusual for the times, it featured material that could help children with their homework. In this sense, *MI* was closer to the new generation of Argentine children's magazines that would emerge in the 1960s than to its predecessors.

Unlike *Billiken*, *MI* stressed the importance of the relative autonomy of children, encouraging them to choose their own future, even if it contradicted the wishes of their parents. *MI* featured a section suggestively called "Su Majestad el Niño" (Your Majesty the child), in which outstanding children were presented. It is worth noting the development of this section. In the first twenty-five issues of the magazine, following the traditional pattern of what constituted a "model child," we find children who had found and returned money (eight cases) or who had engaged in acts of charity (three cases). But together with those models, we find children who deserved to be included in this section because they had excelled in artistic or technical tasks. Even more interesting were the cases of six children who were included because they continued to study while they worked as newspaper sellers.

For *Billiken*, work on the streets was incompatible with morality. For the Peronist magazine (as for the Peronist texts analyzed in Part III), on the contrary, work in all its forms was exalted as a positive value. Far from being portrayed as the prey of all sorts of vices, children who worked to help their parents were held up by *MI* as models. Those who had to work in order to help their families or support their widowed mothers were no longer presented as objects of pity or charity. This new perception of work was also present in other ways. In order to celebrate the anniversary of the Seventeenth of October, students of the school bearing that name dressed up as workers, just as schoolchildren usually dressed up as soldiers during national holidays. This image, however, was less of a complete break with the past than a superficial reading might suggest. Middle-class values of a "well-constituted family" where "nothing is lacking" were still stressed. One newspaper boy was singled out for praise because "he was not a child deformed by his contact with the street, or with grownups. He still knew how to blush timidly. And [when spoken to], he answered as we like to hear: 'Yes, sir!' "[86]

Ideologically, *MI* presented the usual topics of Peronist propaganda. It was assumed that the children presented in the section "Su Majestad el Niño," beyond their other virtues, possessed one of crucial importance: their Peronist fervor. The magazine stressed patriotic and nationalistic topics, which had been absent from the magazines of the previous period. *MI* also included elements of the Peronist imagery: Perón, Eva, the Second Five-Year Plan, and the "recovery" of public services.

There was, however, an evolution of these themes. The first issues of *MI* made no mention of Perón's government. Only after the eighth issue did a fixed page showing the achievements of the government appear. From the first issue, *MI* included a regular section on national holidays. "October Seventeenth" was highlighted in red, but in the explanation underneath, we learn that what was being commemorated was October 17, 1858, the death of Félix Olazábal. After 1950, the Seventeenth of October would acquire its familiar Peronist meaning. In 1951, for instance, the article dealing with the Seventeenth of October read: "The people have in Perón and Evita their spiritual parents, and the Seventeenth of October was a day of family council when the people dedicated the occasion to the *dueña de casa*—who was sick because of her hard work—and the Leader asked his children if they were happy with his work. All of us answered with a 'yes' that must have been heard from Quiaca to Antarctica."[87] In the issues published in 1952, one finds such statements as: "To look after Perón is to look after the fatherland." By then, even crossword puzzles included references to Perón, Eva, and Governor Aloé, who was known for his blind loyalty to the Peróns.[88]

The magazine also presented other topics of interest for the regime, such as the supposed experiments with atomic energy carried out by Professor Ronald Richter in Patagonia. Richter was a Bohemian physicist who emigrated to Argentina after World War II. He managed to convince Perón that he was able to provoke controlled nuclear explosions—that is, he could control the intensity of the explosion while it was taking place. Perón gave Richter unlimited funding and had research facilities built for him in Patagonia. It took more than a year from the time the project was publicly announced in March 1951 to the final realization that Richter was a fraud. After the fiasco was discovered, the topic of atomic energy disappeared from the pages of *MI* as suddenly as it did from other official publications. In general, *MI* was consistent with the official discourse, even reproducing its contradictions. For example, after a long series of articles in which the equality of the sexes was stressed, we find:

[Women have their natural activities such as teaching young children, tending the nursery, and others. They also participate alongside men in other activities.] But the most wonderful thing is that women do not abandon their traditional functions, those which God commanded them to perform when He linked their fate to men's, and they [women] are still mothers and devoted and faithful wives. What is truly wonderful and worthy of real admiration is seeing women who, tired, leave their jobs every day and return promptly to their homes, where they still carry out their tasks efficiently.[89]

Likewise, *MI* presented a vision of politics similar to the one we saw when discussing the PPF: "You know that all children of the neighborhood go there [to the UBs]. Everybody goes, parents and children alike. The very name has changed, and [the UBs] are not like the *comités*, where they gave and sold [official] posts, and where people gambled. No. Today, [the UBs] are healthy places, where your parents go because there are books, and where men do not have those congested faces that the ambitious used to have. . . . Nobody wants to step on anyone else. Today, they devote themselves . . . to praying for Evita's health, and to providing entertainment to all children."[90] Peronist politics was virtuous in contrast to "traditional politics," which was presented as immoral, and therefore illegitimate.

The two main topics of the magazine were the CE and the successful activities of the FEP. The CE were presented in the same way that commercial sports magazines presented professional matches. The participants were interviewed, stars were idealized, and a schedule of the competitions was featured in every issue. *MI* was one of the media tools used by the regime to advertise the competitions.

MI served the regime's purpose as a means to "Peronize" youth by transmitting the elements of the official propaganda in an attractive package. Moreover, the magazine presented Perón's government as an endless source of favors and benefits. In this sense, the message transmitted by *MI* was similar to the one adults received through official propaganda. For adults, the regime dispensed social justice, which, on a less abstract level, translated into concrete social benefits and better salaries. For the children, beyond the rhetoric of social justice and nationalism, there was the concrete reality of a regime that offered such interesting incentives as the CE and was, according to *MI*, an endless source of toys, games, shows, sports, and entertainment.

MI also stressed the Peróns' proximity to the people: they were easily available to anyone in need. In an article in *MI* we read: "Aren't we aware that for the first time in the history of our country THERE IS NOT ONE SINGLE

CHILD who, even if he does not go to school, DOES NOT KNOW WHO HIS GOVERNMENT OFFICERS ARE AND, EVEN MORE, COULD NOT RECOGNIZE THEM?"[91] Stories were repeated of children who found it easy to approach Perón or Eva on different occasions. Every time a child was successful in contacting Perón or Eva, that child was usually rewarded with a gift from the ruling couple.[92] The image of an ever-present and caring power was essential for the creation of Perón's charisma. *MI* contributed to the creation of such an image in the minds of children.

This kind of image was also used by *MI* with openly manipulative purposes. In August 1951, *MI* began to publish invitations for a children's festival of music and theater at Luna Park. The main attraction of the party was to be the distribution of toys among the children. "Twenty bicycles! One hundred dolls! One hundred soccer balls!" plus candy and other gifts would be given away. Although the fact that the prizes had been donated by Perón and Eva was mentioned, no further note was made of the ruling couple. On the contrary, the magazine only emphasized the patriotic tributes that would take place, such as the singing of the National Anthem and a tribute to San Martín.[93]

But after the festival, the meaning of the party was presented in a completely different way. *MI* tells us that the children had gathered in Luna Park for the sole purpose of paying tribute to Perón and supporting his reelection. The magazine used eleven pages to show the children's enthusiasm for the presidential reelection.[94]

We can only speculate on the success of *MI* in its objective of "Peronizing" childhood. We do not know, for example, how many copies were printed— or how many were sold. It is possible that children belonging to anti-Peronist families bought *MI* behind their parents' backs, or even borrowed it (I personally know of two cases) simply out of curiosity or because it was useful for homework.[95] If, as Kristen Drotner points out, "juvenile magazines must be understood and interpreted as emotional interventions into the everyday lives of their readers,"[96] then we can assume that those readers must have absorbed at least part of the message that the magazine tried to transmit, especially since it was consistent with the message conveyed by the educational system.

There is, however, some evidence (indirect in this case as well) that might suggest a quite limited success in this regard. *MI* featured two fixed sections: "First Steps," where readers could publish short poems; and "This Is My Corner," where drawings were published. The topics of the works included in both sections were of the children's choosing. Most drawings and poems were related to popular figures, such as sport stars (Fangio was a favorite), Walt Disney characters, or traditional patriotic themes. Only a very small percentage of the poems and none of the drawings touched on Peronist topics. From a small but representative sample, we find that in four issues of the magazine published between 1953 and 1954, only four (one in each) out of twenty-eight contributions in "First Steps" dealt with Peronist topics. It is fair to think that the magazine was publishing all of the contributions dealing with Peronist themes, particularly because, by then, the content of *MI* was openly propagandistic. This lack of interest in spontaneous tributes to Perón and Eva is consistent with the evidence shown by the sources discussed above and with the hypothesis presented by Julie Taylor in her book on the myths of Eva Perón.

In its attempts to generate an image of the existence of consensus in society, the Peronist regime needed to broaden its social base. After securing the support of the organized working class, Perón sought to obtain the support of other less-structured sectors of society that could eventually function as a counterbalance to the power of the unions. These sectors were women, marginal rural and urban groups, the aged, and nonunionized workers. The regime also attempted to attract the children and youth who would be the seeds for the Peronization of all society. As Perón liked to say, he had won the first election with the vote of men, the second with the women's vote, and he would win the third with the support of the children.

To attract those nonorganized sectors, Perón set up a complex system of symbolic and material exchange. The FEP provided concrete benefits to the poor, but at the same time it was instrumental in the creation of some aspects of the Peronist political imagery. The FEP was perhaps the most visible evidence of the accessible and dedicated nature of the government. Moreover, the FEP contributed to the process of the politicization of everyday life. Going to an FEP hospital or participating (or allowing your child to participate) in the CE could be seen as an act of—if not support for—at least benevolent neutrality toward the regime (which we call passive consensus). In the context of a society profoundly polarized along the lines of "Peronism" and "anti-Peronism," this was an important achievement.

Through the PPF, the regime sought to incorporate women into political life. In doing so, however, Peronism tried not to depart from some crucial aspects of the traditional perception of the "natural" role of women in society. In this sense, Peronist women did not participate in politics, but provided social assistance. The PPF and the FEP became indistinguishable. Consistent with the traditional vision of women's work as "nondifferentiated" activities, the women of the PPF and the FEP had to be available for all kinds of tasks.[97] Nurses of the FEP in uniform could be seen parading during national holidays, the next day cleaning the floors of the Ciudad Infantil, or enlisting other women for the PPF. Peronist women not only provided votes, but also provided (and in this sense their role was similar to the one assigned to children) an open door through which Peronist doctrine could enter the family home.

Children were also targeted by the Peronist propaganda. Children and youth were a captive audience at school. However, the regime also tried to attract them through voluntary activities and offered them material and symbolic rewards. Although the government tried to generate active and visible support through political rituals, the mechanisms analyzed in this part of the book were aimed at generating passive consensus. People were encouraged to use the services of the FEP or to enjoy attractions provided by the regime that had an implicit political meaning but that did not require—with the possible exception of the UBs of the PPF—an active show of support for the regime. Even with the PPF, although its UBs were obvious political centers, its nonpolitical character was emphasized in the official propaganda.

It is difficult to evaluate the degree of success that the regime had in its attempts to attract and incorporate new sectors of the population into the Peronist machinery. The evidence available suggests, however, a change over time in the composition of the Peronist constituency. In 1951 most of the women who voted for the first time supported Perón, and by 1954, Peronism seems to have succeeded in attracting previously marginalized sectors.

In terms of children, it is even more difficult to evaluate the success of Peronist policies. Although the evidence seems to suggest that publications such as *Mundo Infantil* failed in their attempt to generate an almost religious loyalty toward Perón and Eva, it is also true that the magazine was instrumental in bringing Peronism into non-Peronist homes. In the context of a polarized society, children were an important link between the regime and the family. Through them, Peronsim could permeate the private sphere, making the distinction between it and the public sphere more blurred.

CONCLUSION: PERONISM—
WAS IT TOTALITARIAN?

In the Peronist political order, the state, embodied in Perón, would work as the absolute arbiter in political and social conflicts. Unanimity, or at least broad consent, was a precondition for the fulfillment of this model. Perón tried to generate the illusion that the legitimacy of his regime was based on the unanimous support of "the people."

A strong confidence in the existence of a broad political consensus long had been a tradition in Argentine political culture. Certainly, Peronism was not the first political movement to proclaim that it embodied "the fatherland itself."[1] But by the time Perón took power, the level of polarization in society was such that it quickly became evident that the existence of consensus was illusory. The liberal consensus, which had been one of the essential components of the Argentine political culture for more than half a century, was in crisis. Peronism, incapable of generating an alternative ideology that would bring together diverse social sectors, instead sought to create a system of myths and symbols in order to maintain the appearance of "spiritual unity" by attempting to incorporate new social sectors into the machinery of the regime.

This policy of incorporation and symbolic interchange was completed with the repression of all those who refused to participate in Perón's artificial movement. The illusion of unanimity was based on a redefinition of "the people," which now included only those who supported Peronism. Those who did not support it became part of "the antipeople" or "antifatherland" and were therefore excluded from participating as legitimate actors in the political arena. Gradually, Peronism monopolized the public symbolic space, delegitimizing alternative symbolic systems. This process made problematic the relationship between the regime and the Catholic Church, which had supported the regime at the beginning. Although the origins of the tensions

between the Peronist government and the Church existed from the beginning of the regime, open conflict only exploded at the end of the Peronist
decade.

Throughout this work, we have mentioned the "Peronist doctrine" and have
made reference to its ambiguous and sometimes contradictory content. Let
us remember that the "doctrine" constituted an essential part of the Peronist
political imagery. How can we characterize this doctrine? In many aspects,
Peronism was much less innovative than it claimed. Perón's initial policies
and his original model of social organization were essentially conservative,
and they may be characterized as a deepening of already existing tendencies,
rather than as a true break with those tendencies. However, the fact that
many sectors of the society, such as the business sector and the middle class,
did not react as he had expected and rejected his discourse and program,
forced Perón to redefine his relationship with sectors connected to the world
of work. This, in turn, changed the political culture by incorporating and
providing a new (Peronist) identity to groups that had until that point occupied only a marginal place in the political system. The paradoxical result
was that the program that originally had been conservative ended up being
revolutionary in many aspects. Later, as we have seen, Perón was forced to
incorporate other even more marginal sectors in order to offset the excessive
weight the trade unions had acquired.

As Halperín Donghi correctly points out, Perón's interest in theoretical
questions was very limited, and thus the "doctrine" was in no sense the
result of theoretical considerations.[2] In fact, the "doctrine" was not even
formulated as a doctrine per se. The books published as *Peronist Doctrine* (of
which there are various distinct editions) are in fact compilations of fragments of Perón's speeches on the most diverse topics. These fragments are in
some cases contradictory and therefore do not constitute a coherent corpus
of thought. Perón—especially at the beginning—adapted his discourse to
his audience, leaving intact only a collection of very basic concrete ideas on
how to deal with politics and society (Chapter 2).

It should come as no surprise, then, that people holding diverse ideologies read the Peronist discourse differently, and they were attracted to it for
diverse and at times antithetical reasons. Joaquín Díaz de Vivar, for example,
an aristocrat who had been an *antipersonalista* Radical in his home province
of Corrientes, and for whom national history was little more than his own
family's history, became attracted to Peronism because, to him, Perón spoke
the same nationalist and Catholic language. According to Díaz de Vivar,
Perón's discourse also made reference to other principles and policies, such

as social justice or the economy, but these were not the tenets that had inspired his interest in Peronism.[3] Díaz de Vivar, a militant Catholic, remained a loyal Peronist representative until the end, despite the moral conflict he suffered as a result of the clash between the Church and the state.

Manuel Molinari, on the other hand, an adherent of Henry George's economic doctrines, was attracted by Perón's agrarian discourse. Molinari became a Peronist because he believed that Perón would promote agrarian reform and because he assumed that he could lead Perón to establish a single-tax system. As we know, Molinari was one of the founders of the newspaper *Democracia*, and in the years 1944 and 1945 was the editor of *Hombre de Campo*, a Peronist magazine that fervently supported the expropriation of the *latifundias*. He had also served during the military regime preceding Perón as comptroller of the Consejo Nacional Agrario. When it became clear that Perón had no intention of carrying out agrarian reform, Molinari distanced himself from the movement. In 1947 he was forced to sell *Democracia* to Eva.[4] Others, such as Angel Borlenghi, Perón's minister of the interior, or Atilio Bramuglia, who would be Perón's minister of foreign affairs, came from Socialist backgrounds and had very different agendas from either Díaz de Vivar or Molinari. Their reading of Peronism was also distinct.

Those who were attracted to Peronism for different reasons not only read Peronist discourse in their own ways but also contributed to shaping it, giving the Peronist doctrine what we can call an "alluvial" character. Peronism absorbed ideas from the different ideological systems that had contributed to the formation of its heterogeneous movement, and this perhaps explains the tensions within the doctrine. One of the tensions permeating various aspects of the Peronist discourse we have discussed throughout was the polarity between modernity and traditionalism. Peronism presented itself simultaneously as a complete and revolutionary rupture with the past and as a conservative force preserving the most traditional national values (defined in different ways, but in general linked to the Hispanic-Catholic tradition). Perón was unable to break completely with the powerful liberal tradition of the country. Therefore, the policies analyzed in this study should be understood as attempts, sometimes rather erratic, at applying Perón's most basic ideas on how to handle society and not as the result of a coherent and structured ideology.

At this point, is it possible to characterize the Peronist regime as totalitarian? Certainly, the Peronist government could not be even remotely compared in terms of brutality to the Fascist or Nazi regimes. Perón respected, at least in form, the republican institutions of the country, including Congress and the judicial system. Anti-Peronist opponents were persecuted and their freedom of expression was not respected, but they did not have to suffer anything comparable to the horrors of German concentration camps or the forced dosing of castor oil, not to mention other horrible experiences lived through by Argentines decades later. After his fall from power, Perón could still claim that during his government he had never ordered the shooting of a political opponent, something the "liberators" of the 1955 revolution could not say.

However, and in spite of the above, Perón certainly had a totalitarian conception of politics: "The state has to give each man the orientation of how to think as an Argentine."[5] He never hid his admiration for Mussolini or even for Hitler.[6] For Perón, as for the European dictators, the state had to occupy all spaces of social life, and nothing was to be left outside its reach. At the end of the regime, there was a clear tendency toward the establishment of a semicorporative state, which shared many characteristics with the interwar European totalitarian regimes. Perón, moreover, saw his opponents as enemies. As he said in his speech opening the congressional session in 1954: "It is no secret that the Republic now has only two sectors: the national Peronist movement and the anti-Peronists; *justicialismo* and *antijusticialismo*; the revolution and the counterrevolution; constructive action and destructive reaction; [the sector] that wants a New Argentina and the one that is nostalgic for the other."[7] Jürgen Habermas defines "public sphere" as the "realm of our social life in which something approaching public opinion can be formed . . . 'public opinion' refers to the tasks of criticism and control which a public body of citizens informally . . . practices vis-à-vis the . . . state."[8] Like the totalitarian regimes, Perón made an effort to erase the public sphere.

Despite the totalitarian tendencies inherent in Peronism, there are a number of important differences between Peronism and the European interwar regimes that precluded Peronism from becoming a vernacular version of fascism. In the first place, there is the issue of the social base. Although recent historiography has demonstrated that the impoverished middle class, war veterans, and business groups were not the only social groups to support the Nazi and Fascist regimes, these were nevertheless their main constituency.[9] Peronism, in contrast, drew its support from the unionized working class, and later, as we have seen, from more marginal groups. Businessmen as a class were not part of the original Peronist coalition.[10] Although Perón never tired of mentioning that his movement was not "class based," the predominantly working-class character of his followers, and the intransigent opposition of the middle class, forced him against his wishes to create a harmonious society, to take sides within the class conflict. This was incompatible with a Fascist orientation.

Conservative groups had supported both the Fascist and Nazi regimes against what was perceived as "the Red threat." Although some conservative sectors had supported Perón in the beginning, and in spite of the fact that Perón sought the support of those same sectors, Peronism was forced to present itself as a reaction against those sectors.[11] Perón was partially correct in claiming that he had dismantled the system of social hierarchy.[12] Philippe Burrin concludes that the strong support provided by conservative forces was a burden that the German and Italian regimes had to bear throughout their existence, which limited their freedom of action. The same can be said, although with opposite consequences, about working-class support for Peronism.[13]

Furthermore, there was a fundamental difference between the foundational moment of Peronism and that of the totalitarian regimes. Both Mussolini and Hitler came to power as a result of serious crises in the existing political systems of their countries, crises that they had decisively helped to provoke. Yet both dictators became leaders of their governments by means of the very constitutional forms that they planned to destroy. Mussolini did not become head of the Italian government as a direct consequence of the March on Rome. Rather, the March added one more element to the crisis that the Giolitti-Facta government was already undergoing.[14] Moreover, by the time of the March, Mussolini had already been a member of the Italian Parliament for two years. Only after the Matteotti Affair in 1925 did the Fascist government become a truly totalitarian regime. Hitler, for his part, was named chancellor in 1933 as a consequence of obscure, though clearly constitutional, political negotiations. The Nazi Party was the senior partner in a conservative coalition that took power. Only after the burning of the Reichstag was Hitler able to obtain a change in the Constitution empowering him to legislate on his own authority, and only in December 1933 was the Nazi Party declared the only legal party in Germany. Hitler still had to wait for President Paul von Hindenburg's death in 1934 to assume total power. Therefore, we can say that if there was a Fascist or Nazi "revolution," it happened after Mussolini and Hitler came to power. These "revolutions" were intended to destroy the very constitutional frameworks that had placed both leaders in power.

Peronism's route to power was directly the opposite. Perón emerged as "the leader" as a consequence of the popular movement of October 17, 1945. What that movement made possible was the election on February 24,

1946, that placed Perón in the government palace. Therefore, the founding moment of Peronism was closely linked to the restoration of the democratic system, not to its elimination. Even the coup of 1943, another symbolic landmark in the history of Peronism, was presented in the Peronist imagery as a milestone in the restoration of the "true democracy" that had been mocked during the *década infame*. Peronism's democratic "birthmark" strongly conditioned the Peronist imagery. Perón never tired of claiming that he had come to power through the cleanest election in the history of the country.

Finally, another important difference between Peronism and the totalitarian European regimes was Perón's ambiguous position vis-à-vis the liberal tradition of the country. Although, as we have seen, Peronism presented itself as a complete rupture with the past, in more than one aspect it was firmly rooted in the liberal tradition. While Perón constantly proclaimed that Peronism had overcome the liberal past, the truth is that it could never entirely detach itself from this tradition. Moreover, Perón, as an officer of an army organized by the founding fathers of Argentine liberalism, saw himself in some way as the heir to that tradition. Only after his fall could Perón openly proclaim his absolute contempt for the liberal tradition, but even this change was probably due more to brazen opportunism than to a true change in his ideology.[15]

Perón was overthrown in September 1955. After the short conciliatory interregnum of General Eduardo Lonardi, the new government headed by General Pedro Aramburu began a policy of harsh repression against the Peronists. For the new government, Peronism was an aberration that had to be rooted out. Following the policies of "denazification" carried out by the Allied forces in Germany, Aramburu's government issued a decree making it a criminal offense to display any Peronist symbol.

Although the formal structure of the Peronist Party did not survive Perón's fall, Peronist unionism did. Very quickly, Peronist militants, mostly from the unions, began to organize themselves into groups of commandos and initiated a wave of terrorist attacks and sabotage, in what came to be known as the Resistencia Peronista.[16] Peronism became the bête noire of Argentine politics and remained so for the next eighteen years. But eventually it became clear that no political regime could be established in Argentina without the participation of Peronism.

During the 1960s, radicalized sectors of predominantly middle-class youth became attracted to Peronism, seeing in it a revolutionary alternative. Once again, Peronism symbolized different things to different sectors, and once again Perón tried to incorporate in his movement as many sectors as possible, shaping his discourse according to his audience. By the early 1970s, Peronism covered a wide range of ideologies—from ultraright-wing nationalism to that of the ultraleftist Marxist urban guerrillas. What gave cohesion to this heterogeneous mass was its powerful Peronist identity and its loyalty to a group of Peronist symbols, including Perón himself. Each sector within Peronism appropriated the part of the Peronist imagery that best served its political orientation.[17] However, the base of the imagery had been created during Perón's government. Its existence was crucial for the survival of Peronism after his fall.

Finally, in 1973, after eighteen years in exile, Perón was inaugurated as president for the third time. After a period of bloody political violence, it became evident that Peronism had become a permanent and necessary actor in Argentine political life. Just as a stable political system was not possible without Peronism, neither was it possible to have "Peronism without Perón." The same political actors, including the military, who had tried to exclude the leader and his movement from the political life of the country, admitted that only Perón could bring order to the chaos of Argentine political life. This time he came closer than ever to fulfilling his dream of turning Peronism into a true "national movement." He had never been so close to obtaining the unanimity he had so desperately sought during his first two terms. The Peronist movement and the country's reality had changed more than had Perón's ideas. In 1973, Perón was even able to do something he had not been able to do in 1951—appoint his wife (now Isabel, whom he had married in 1961) vice president.

When Perón died in 1974, at the age of seventy-eight, after being in power for less than a year, it became clear that a crucial period in the history of Argentina was closing forever. A new and terrible decade was just beginning. Perón's death had orphaned the Peronist masses. Tomás Eloy Martínez captured this feeling at the end of his 1985 *Novela de Perón*, when Doña Luisa, watching Perón's televised funeral, embraces the television set and says: "Come back to life, *machito*, is that too much to ask?"

Peronism introduced deep changes into the Argentine political culture and into its social, economic, and political structures. It also redefined the relationship among social classes and between the state and the society. In this sense, we can say that Peronism was a revolutionary movement. But this same revolutionary character was what, on the one hand, impeded the general from generating consensus and, at the same time, was what made possible the durability of Peronism. The Peronist experience and the survival of Peronism after the leader's fall shaped Argentine political development for almost forty years. Given the ambiguities of the "Peronist doctrine," it should seem less paradoxical that it was another Peronist government—this time without Perón—that recently took upon itself the task of undoing most of the "Peronist achievements."

NOTES

Introduction, Pages ix–xiv

1. José Murilo de Carvalho, *A formação das almas: O imaginario da república no Brasil* (São Paulo, 1990), 10. The literature on political rituals and myths is considerable. See, for instance, Sean Wilentz, ed., *Rites of Power: Symbolism, Ritual, and Politics since the Middle Ages* (Pittsburgh, 1985); Claude Rivière, *Les liturgies politiques* (Paris, 1989); Raoul Girardet, *Myths et mythologies politiques* (Paris, 1986); Broneslaw Baczko, *Les imaginaires sociaux: Mémoires et espoirs collectifs* (Paris, 1984).

2. On the "creation of charisma," see B. Baczko, "Staline: Fabrication d'un charisme," in B. Baczko, *Les imaginaires sociaux*; Clifford Geertz, "Centers, Kings, and Charisma: Reflections on the Symbolics of Power," in C. Geertz, ed., *Local Knowledge: Further Essays in Interpretative Anthropology* (New York, 1983); Ian Kershaw, *The "Hitler Myth": Image and Reality in the Third Reich* (Oxford, 1987); and Ronald Glassman, "Legitimacy and Manufactured Charisma," in *Social Research: An International Quarterly of the Social Sciences* (Winter 1975). See also Dominique Rossignol, *Histoire de la propagande en France de 1940 á 1944: L'utopie Pétain* (Paris, 1991).

3. For a summary of the literature on Peronism, see Mariano Plotkin, "Perón y el peronismo: Un ensayo bibliográfico," in *Estudios Interdisciplinarios de América Latina y el Caribe* 2:1 (January–June 1991).

4. Gino Germani, *Política y sociedad en una época de transición: De la sociedad tradicional a la sociedad de masas* (Buenos Aires, 1962).

5. Miguel Murmis and Juan Carlos Portantiero, *Estudios sobre los orígenes del peronismo* (Buenos Aires, 1971).

6. Some of the most relevant articles generated by this debate were later collected in Manuel Mora y Araujo and Ignacio Llorente, comps., *El voto peronista: Ensayos de sociología electoral argentina* (Buenos Aires, 1980). See also Juan Carlos Torre, *La vieja guardia sindical y Perón: Sobre los orígenes del peronismo* (Buenos Aires, 1990); and Douglas Madsen and Peter Snow, *The Charismatic Bond: Political Behavior in Times of Crisis* (Cambridge, MA, 1990).

7. See, among others, J. C. Torre, *La vieja guardia sindical*; Hugo del Campo, *Sindicalismo y peronismo: Los comienzos de un vínculo perdurable* (Buenos Aires, 1983); Louise Doyon, "La organización del movimiento sindical peronista, 1946–1955," in *Desarrollo Económico: Revista de Ciencias Sociales* 94 (July–September 1984); L. Doyon, "Conflictos obreros durante el régimen peronista," in ibid., 67 (October–December 1977); Walter Little, "La organización obrera y el Estado peronista, 1943–1955," in ibid., 75 (October–December 1979).

8. Fortunately this situation is now starting to change. See the new works by Daniel James, *Doña Maria's Story: Life History, Memory, and Political Identity* (Durham, NC, 2000); and Javier Auyero, *Poor People's Politics: Peronist Survival Networks and the Legacy of Evita* (Durham, NC, 2001).

9. For a perceptive analysis of the "Peronist identity," see Daniel James, *Resistance and Integration: Peronism and the Argentine Working Class, 1946–1976* (Cambridge, MA, 1988).

10. See, among others, Julie Taylor, *Eva Perón: The Myths of a Woman* (Chicago, 1979); Alberto Ciria, *Política y cultura popular: La Argentina peronista* (Buenos Aires, 1984); Aníbal Viguera, "El primero de mayo en Buenos Aires, 1890–1950: Evolución y usos de una tradición," in *Boletín del Instituto de Historia Argentina y Americana Dr. Emilio Ravignani*, 3d series, 3 (1991).

11. See D. James, *Resistance and Integration*; and Susana Bianchi and Norma Sanchís, *El Partido Peronista Femenino* (Buenos Aires, 1986). For the impact of Peronism in more recent times, see J. Auyero, *Poor People's Politics*.

Part I and Chapter 1, Pages 1–18

1. For an analysis of liberalism as a unifying myth in Latin America, see Charles Hale, "Political and Social Ideas," in Leslie Bethell, ed., *The Cambridge History of Latin America*, vol. 4 (Cambridge, England, 1986). See also Ernest Laclau, *Politics and Ideology in Marxist Theory: Capitalism, Fascism, Populism* (London, 1977).

2. For an overview of this period, see Ezequiel Gallo and Roberto Cortes Conde, *Argentina: La república conservadora* (Buenos Aires, 1972). See also Natalio Botana, *El orden conservador: La política argentina entre 1880 y 1916* (Buenos Aires, 1977).

3. C. Hale, "Political and Social Ideas." For the evolution of liberalism in Mexico, see Charles Hale, *The Transformation of Mexican Liberalism in Late Nineteenth-Century Mexico* (Princeton, 1989). For Argentina, see N. Botana, *La tradición republicana: Alberdi, Sarmiento y las ideas políticas de su tiempo* (Buenos Aires, 1984). See also Tulio Halperín Donghi, "Liberalismo argentino y liberalismo mexicano: Dos destinos divergentes," in T. Halperín Donghi, ed., *El espejo de la historia: Problemas argentinos y perspectivas latinoamericanas* (Buenos Aires, 1987).

4. Cristián Buchrucker, *Nacionalismo y peronismo: La Argentina en la crisis ideológica mundial (1927–1955)* (Buenos Aires, 1987), 28.

5. On the Socialist Party, see the classic work by Richard Walter, *The Socialist Party of Argentina, 1890–1930* (Austin, TX, 1977). See also Jeremy Adelman, "Socialism and Democracy in the Age of the Second International," in *Hispanic American Historical Review* 72:2 (1992).

6. Cited in David Viñas, *Literatura argentina y realidad política* (Buenos Aires, 1982), 236.

7. On patriotic education, see Carlos Escude, *El fracaso del proyecto argentino: Educación e ideología* (Buenos Aires, 1990), esp. chap. 2; and Hobart Spalding, "Education in Argentina, 1880–1914: The Limits of Oligarchic Reform," in *Journal of Interdisciplinary History* 3:1 (1972).

8. Many teachers who participated in "rationalist schools" linked to anarchist groups, which were supposed to provide alternative nonpatriotic education, simultaneously held posts in the Consejo Nacional de Educación. On anarchist education, see Dora Barrancos, *Anarquismo, educación y costumbres en la Argentina de principios de siglo* (Buenos Aires, 1990).

9. On the evolution of the Unión Cívica Radical, see David Rock, *El radicalismo argentino: 1890–1930* (Buenos Aires, 1977) and Paula Alonso, *Entre las urnas y la revolución: Los orígenes de la Unión Cívica Radical y la política argentina en los años '90* (Buenos Aires, 2000).

10. José Luis Romero, *El desarrollo de las ideas en la sociedad argentina del siglo XX* (Buenos Aires, 1983), 57–58.

11. C. Buchrucker, *Nacionalismo y peronismo*, 32ff.

12. See T. Halperín Donghi, *Vida y muerte de la República verdadera (1910–1930)* (Buenos Aires, 1999).

13. It is interesting to mention that the tone of the *yrigoyenista* newspaper *La Epoca* was not significantly different in its praise for the Radical president and its insults for the opposition than it would be later when it became a Peronist newspaper.

14. See Ana María Mustapic, "Conflictos institucionales durante el primer gobierno radical: 1916–1922," in *Desarrollo Económico: Revista de Ciencias Sociales* 24:93 (1984); and Peter Smith, "The Breakdown of Democracy in Argentina, 1916–1930," in Juan Linz and Alfred Stepan, eds., *The Breakdown of Democratic Regimes: Latin America* (Baltimore, 1978).

15. On the nationalists of the 1920s and 1930s, see Marysa Navarro Gerassi, *Los nacionalistas* (Buenos Aires, 1969); Enrique Zuleta Alvarez, *El nacionalismo argentino* (Buenos Aires, 1975); C. Buchrucker, *Nacionalismo y peronismo*; and David Rock, *Authoritarian Argentina: The Nationalist Movement, Its History and Its Impact* (Berkeley, 1993).

16. See Sandra McGee Deutsch, *Counterrevolution in Argentina, 1900–1932: The Argentine Patriotic League* (Lincoln, NE, 1986).

17. See, for example, Ricardo Rojas, *La restauración nacionalista: Crítica de la educación argentina y bases para una reforma del estudio de las humanidades modernas* (Buenos Aires, 1909). On nationalism in the 1910s, see David Rock, "Intellectual

Precursors of Conservative Nationalism in Argentina, 1900–1927," *Hispanic American Historical Review* 67:2 (1987). On the reaction of the nationalists to immigration, see T. Halperín Donghi, "¿Para qué la inmigración? Ideología y política inmigratoria en la Argentina (1810–1914)," in T. Halperín Donghi, ed., *El espejo de la historia*.

18. See Loris Zanatta, *Del Estado liberal a la nación católica. Iglesia y ejercito en los orígenes del peronismo (1930–1943)* (Bernal, 1996).

19. Juan D. Perón, *Tres revoluciones militares* (Buenos Aires, n.d.).

20. T. Halperín Donghi, "El lugar del peronismo en la tradición política argentina," in Samuel Amaral and Mariano Plotkin, comps., *Perón, del exilio al poder* (Buenos Aires, 1993).

21. Diana Quattrocchi-Woisson, *Los males de la memoria. Historia y política en la Argentina* (Buenos Aires, 1995).

22. Cited by Miguel Angel Scenna, *FORJA: Una aventura argentina (de Yrigoyen a Perón)* (Buenos Aires, 1972), 2:387. For a good overview of the politicization of history, see Quattrochi-Woisson, *Los males de la memoria*.

23. Jesús Mendez, "Argentine Intellectuals in the Twentieth Century, 1900–1943" (Ph.D. diss., University of Texas, Austin, 1980).

24. In spite of his influence, Scalabrini Ortiz was not a member of FORJA because he had refused to join the UCR, one of the requirements for joining FORJA.

25. On FORJA, see M. A. Scenna, *FORJA: Una aventura argentina*; and Buchrucker, *Nacionalismo y peronismo*.

26. Letter to José Avalos, cited in M. A. Scenna, *FORJA*, 2:517.

27. Ernesto Laclau, "Politics and Ideology," in *Politics and Ideology in Marxist Theory: Capitalism, Fascism, Populism* (London, 1977), 180.

28. Scenna, *FORJA*, 152.

29. Letter to Avalos, cited in Scenna, *FORJA*, 2:519.

30. *La Vispera*, January 27, 1945, cited in ibid., 611.

31. Ibid., 194–95.

32. A. Ciria, *Partidos y poder en la Argentina moderna (1930–1946)* (Buenos Aires, 1975).

33. Carlos Díaz Alejandro, *Essays on the Economic History of the Argentine Republic* (New Haven, 1970); Javier Villanueva, "Economic Development," in Mark Falcoff and Ronald Dolkart, eds., *Prologue to Perón: Argentina in Depression and War, 1930–1943* (Berkeley, 1975). See also Peter Alhadeff, "The Economic Formulae of the 1930s: A Reassessment," in Guido Di Tella and D. C. M. Platt, eds., *The Political Economy of Argentina: 1880–1930* (London, 1985).

34. See, among others, Marcos Rouges, "¿Está el horizonte tan oscuro?" *Revista de Economía Argentina* (hereafter *REA*), 30:179–80 (1933); Alejandro Bunge, "A propósito de la participación del Estado en la industria y el comercio," ibid., 34:204 (1935); "El Estado industrial, dos experimentos," ibid., 34:10–12; and ibid., 41:292 (1942), an issue entirely dedicated to the role of the state in the economy.

35. D. James, *Resistance and Integration*.

36. J. C. Torre, "Interpretando (una ve más) los orígenes del peronismo," in *Desarrollo Económico: Revista de Ciencias Sociales* 29:112 (1989).

37. Luis Colombo, speech given April 16, 1943, and reproduced in *REA*, 42:299 (1943).

38. The debate over Di Tella's plan may be followed in the pages of *REA* throughout 1942.

39. Alain Rouquie, *Poder militar y sociedad política en la Argentina* (Buenos Aires, 1982), 1:333; and J. D. Perón, *Tres revoluciones militares*, 97.

40. A. Rouquie, *Poder militar*, 1:333.

41. E. Laclau, *Politics and Ideology in Marxist Theory*, 188.

42. "Speech of General Justo at a Lunch Meeting of Secondary Schoolteachers from Capital Federal, September 21, 1934," *Monitor de Educación Común* 714 (September 1934).

43. Carlos Ibarguren, *La historia que he vivido* (Buenos Aires, n.d.), 465.

44. Cited in J. L. Romero, *El desarrollo de las ideas*, 166.

45. Néstor Tomás Auza, *Católicos y liberales en la generación del ochenta* (Buenos Aires, 1981).

46. "Do not attack [the Catholic]; and when you feel inclined to do so, think that each of those attacks aimed against his truths and principles, against his practice and morals, will be like striking at the very bases of the social building on which you rest. . . . These precious energies which are aimed against us for no reason, apply them with resolve to counteract the demolishing influence of the dissolvent ideologies." Miguel de Andrea, "Oración patriótica de acción de gracias por el éxito de las Fiestas del Centenario" (Buenos Aires, 1910).

47. Cited by J. L. Romero, *El desarrollo de las ideas*, 109.

48. The two best analyses of the role of the Catholic Church in those years are L. Zanatta, *Del Estado liberal a la nación católica*, and Lila Caimari, *Perón y la Iglesia Católica* (Buenos Aires, 1995).

49. Gustavo Franceschi, *Totalitarianismo, liberalismo, catolicismo* (Buenos Aires, 1940), 34, cited in M. Navarro Gerassi, *Los nacionalistas*, 116.

50. Julio Meinvielle, "Sobre la Iglesia y la política," *Criterio* 110 (1930), cited in Carlos Wirley, *Vida cultural e intelectuales en la década de 1930* (Buenos Aires, 1985).

51. M. Navarro Gerassi, *Los nacionalistas*, 109–10.

52. *L'Osservatore Romano*, November 4, 1934, reproduced in *Criterio* 359 (1935); cited in Noreen Stack, "Avoiding the Greater Evil: The Response of the Catholic Church to Juan Perón" (Ph.D. diss., Rutgers University, 1976), 57.

53. T. Halperín Donghi, *Argentina en el callejón* (Montevideo, 1964), 37.

54. According to *Criterio*, 1.5 million people attended the events of the Eucharistic Conference. *Criterio* 345 (1934), cited in Fortunato Mallimaci, *El catolicismo integral en la Argentina (1930–1946)* (Buenos Aires, 1988), 9.

55. N. Stack, "Avoiding the Greater Evil," 77. According to T. Halperín Donghi, "Adherence to the Church as a social glue [during the 1930s] meant at the same

time a disgust with the present reality . . . and a resigned acceptance of its fundamental elements" (*Argentina en el callejón*, 38).

56. In *Criterio* 432 (1936), Franceschi aimed his criticism at those who drew
near to the Church because it was fashionable, as seventy years earlier it had been
fashionable to be a Positivist.

57. In 1932, *Criterio* complained that "the great majority of the people were
no longer Catholic; least of all, the Argentine working class." Seven years later, in
1939, the situation, according to the same magazine, had changed favorably, as it
happily announced that "just now a new Middle Ages is born. Catholicism in 1939
is a spiritual spring. The wind has taken away the dead leaves, but the tree shows all
its luxuriance." Cited in F. Mallimaci, *El catolicismo integral*, 28–29.

58. *Monitor de Educación Común* 774 (1937).

59. In 1939, Cardinal Copello attended one of these celebrations personally.

60. Juan Nissen, "Grave regresión cultural y derroche de caudales públicos," in
Orientación, October 31, 1945.

61. On the impact of the Spanish Civil War on Argentina, see M. Falcoff,
"Argentina," in M. Falcoff and Frederick Pike, eds., *The Spanish Civil War, 1936–
1939: American Hemispheric Perspectives* (Lincoln, NE, 1982). See also the excellent
analysis by Federico Neiburg, *Los intelectuales y la invención del peronismo* (Buenos
Aires, 1998).

62. Julio Irazusta, *Memorias* (Buenos Aires, 1974), 227; cited in John King,
*Sur: A Study of the Argentine Literary Journal and Its Role in the Development of a
Culture, 1930–1970* (Cambridge, Eng., 1986), 74.

63. B. Sarlo, *Una modernidad periférica: Buenos Aires, 1920 and 1930* (Buenos
Aires, 1988), 133.

64. J. Méndez, "Argentine Intellectuals in the Twentieth Century," 358.

65. Euardo Mallea, "El escritor de hoy frente a su tiempo," in *Sur* 12 (1935).
For an overview of the intellectual currents of the period, see M. Falcoff, "Intellectual Currents," in M. Falcoff and R. Dolkart, eds., *Prologue to Perón*.

66. B. Sarlo, *Una modernidad periférica*, 242.

67. Ibid. The idea of "structure of feelings" is borrowed from Raymond Wil-
liams, *Marxism and Literature* (Oxford, 1977), 131–32.

Chapter 2, Pages 19–38

1. See the collection of GOU documents edited by Robert Potash, *Perón y el
GOU: Los documentos de una logia secreta* (Buenos Aires, 1984).

2. Document reproduced in ibid., 202.

3. Ibid.

4. The complete text may be found in *La Prensa*, June 5, 1943, 6.

5. See C. Buchrucker, *Nacionalismo y peronismo: La Argentina en la crisis ideológica mundial (1927–1955)* (Buenos Aires, 1987), 301.

6. For accounts of Perón's life, see Joseph Page, *Perón: A Biography* (New York, 1983); and Robert Crassweller, *Perón and the Enigmas of Argentina* (New York, 1987).

7. León Rozitchner, *Perón entre la sangre y el tiempo: Lo inconsciente y la política* (Buenos Aires, 1985). See also Peter Ranis, "Early Peronism and the Post-Liberal Argentine State," in *Journal of Inter-American Studies and World Affairs* 21:3 (1979).

8. Some authors argue that the birth of Peronism can in fact be explained as the result of the elites' fears of a social revolution. See Carlos Waisman, *Reversal of Development in Argentina: Postwar Counterrevolutionary Policies and Their Structural Consequences* (Princeton, 1987).

9. See Torcuato Luca De Tena, Luis Calvo, and Esteban Peicovich, comps., *Yo, Juan Domingo Perón: Relato autobiográfico* (Buenos Aires, 1986), 28–29.

10. T. Halperín Donghi, "El lugar del peronismo en la tradición política argentina," in S. Amaral and M. Plotkin, comps., *Perón, del exilio al poder* (Buenos Aires, 1993).

11. J. D. Perón, *Conducción política* (Buenos Aires, 1952), 105. Emphasis in original.

12. J. D. Perón, *Apuntes de historia militar* (Buenos Aires, 1984), 243. Emphasis in original.

13. Cited by L. Rozitchner, *Perón entre la sangre y el tiempo*, 124.

14. J. D. Perón, "Significado de la defensa nacional desde el punto de vista militar," in J. D. Perón, *El pueblo quiere saber de qué se trata* (Buenos Aires, 1944), 79.

15. Peronist Party, Consejo Superior Ejecutivo, *Manual del peronista* (Buenos Aires, 1954), 22.

16. Ibid. (1948), 96.

17. Ibid. (1954), 20–21.

18. The idea of a third position between capitalism and collectivism had been developed by Mussolini and Franco in Europe. In Argentina, during the 1930s, this position had been adopted by the Catholic right. See F. Mallimaci, *El catolicismo integral en la Argentina (1930–1946)* (Buenos Aires, 1988), 42.

19. J. D. Perón, *Conferencia del Excmo. Señor Presidente de la Nación Argentina, Gral. Juan Perón, pronunciada en la ciudad de Mendoza el 9 de abril de 1949 en el acto de clausura del Primer Congreso Nacional de Filosofía* (Buenos Aires, 1952).

20. Lila Caimari, *Perón y la Iglesia Católica* (Buenos Aires, 1995).

21. Throughout this work I follow the distinction between "political religions" and "civil religions" presented by Claude Rivière. The main differences between the two are: (a) in political religions, the religious elements are found in the sacralization of the political order, while in civil religions, the religious elements derive from a link between the political order and a transcendental power based on the religious

beliefs of society; (b) in political religions, political power exercises its authority not only in the political sphere but over the whole social life, while in civil religions, political power is exercised in the political sphere; (c) in political religions, there is a specific system of norms and values defined by the political power, while in civil religions the contents of those values are general enough so that they cannot conflict with religious values or beliefs. C. Rivière, *Les liturgies politiques* (Paris, 1988), 136–37. See also Jean Pierre Sironneau, *Secularisation et religions politiques* (Paris, 1982), 557–58.

22. *Manual del peronista* (1948), 60.

23. The use of "recent European experiences of social organization according to natural law" as a source of inspiration was explicitly recognized in some official documents. See, for example, *Plan político orgánico, 1952–1958: Situación, apreciación, resolución* (Buenos Aires, n.d.).

24. On the relationship between Perón and the unions during Peronism's beginnings, see Hugo del Campo, *Sindicalismo y peronismo: Los comienzos de un vínculo perdurable* (Buenos Aires, 1983); and Juan Carlos Torre, *La vieja guardia sindical y Perón: Sobre los orígenes del peronismo* (Buenos Aires, 1990).

25. On the relationship between the unions and the state before Perón, see Joel Horowitz, *Argentine Unions, the State, and the Rise of Perón, 1930–1945* (Berkeley, 1990); and Hiroshi Matsushita, *El movimiento obrero argentino, 1930–1943: Sus proyecciones en los orígenes del peronismo* (Buenos Aires, 1983).

26. Perón also tried unsuccessfully to obtain support from the Radical Party. He became more militant in his attempts to attract the support of labor only when he failed to attract other sectors. See Félix Luna, *El 45: Crónica de un año decisivo* (Buenos Aires, 1969), chap. 1; and J. C. Torre, *La vieja guardia sindical*, chap. 2.

27. "Discurso del Coronel Perón en la Bolsa de Comercio de Buenos Aires, el 25 de agosto de 1944," in J. D. Perón, *Obras completas*, 7:3 (Buenos Aires, 1985).

28. "Discurso de Perón en la Academia Argentina de Letras con motivo del IV centenario del nacimiento de Cervantes," Ministerio de Educación, Dirección de Documentación y Estadísticas, Archive.

29. Cited by J. C. Torre, *La vieja guardia sindical*, 94.

30. Ibid., 95.

31. J. Horowitz, "Industrialists and the Rise of Perón, 1943–1946: Some Implications for the Conceptualization of Populism," in *The Americas* 47:2 (1990).

32. Testimony of an engineer of SIAM, the most important Argentine industrial firm, in Thomas Cochran and Rubén Reina, *Entrepreneurship in Argentine Culture: Torcuato Di Tella and SIAM* (Pittsburgh, 1962), 162.

33. See, for instance, Daniel James, *Doña Maria's Story: Life History, Memory, and Political Identity* (Durham, NC, 2000).

34. F. Luna, *El 45*, 162.

35. T. Halperín Donghi, *Historia de la Universidad de Buenos Aires* (Buenos Aires, 1962), 178.

36. Ibid.

37. The ideological changes within the UIA can be followed in the *Revista de la UIA* throughout the 1930s and 1940s.

38. F. Luna, *El 45*, 199.

39. *La Nación*, September 20, 1945, 1.

40. The participants yelled: "Mitre, yes; Rosas, no! Sarmiento, yes; Rosas, no! Urquiza, yes; Rosas, no!" Ibid.

41. A year later, Peronist deputy Albrieu would say in Congress: "We . . . in 1810, would have been supporters of Moreno; if we had been alive in the year [18]60, we would have been followers of Sarmiento; if we had been alive in 1916, we would all have been *yrigoyenistas*, and because of that same passion for the fatherland, in 1945 we are all Peronists." *Diario de Sesiones de la Cámara de Diputados* (1946) 6:90, session of October 1, 1946 (hereafter *DSCD*).

42. *La Epoca*, November 10, 1945, 3.

43. Ibid., October 17, 1945, 1.

44. In its edition of October 18, 1945, 4, *La Epoca* reported: "Last night was an Argentine night. Essentially Argentine, because during last night, the destiny of the nation was at stake."

45. *Democracia*, October 16, 1949, 3.

46. From a speech by Perón announcing his candidacy on February 12, 1946, in J. D. Perón, *El pueblo ya sabe de qué se trata*, 189.

47. *Plan político año 1951: Orientación a los señores gobernadores*, cited in F. Luna, *Perón y su tiempo*, vol. 2, *La comunidad organizada* (Buenos Aires, 1987), 160.

48. Interview with Fermín Chávez, Buenos Aires, June 15, 1990.

49. H. Del Campo, *Sindicalismo y peronismo*, passim.

50. D. James, *Resistance and Integration: Peronism and the Argentine Working Class, 1946–1976* (Cambridge, MA, 1988), 16.

51. On the relationship between Braden and Perón, see Gary Frank, *Juan Perón vs. Spruille Braden* (Lanham, MD, 1980).

52. See J. C. Torre, *La vieja guardia sindical*; F. Luna, *Perón y su tiempo*, vol. 1: *La Argentina era una fiesta* (Buenos Aires, 1984); P. Smith, "Party and State in Peronist Argentina, 1945–1955," in *Hispanic American Historical Review* 53:4 (1973).

53. Details of the political campaign may be found in R. Potash, *The Army and Politics in Argentina*, vol. 1, *From Yrigoyen to Perón* (Stanford, CA, 1969).

54. Habermas, *Legitimation Crisis* (London, 1988), 101.

55. For a complete list of materials published by the Subsecretaría, see Vicepresidencia de la Nación, Comisión Nacional de Investigaciones, *Documentación, autores y cómplices de las irregularidades cometidas durante la segunda tiranía* (Buenos Aires, 1958), 2:487 ff. It is interesting to point out that the use of this kind of mass propaganda was only possible because Argentina was a country with a high literacy rate. On the relationship between literacy and political propaganda, see B. Baczko, *Les imaginaires sociaux: Mémoire et espoirs collectifs* (Paris, 1984), 36.

56. Ernesto Goldar, *Vida cotidiana en la década del 50* (Buenos Aires, 1980).

57. *Sábado de gloria* was written in 1944. According to Rodolfo Borelo, "For Martínez Estrada, Peronism was not a unique phenomenon, but the augmented and more successful reappearance of this negative period in the historical life of a young but sick country. . . . Peronism [is] one of the faces of Evil." R. Borelo, "Martínez Estrada: Una visión fictiva del período peronista," in *Hispanoamérica* 8:23–24 (1979).

58. Andrés Avellaneda, *El habla de la ideología: Modos de réplica literaria en la Argentina contemporánea* (Buenos Aires, 1983).

59. See, for instance, the two short stories written in collaboration with Adolfo Bioy Casares under the pen name Honorio Bustos Domecq: "La fiesta del monstruo," originally published in *Marcha* (Montevideo), September 30, 1955, 20–21, 23; and "El hijo de su amigo," published in *Número* (Montevideo) 19 (1952): 101–19.

60. Jorge Luis Borges, "L'illusion comique," in *Sur* 237 (1955).

61. J. King, *Sur: A Study of the Argentine Literary Journal and Its Role in the Development of a Culture, 1931–1970* (Cambridge, 1986).

62. According to Ernesto Goldar, the more or less exhaustive list of Peronist intellectuals includes Leopoldo Marechal, Ignacio Anzoategui, Tulio Carella, Arturo Cambours Ocampo, Leonardo Castellani, Elías Castelnuovo, Arturo Carretani, Fermín Chávez, Ramón Doll, Ricardo Furlong, José Gobello, Tomás de Lara, Homero Manzi, Horacio Rega Molina, Elbia Rosbaco de Marechal, Constancio C. Vigil, Alberto Vanasco, Juan José de Soiza Reilly, Luis Horacio Velázquez, Jorge Newton, Claudio Martínez Paiva, Lizardo Zía, Nicolás Olivari, Julia Pritzlutzky, Cátulo Castillo, César Tiempo, Arturo Jauretche, María Granata, Roberto Vagni, Juan Ponferrada, Eduardo Astesano, Dalmiro Ayala Gauna, Ernesto Barreda, Juan Carlos Davalos, Héctor Lafleur, Salvador Merlino, Miguel Angel Speroni, Antonio Nello Castro, José María Castiñeira de Dios, José Luis Muñoz Aspiri, Juan Pinto, Enrique Pavón Pereyra, Jorge Perrone, Luis Soler Cañas, Arturo Berenguer Carisomo, Pablo Carvallo, Juan José Hernández Arregui, and Raúl Scalabrini Ortíz. E. Goldar, *El peronismo en la literatura argentina* (Buenos Aires, 1971). See also his "La literatura peronista," in Gonzalo Cardenas et al., eds., *El peronismo* (Buenos Aires, 1969); Martin Stabb, "Argentine Letters and the Peronato: An Overview," in *Journal of Inter-American Studies and World Affairs* 13:3–4 (1971); Pedro Orgambide, "Peronismo y antiperonismo en la literatura argentina (1945–1955)," in *Cambio* (October 1978–March 1979); and J. C. Portantiero, "La literatura argentina después del 43," in *Lyra* 20:189–91 (1963).

63. "El Presidente de la Nación Argentina Gral. Juan Perón se dirige a los intelectuales, escritores, artistas pintores y maestros" (1947), in Harvard University, *A Collection of Pamphlets on or by Juan and Eva Perón* (hereafter HUCP).

64. Ibid.

65. Ibid.

66. Manuel Gálvez, *Recuerdos de la vida literaria*, vol. 4 (Buenos Aires, 1965), 176, cited in Andrés Avellaneda, *El habla de la ideología*, 21.

67. *Sexto Continente* 1 (July 1949): "El sexto continente."

68. See, for example, the article entitled "Un rasgo revolucionario del gobierno del Cnel. Mercante: El turismo social," in ibid. The magazine published a large quantity of official propaganda, especially from the province of Buenos Aires.

69. Ibid., 2 (August–September 1949).

70. Ibid., 3–4 (October–November 1949).

71. For a discussion of "intellectual fields" and the struggle over symbolic capital, see Pierre Bourdieu, "Quelques propriétés des champs," in his *Questions de sociologie* (Paris, 1980). See also P. Bourdieu, "Le champ intellectuel: Un monde à part," in his *Choses dites* (Paris, 1987).

72. See Centro Universitario Argentino, *Tribuna de la revolución (conferencias)* (Buenos Aires, 1948).

73. *Argentina* 2 (1948), 18.

74. "El árbol exótico," in ibid. (1950).

75. Ibid., 12.

76. Ramón Asís, "Hacia una arquitectura simbólica justicialista" (Buenos Aires, 1953).

77. See, for example, October 13, 1955, articles written by Gustavo Franceschi in *Criterio* immediately after the fall of Perón with headlines such as "Freedom!" or "A Dictatorship," among others.

78. Oscar Terán, *En busca de la ideología argentina* (Buenos Aires, 1986).

79. The publication of these articles resulted in a crisis involving the governor of Entre Ríos, who found the references to Urquiza offensive. After the incident, and probably as a partial result of this crisis (although there were undoubtedly other causes), Colom was forced to sell *La Epoca* to the official media network. On this topic, see the interview of Eduardo Colom in Instituto Torcuato Di Tella, *Proyecto de historia oral.*

80. This phrase was used as the motto for the newspaper. The article on *Facundo* appeared in *La Epoca,* July 6, 1950.

81. "La historiografía. La crónica. La historia erudita. El ensayo." Talk given by Dr. Tomás Bernard on May 19, 1949, in the "Ciclo Annual de Conferencias de la Subsecretaría de Cultura de la Nación," Ministerio de Educación, Dirección de Documentación y Estadísticas, Archive.

Part II and Chapter 3, Pages 39–58

1. Cited in Carlos Fayt, *La naturaleza del Peronismo* (Buenos Aires, 1967), 92.

2. Cited in Anibal Viguera, "El primero de mayo en Buenos Aires, 1890–1950: Evolución y usos de una tradición," *Boletín del Instituto de Historia Argentina y Americana "Dr. Emilio Ravignani,"* 3d series, no. 3 (1st semester, 1991).

3. *La Prensa,* May 2, 1943, 7.

4. The same happened at the celebration organized by the pro-Communist CGT 2, which also had a patriotic tone.

5. *La Prensa*, May 2, 1943, 6.

6. Viguera, "El primero de mayo en Buenos Aires."

7. Mona Ozouf, *Festivals and the French Revolution* (Cambridge and London, 1988), 9.

8. Max Weber defines "charisma" as a personal quality believed to be extraordinary and as a result of which its possessor is considered to have supernatural powers, or at least powers not available to ordinary people. See Max Weber, *Economía y sociedad*, 2 vols. (Bogotá, 1977), 1:193. For Clifford Geertz's discussion on charisma, see "Centers, Kings, and Charisma: Reflections on the Symbolics of Power," in his *Local Knowledge: Further Essays in Interpretative Anthropology* (New York, 1983), 124. See also Bronislaw Baczko, *Les imaginaires sociaux: Mémoire et espoirs collectifs* (Paris, 1982), esp. the chapter "Staline: Fabrication d'un charisme."

9. On political religions, see note 21 in Chapter 2.

10. The manufacturing of a myth around a charismatic leader in order to generate consensus (or the illusion of it) in a divided society was a device used consistently by prewar European totalitarian and authoritarian regimes. See, among others, Ian Kershaw, *The "Hitler Myth": Image and Reality in the Third Reich* (Oxford, 1987).

11. This assertion was not completely true, since people were mobilized either in the streets or in the Plaza de Mayo on various occasions. It is true, however, that the only two fixed and ritualized celebrations of the Peronist regime were May Day and the Seventeenth of October.

12. The invention of traditions has been used as a political tool for the generation of loyalty and in establishing and legitimizing relations of authority since antiquity. See Eric Hobsbawm, "Introduction: Inventing Traditions," in Eric Hobsbawm and Terence Ranger, eds., *The Invention of Tradition* (New York, 1983).

13. Ozouf, *Festivals*, 25.

14. Pierre Nora, ed., *Les lieux de mémoire*, vol. 1, *La République* (Paris, 1984), Intro.

15. For a history of May Day in France, the classic *Histoire du Premier Mai* by Maurice Dommanget (Paris, 1972) is still useful. For Italy, see, among others, Massimo Massara, Claudio Schirinzi, and Maurilio Sioli, *Storia del Primo Maggio* (Milan, 1978). For a comparative view of the early May Days, see Andrea Panaccione, ed., *May Day Celebration* (Venice, 1988).

16. The reaction of the press in France can be seen in M. Dommanget, *Histoire du Premier Mai*. For press reaction in Argentina, see Jacinto Oddone, *Gremialismo proletario argentino* (Buenos Aires, 1975), 93ff., and Sebastian Marotta, *El movimiento sindical argentino: Su génesis y desarrollo* (Buenos Aires, 1960), vol. 1, passim.

17. Oddone, *Gremialismo proletario*, 98.

18. Viguera, "El primero de mayo en Buenos Aires."

19. On the three occasions in which there was bloody repression—1901, 1904, and 1909—police efforts were directed mostly against Anarchist demonstrations. There were several cases of police repression of the Socialist demonstrations, but these were not notably violent.

20. Cited in Oddone, *Gremialismo proletario*, 88.

21. *La Nación*, May 1, 1926. See also ibid., May 1, 1934: "We are already far from the time in which this date caused anxiety in the government and dread in the population."

22. Viguera, "El primero de mayo en Buenos Aires."

23. *La Prensa*, May 3, 1926, 7.

24. At the beginning, even the ultraright organizations made reference to the Constitution in their celebrations of the First of May. During the 1930s, however, the references to the Constitution disappeared from the nationalist meetings. In 1938 the Alianza Libertadora Nacionalista called its May First demonstration the "Marcha de la Libertad" (March of freedom). During the war, the parades would be renamed "Marcha de la Neutralidad" (March of neutrality).

25. On the divisions within the Socialist Party, see Richard Walter, *The Socialist Party of Argentina, 1890–1930* (Austin, TX, 1977).

26. *La Vanguardia*, May 3, 1932, cited in Viguera, "El primero de mayo en Buenos Aires."

27. *La Prensa*, May 2, 1934, 9.

28. *La Nación*, May 2, 1938, 11.

29. Ibid. As early as 1934, when a participant in the demonstration pulled out a red flag, it was immediately confiscated by the police. The demonstrator was also reprimanded by the party authorities, since the red flag had also been banned in Socialist demonstrations by internal regulations of the party.

30. *La Prensa*, May 2, 1940, 10.

31. For details, see Oddone, *Gremialismo proletario*, 517ff.

32. Unlike Alvear's decree, the holiday declared by military authorities was not limited to public officials. May Day was made a national holiday, giving it the same status as May 25, 1810 (beginning of the revolution against the Spaniards) and July 9, 1816 (beginning of independence). Workers received full pay for this day off.

33. "All the unions" participated in the official ceremony, according to *La Nación*, but only "many unions" took part, according to *La Prensa*.

34. Perón said, "As was promised at the beginning of this crusade of work, we have defended the unity and harmony of objectives among employers, workers, and the state as the only way to combat the real social enemies represented by false policies and foreign ideologies, which were the false apostles introduced into the union movement to thrive on deceit and the betrayal of the masses and the hidden powers of disturbance in the field of international politics."

35. At one point in his speech, for example, Perón said: "We are searching for the union of all Argentines and, because of that, we wish to have Argentine capital

that, in harmony with work, will form the basis of our great industrial and collective well-being."

36. In November 1944, Perón called the workers to a meeting organized to celebrate the first anniversary of the Secretariat of Labor and Welfare. According to one witness, "Had we paid one hundred pesos to each one of the attendants at the meeting, it would have been cheaper than the propaganda we made." Cited in Félix Luna, *El 45: Crónica de un año decisivo* (Buenos Aires, 1986), 42.

37. During his speech, Perón went to great lengths to distinguish between those who "openly—although using misconstrued events—had been able to express dissent or disagreement with the economic and social policy" and those who "hiding, had maneuvered without showing their faces, cheating and confusing the conscience, and trying to discredit the work of the government in order to create a favorable climate for a rebellion." Apparently, Perón repeated the words that he had used the day before when talking to the Post-War National Council, an organization over which he presided. See *La Nación*, May 1, 1945, 5.

38. Interestingly, the only concrete "social conquest" mentioned by the article was the pension system obtained for the Commercial Employees in November 1944, when this union was not a member of the CGT.

39. See, among others, F. Luna, *El 45*; J. C. Torre, *La vieja guardia sindical*; R. Potash, *El ejército y la política en la Argentina, 1928–1945*, vol. 1, *De Yrigoyen a Perón* (Buenos Aires, 1981), chap. 9; D. James, "17 y 18 de octubre de 1945: El peronismo, la protesta de masas y la clase obrera argentina," in *Desarrollo Económico: Revista de Ciencias Sociales* 107 (October–December 1987). For personal recollections of the events of October 17, see Cipriano Reyes, *Yo hice el 17 de Octubre: Memorias* (Buenos Aires, 1973); Angel Perelman, *Cómo hicimos el 17 de Octubre* (Buenos Aires, 1961); and Eduardo Colom, *El 17 de Octubre* (Buenos Aires, 1946).

40. Given this opportunity, Perón also announced that he had left for the signature of the president two important decree–laws establishing important improvements for workers: one setting a minimum wage, and another issuing new regulations for unions.

41. During the meeting, workers cried, "A million votes; Perón for President!" Throughout 1945, the relationship between Perón and the unions solidified. See J. C. Torre, *La vieja guardia sindical*.

42. See Emilio De Ipola, *Ideología y discurso populista* (Mexico City, 1982), chap. 6.

43. Ibid., 148–49.

44. Perón even glossed a phrase from Marx: "The emancipation of the working class is in the hands of the working man."

45. This meeting in the Plaza San Martín was presented afterward by the Peronist propaganda machine as a gathering of the worst of the Argentine oligarchy, even suggesting that there had been an orgy there. See, for example, E. Colom, *El 17 de Octubre*.

46. F. Luna, in *El 45*, reproduces a letter sent by Perón to his then-girlfriend, Eva Duarte, from Martín García Island in which he made clear that as far as he was

concerned, his political career was over. On October 13 an editorial in *La Prensa* exulted: "A new regime centered around the cult of a person has been destroyed; although it has had access to all the government resources in a measure so far unknown in Argentina, and has deprived the people of their rights, freedoms, and guarantees in a measure equally unknown in this land after the battle of Caseros, . . . it has only managed to trick those who were totally ignorant of reality" (p. 4).

47. Among other decrees that they refused to follow was the one stipulating that they should pay full salaries for October 12.

48. On the other hand, President Farrell had commissioned Attorney General Juan Alvares to form a conciliatory cabinet with the opposition. Alvares took his time, and by October 17 had not fulfilled his mission.

49. Juan Carlos Torre shows that although the pressure for the strike came from the rank and file, the final decision was made by the leaders of the CGT. Although the CGT did not yet have the relevance it would later, its approval was necessary, even at this point, for any coordinated action attempted by the unions. See J. C. Torre, *La vieja guardia sindical*.

50. Ibid., 133.

51. Ibid., 134. A similar perception of the relationship between Perón and the unions was expressed one year later, although in a very different context, by S. Pontieri, then secretary general of the CGT and also a congressman, in the parliamentary debates over whether to make October 17 a national holiday: "I am sure that if Colonel Perón had given his word as a simple citizen he wouldn't have succeeded because many of the things that he said had been said by the workers for a long time. However, he spoke not only as a colonel, but also as a member of the government. This the working class in the whole country saw. . . . I don't know what happened on the 9th of October. . . . What I do know is that on the 9th of October Colonel Perón fell. We know, yes, that on the next day, just like that, the curve marking the standard of living began to fall. On the next day, the government started telling the Argentine workers in the factories and workshops: let Colonel Perón pay you all these improvements; it is all over, say good-bye to social justice." *DSCD* 4 (1946): 107.

52. D. James, "17 y 18 de octubre."

53. This last part does not appear in the official version of the speech. See E. De Ipola, *Ideología y discurso populista*, 185.

54. Roberto Da Matta, *Carnavais, malandros e herois: Para uma sociologia do dilema brasileiro* (Rio de Janeiro, 1979), 62.

55. J. C. Torre, "Interpretando (una vez más) los orígenes del peronismo," in *Desarrollo Económico* 112 (January–March 1989).

56. C. Geertz, "Centers, Kings, and Charisma: Reflections on the Symbolics of Power."

57. *La Epoca*, October 18, 1945, 1.

58. Ibid., October 20, 1945, 3.

59. Ibid., 6.

60. Ibid., October 18, 1945, 2.

61. *La Nación*, October 19, 1945, 5.

62. *Crítica*, October 17, 1945, cited in F. Luna, *El 45*, 286.

63. *La Nación*, October 19, 1945, 5.

64. In contrast, when the same newspaper had characterized the participants in the Marcha de la Constitución y la Libertdad, it had used the following words: "There, the painters and sculptors who show their work in the Independents' Salon; there, those whose voices are broadcast on the radio, and the beauty and sympathy of our movie stars; over there, the dean of the University of Buenos Aires, and the teachers who give classes in their institutes, and the students; there, the lawyers and engineers and architects; over there, the doctors and industrialists and merchants. And also the strong-handed worker with an honest look, and the high-school student and the girls who opted for school uniforms over their spring attire. . . . These are the people!" *La Nación*, September 20, 1945, 1.

65. Diverse sectors saw the Seventeenth of October as an invasion of people perceived as "the others," making it difficult for them to assimilate what was really happening. Cardinal Copello, archbishop of Buenos Aires, watching the spectacle of the masses of workers (many of whom crossed themselves when passing in front of the Cathedral) gathering in the Plaza de Mayo, went down to the Plaza and began handing out religious stamps to the people in order to "convert them." Telephone interview of Father Hernán Benítez by the author, October 17, 1989. The presence of Copello in the Plaza is also mentioned in C. Reyes, *Cómo hice el 17 de Octubre*.

66. *Orientación: Organo oficial del Partido Comunista*, October 24, 1945, 1; *La Vanguardia*, October 23, 1945, 7.

67. See, for example, ibid., 4.

68. See *CGT: Periódico de la Confederación General del Trabajo*, November 1, 1945. Although it was not mentioned in the headlines on page 1 (which dealt with the intrigues of Vicente Lombardo Toledano in Mexico, and with a critique of the United States), the strike of October 18 occupied a prominent space in the inside pages of the journal. The only mention of the Seventeenth of October was in the "Declaración Pública de la CGT," reproduced on pages 4 and 5, which commented that the worker complaints that had led to the calling of the strike had been addressed by the government, as was clear from President Farrell's speech.

69. "Saint Perón" came from a chant of the workers gathered in the Plaza that declared, "Mañana es San Perón, que trabaje el patrón" (Tomorrow is Saint Perón Day, let the boss work").

Chapter 4, Pages 59–82

1. It was clear, however, that the celebration had been organized by the CGT; the political parties had only given their support.

2. There are discrepancies in the versions of the speech as presented by *La Nación* and *La Prensa*. According to *La Nación*, Perón began his speech by saying: "Workers, we arrive at this joyous May Day as our ancestors did when on that magnanimous date in 1810, they gathered in the Plaza Mayor." According to *La Prensa*, the reference had been not to May 25, but to the Seventeenth of October. The latter version matches the one provided by *El Laborista*, May 3, 1946, 9. However, neither *El Laborista* nor *La Prensa* printed the speech verbatim.

There are other discrepancies. According to *La Nación*, Perón continued his speech with: "The meaning of this day extends now to all classes in society. This celebration of the worker finds echoes in all sectors of Argentine society. And all of them now agree on the need to humanize work, considering labor to be the logical and principal helper of capital." This portion of the speech is missing in the versions published by *El Laborista* and *La Prensa*. See *La Nación*, May 3, 1946, 5.

3. It is interesting to compare Perón's speech, which hinged on the benefits his government would grant the workers, with that of the Socialists, which only criticized the elected authorities (calling them Nazis) and requested confidence in the "scientific, progressive, and democratic methods" supported by the party. Alfredo Palacios, the only speaker to mention a concrete program, sounded like a Peronist: "[The workers] will fight so that our country does not become a simple market for antagonistic imperialist powers, and we can acquire our economic emancipation. They should work for a policy that leads towards the domination of the domestic market and a larger capacity for consumption. They should demand . . . the granting of land in 'emphyteusis' or as private property to those who work it. . . . They will fight for the nationalization of basic national industries. . . . They will fight to suppress the privileges of foreign capital and the exploitation of man by man. But they should also get over the materialist conception of history, upholding the ideal of justice." *La Prensa*, May 2, 1946, 12.

4. "We find it to our advantage to make public now . . . our total independence from the authorities and the government of the Republic, and to stress our organic and disciplined attitude to maintain [*sic*] ourselves aloof from philosophical, political, or religious questions." However, in their edition of May 16, *CGT* characterized May Day 1946 as the last in a series of occasions in which the CGT showed its support for the secretary of labor and welfare. These included November 27, 1944 (when, as we have seen, the CGT did not show any enthusiastic support), July 10, 1945, and October 17, 1945.

5. *CGT*, May 16, 6ff. Significantly, this portion of the speech was omitted from the version presented by *El Laborista*, May 3, 1946, 9.

6. After Perón dissolved the party in May 1946, the newspaper was taken over by Mercante and his associates.

7. *El Laborista*, April 23, 1946, 7.

8. *La Epoca* stressed that the meeting had been organized by the CGT, while the political parties had given only support and assistance.

9. *La Epoca*, April 23, 1946, 5.

10. Several unions held meetings at which the "real" significance of May Day was explained, "undermining the value of the Communist and Socialist campaign that wished to give it sectarian class tones." Ibid., April 25, 1946, 5.

11. "Numerous student centers have sent their support, just as have men of letters, professionals, and technicians, giving this gathering an unfamiliar aspect if compared to the May Days of other years, which had a clear class content." *La Epoca*, April 21, 1946, 4.

12. *El Laborista*, May 1, 1946, 10.

13. *La Epoca*, May 3, 1946, 3.

14. Ibid., April 19, 1946, 1.

15. This idea of the existence of a "dual" working class would be the basis for the standard sociological interpretation of Peronism in Argentina in the 1960s.

16. *El Laborista*, May 1, 1946, 1. The editorial note for May 3 was titled, "¡Perón, Perón!"

17. *La Epoca*, May 3, 1946, 3.

18. See P. Smith, "Party and State in Peronist Argentina, 1945–1955," *HAHR* 53 (November 1973): 4; and F. Luna, *Perón y su tiempo*, vol.1, *La Argentina era una fiesta* (Buenos Aires, 1984), chap. 2.

19. *DSCD* 6 (1946): 356.

20. Ibid., 398–99.

21. Ibid., 94.

22. After being shelved for almost three months, the bills were suddenly reintroduced by a Peronist representative. The debate was closed abruptly when, using a typical Peronist tactic, the Peronist majority voted to end the debate.

23. *La Nación*, October 18, 1946, 5.

24. Ibid., 6.

25. Numerous schools were renamed "Seventeenth of October" or something similar in the years that followed.

26. *La Prensa*, October 16, 1946, 12.

27. *CGT*, this time, gave a version of events different from the one given in the previous year. According to the new version, the trade unions had paralyzed all productive activity on October 17 following an order issued by the CGT. Remember, however, that the strike had been declared for the eighteenth, and that, in 1945, *CGT* had not mentioned the seventeenth, concentrating all its attention on the eighteenth. According to the new version, the workers had mobilized because "they would prefer their leader to be free from all official ties. That he be theirs, totally theirs, to make of him what his enemies did not want him to be." *CGT*, October 16, 1946, 2.

28. *La Prensa*, October 18, 1946.

29. The speaker who had made the announcements in the Plaza de Mayo finished his remarks by saying, "And this is the end of this broadcast, which has taken place on the same balcony to which, on October 17, 1945, the then Colonel Perón returned; this time, forever to lead the destiny of this people." *La Nación*,

October 18, 1946, 5. The word "*descamisado*" was used for the first time in a pejorative manner by the newspaper *El Mundo* to describe the participants of the events of October 17, 1945. Later it was adopted as a sort of "trademark" by the Peronist movement.

30. As Sigal and Veron point out, Perón identified the *descamisados* as the "real" people, standard-bearers of the true nationality: "the only authentic people of the nation are the ones that are here," he would say. At the same time, Perón used a rhetorical resource that would be used in the 1970s: the *descamisados* had been eternal protagonists in the history of the country. "This *descamisado*, who was cannon fodder during the struggle for Independence, was the gaucho of knives and long hair of the national organization period." See Silvia Sigal and Eliseo Veron, *Perón o muerte: Los fundamentos discursivos del fenómeno peronista* (Buenos Aires, 1986).

31. *La Prensa*, October 18, 1946, 8.

32. Ibid.

33. This gesture resembles San Martín bequeathing his sword to Rosas. The comparisons between Perón and San Martín can be found elsewhere in the pages of *El Laborista*. In a cartoonlike narration of the events of the "Week of October," when Perón is taken to Martín García Island, the story reads: "The scene on the immortal canvas that shows the Father of the Nation was repeated: San Martín in Boulogne-sur-Mer." *El Laborista*, October 17, 1946, special supplement.

34. *El Líder*, October 17, 1946, 4.

35. Remember that the CGT had elections in November to elect the general secretary, and that Borlenghi, Perón's candidate for the position, was defeated by Luis Gay.

36. As a matter of fact, there were several comments on the role played by the CGT. See, for example, *El Líder*, October 17, 1946, 14, 15, and 17.

37. *Democracia* had been created in December 1945 in order to support Perón in the electoral campaign. Its owner, Manuel Molinari, was an economist influenced by the doctrines of Henry George. Molinari, who had been named head of the National Agrarian Council during the military government, had supported Perón because he had believed in his promise to carry out an agrarian reform. When, in 1947, it became evident that Perón would not put the reform into practice, Molinari and *Democracia* became more critical until Perón forced him to sell the newspaper.

38. Alfredo Fernandez, "La Revolución debe seguir avanzando," in *Democracia*, October 19, 1946, 5.

39. Ibid., October 12, 1946, 9.

40. Ibid., October 17, 1946, 20.

41. *El Laborista*, October 17, 1946, 5.

42. Ibid., October 17, 1945, 2.

43. Ibid., October 16, 1947, 2; and *Democracia*, October 10, 1947, 7. The myth of the participation of Eva in the events of the Seventeenth of October has been studied by Marisa Navarro Gerassi in "Evita and the Crisis of 17 October,

1945: A Case Study of Peronist and Anti-Peronist Mythology," *Journal of Latin American Studies* 12 (1980).

44. *La Prensa*, April 30, 1946.

45. Ibid.

46. Ibid.

47. E. Hobsbawm, "Introduction: Inventing Traditions," 2.

48. Perón began his speech on May Day 1947 by saying "We celebrate [this May Day] as a festivity incorporated into the list of our greatest national celebrations. We celebrate it as the coming of a new era for this much beloved nation."

49. *Clarín*, May 2, 1947, cited by A. Viguera, "El Primero de Mayo en Buenos Aires."

50. Perón's dual character was stressed by *El Líder*: "El Mensaje de Perón en su Doble Carácter de Presidente y de Primer Trabajador" (Perón's message in his double character as president and as "first worker"), *El Líder*, April 21, 1948, 7.

51. Among other things, Perón said: "That's why, in formulating the rights of the worker, we have done so with the conviction that it is necessary definitively to consolidate our victories. . . . For them [the rights], brothers of ours have perished; for them, the leaders of our suffering and hard-working unions have fought their entire lives. For them, we will fight until our last breath." *La Nación*, May 2, 1947, 1.

52. The announcements of the contest were virtually the main theme of all the articles in the newspaper discussing the celebrations of May Day, the first of which appeared at the beginning of March. Although the election of the "Queen of Labor" was supposed to take place immediately after the official celebration of May Day, that year it seems it did not take place. Many important industrial companies, including some multinational ones, had donated money and products for the prizes. Interestingly enough, most of the contests announced by *El Laborista*, including the one for the "Queen of Labor," were prizes for productivity, and not for trade union activity.

53. *El Laborista*, April 30, 1947, 9.

54. "Argentine workers . . . give the May Day celebration a meaning . . . which is anti-Communist, stressing, in contrast, the national and social content of the revolution." *La Epoca*, April 29, 1947, 4. In another issue of the paper: "The May Day celebration, this year, will have a meaning it never had before. Until the Revolution of the 4th of June, the main festivities of May Day had a clear class sense, almost antinational. The only song sung was 'The International,' and the only flag waved was the red one. Now, however, May Day has a national meaning: the recovery of the nation." *La Epoca*, April 28, 1947, 4.

55. *El Líder*, April 27, 1947, 7. In other parts, the newspaper evoked the Chicago Martyrs, a remembrance that, as we have seen, was not part of the original meaning of May Day. Its editorial for April 30, 1947, read: "In this year, as in all years . . . this vision of the blood of Chicago will be with us. . . . Above all, the

people, with the beautiful and undying internationalism of May Day, will this year follow a new road of festivity, painful but festive all the same."

56. "United across the seas, all the workers of the world lived their day." Ibid., May 3, 1947, 2. *El Líder* adopted as its own a more traditional interpretation of May Day by exalting, above all, its working-class character. Unlike the other Peronist newspapers, *El Líder* did not place May Day on the list of "Peronist events," but in a series of more general historic moments that began with the May Revolution and included the Revolution of 1890, the radical uprisings of 1893 and 1905, and the bloody May Day of 1901. Ibid., April 30, 1947, 19.

57. *El Laborista*, April 25, 1947, 8.

58. See the "Manifiesto de la CGT," ibid., April 30, 1947, 9.

59. *Democracia*, October 18, 1947, 2.

60. *La Nación*, October 18, 1947, 5.

61. In addition, shortly before October 17, 1948, Cipriano Reyes was implicated in a supposed plot to assassinate Perón and Eva. Afterward, Reyes would be prosecuted and jailed.

62. *La Nación*, October 18, 1947, 1.

63. *La Prensa*, October 18, 1947.

64. On October 16, 1947, *Democracia* and *El Líder* ran the same headlines: "The Seventeenth of October, Day of Liberation! Today as yesterday the people with Perón!"

65. *Democracia*, October 16, 1947, 1.

66. Ibid., October 11, 1947, 4; *El Líder*, October 10, 1947, 4.

67. See, for example, *El Laborista*, October 16, 1947, 2; *Democracia*, October 16, 1947, 3.

68. The lyrics to the "March of Labor" are as follows: "Today in this celebration of work/ United by the love of God/At the foot of this sacred flag/ Let us pledge to defend with honor/That which is our blue and white flag/ The sublime expression of our love/ For it, for our parents and the children/ For the home which is our tradition/ Our life is ennobled by work/ We love our nation and home even more/ When sweat blesses our effort/ When we earn our bread by working./ San Martín subdued the Andes by working/And crossed its summits toward the sun./ By complying with our Argentine responsibilities/We will have rights and love." The music was composed by Cátulo Castillo.

69. *La Época*, April 30, 1948, 20, and *Democracia*, May 2, 1948, 8 and 9.

70. The official program ran as follows: (a) At 6:00 P.M., the celebration was opened by the singing of the National Anthem played by the orchestra of the Colón Theater; (b) "Canto al trabajo" (Hymn to work) was played by the band of the Military School; (c) Secretary General of the CGT José Espejo delivered his speech; (d) Perón delivered his speech (Eva also gave a speech, although it was not officially scheduled); (e) Performance of folkloric dances; (f) Arrival of carriages with the regional "Queens of Labor"; (g) Allegorical dances by dancers of the Colón

Theater; (h) Election of the national "Queen of Labor"; (i) Parade of floats with the queens.

71. The program for May Day 1949 ran as follows: (a) From April 25 to April 28, schoolchildren all around the country would visit workplaces during class time; (b) On April 29, there would be four large gatherings of students in the interior of the country, particularly in areas of "vast industrial activity." These gatherings would be synchronized with four other gatherings occurring in the province of Buenos Aires; (c) On April 30 there would be a ceremony in each school in which schoolchildren would present a firefighter, a police officer, a mailman, and an industrial worker with books. They would bestow a total of 45,000 books. *Compendio de la Suma Teológica*, *La Anunciación de María* by Paul Claudel, *El secreto del éxito* by Father Ramón Ruiz Amado, and *Todo llega* by Henri Ardel were the titles distributed. *La Prensa*, May 2, 1949, 8.

72. The army and the air force made public their allegiance to the celebration of May Day. At various air force bases there were conferences on the meaning of May Day, and air force officers were invited to the main gathering in the Plaza de Mayo. *El Laborista*, April 29, 1948, 5. The minister of war issued a communication on April 25 stating, "The celebration of May Day will take place on May First with a different meaning from the one given to it up to the present. It will be a patriotic celebration of peace and work by all the Argentine family, which is expressed in the verses of the 'Hymn to Work' that the people will sing on that day." *El Laborista*, April 26, 1948, 5. For its part the Federal Court of Appeals of the Labor Courts also publicly supported the celebration.

73. Perón's speech, according to *La Nación*, May 2, 1948, 8.

74. Given that opportunity, Perón felt compelled to defend the role he had played during the Tragic Week: "It has been said during the electoral campaign that I intervened in that area during that week of January. I was a lieutenant and was in the war arsenal; I stood on duty here precisely the day after the events. I was able to see, then, the true misery of men." The complete text of the speech may be found in *El Líder*, May 2, 1948, 23. The celebration had been planned well in advance. *El Laborista* had announced it on April 10, stating that both Peróns had promised to attend.

75. Speech given by Eva Perón on October 17, 1949.

76. For a general overview of the relations between Perón and the Catholic Church, see Lila Caimari, *Perón y la Iglesia Católica: Religión, Estado, y sociedad en la Argentina, 1943–1955* (Buenos Aires, 1995). See also N. Stack, "Avoiding the Greater Evil: The Response of the Catholic Church to Juan Perón, 1943–1955" (Ph.D. diss., Rutgers University, 1976).

77. See the provocative article by Lila Caimari, "El lugar del catolicismo en el primer peronismo." Paper presented at the International Meeting of Argentine History (1930–1955), organized by the Instituto Universitario José Ortega y Gasset, Madrid, May 1991.

78. *La Prensa*, October 18, 1948.

79. *Democracia*, October 5, 1949.

80. *La Nación*, May 2, 1949, 5.

81. *Democracia*, April 27, 1948, 1.

82. Ibid.

83. *El Líder*, April 28, 1949, 4.

84. It is interesting that this editorial is about Urquiza's *Pronunciamiento*, and it characterizes Rosas in a very favorable manner.

85. A. Ciria, *Política y cultura popular: La Argentina peronista (1946–1955)* (Buenos Aires, 1984), 276.

86. In terms of loyalty to the president and to the Peronist movement. The CGT was becoming the disciplinary arm of the government within the trade unions. The 1950 statutes gave CGT the right to intervene in rebellious unions. See L. Doyon, "Organized Labour and Perón (1943–1955): A Study of the Conflictual Dynamics of the Peronist Movement in Power" (Ph.D. diss., University of Toronto, 1978), 503–10.

87. *The Economist*, April 27, 1950, 895.

88. After reading them, Perón said: "I have wanted to gather them like this, so that each one of you can record them in your minds and hearts, spread them like a message of love and justice, practice them loyally and honorably, live happily by them, and also die happily in their defense if necessary."

89. *Democracia*, October 18, 1951, 3.

90. *La Nación*, October 18, 1951, 5. This symbiosis between the CGT and the state was also evident in the fact that the secretary of labor and welfare participated in the delegation of the CGT that carried the Argentine flag to the Plaza de Mayo at the beginning of the celebration. The participation of the CGT in the decoration of servicemen provoked a minor incident when rumors spread that the CGT had given orders (never specified) to the armed forces. The CGT denied this. *Democracia*, October 18, 1951, 5.

91. The decree declaring the Eighteenth of October a national holiday read: "That the Argentine people has hereby decided to exalt not only the social redemption work that Eva Perón is carrying out for the good of the *descamisados* of the country, but also the gesture of self-denying renunciation which led her to refuse high political office so as to continue fighting from the bottom up for the happiness of this same people. That the overflowing assembly witnessed today constitutes an affirmation of the *justicialista* faith and a clear repudiation of the traitors who did not waiver in raising arms against the constituted order." *La Nación*, October 18, 1951, 1.

92. *Democracia*, October 18, 1951.

93. After CGT leader José Espejo's speech, other speakers distributed the words pronounced by Eva in her May Day speech from the First of May. Afterward, a speaker read a text left by Eva Perón before dying, in which she proclaimed her love for Perón and for the people. Other passages of the text were treated as her will. In it, she left all her property to Perón and the people. During Perón's lifetime he could

dispose of Eva's property, because "everything while he's alive belongs to him . . . even my own life." After the death of Perón, all her property would be inherited by the people. With her jewelry, Eva established a fund to guarantee the granting of loans to the needy. In a very emotional note, Eva asked her *descamisados* to keep sending her letters even after her death.

94. *La Nación*, October 16, 1952, 1.

95. One year later, after the attempted coup, Perón would be even more direct, stating that "each minute that goes by should be devoted to swearing, before the unfading altar of our nation, to defeat our internal and external enemies, to annihilate them, if necessary."

96. *Democracia*, May 2, 1951, 2.

97. Ibid., 1.

98. A typical example of this is the following note appearing in ibid., May 2, 1952, 1. "The Peronist conception of man, in its ecumenical and transcendental sense . . . has the spiritual force to expand throughout the world, supported by our own happy and fecund experience. This has made it dangerous to the powerful imperialist powers, which do not have any other resources but arms to impose their designs of conquest and vassalage on others. For this reason, all the foreign Bradens and their colonial agents are gathering at this point in our national epic to try to frustrate it." In 1953, *Democracia* would go even further: "What is the name of our enemy spelled out in full? THE UNITED STATES OF AMERICA" (May 2, 1953, 4).

Part III and Chapter 5, Pages 83–103

1. Tracy Koon, *Believe, Obey, Fight: Political Socialization of Youth in Fascist Italy, 1922–1943* (Chapel Hill, NC, 1985), xv.

2. Argentina, Subsecretaría de Informaciones de la Presidencia de la Nación, *Segundo Plan Quinquenal de Gobierno* (Buenos Aires, 1952).

3. Michael Conniff, "Introduction: Towards a Comparative Definition of Populism," in M. Conniff, ed., *Latin American Populism in Comparative Perspective* (Albuquerque, NM, 1982), 5.

4. On the organization of the educational system in Argentina, see Juan Carlos Tedesco, *Educación y sociedad en la Argentina (1880–1900)* (Buenos Aires, 1970). See also H. Spalding, "Education in Argentina, 1890–1914: The Limits of Oligarchic Reform," in *Journal of Interdisciplinary History* 3, no. 1 (Summer 1972).

5. On this subject, see, among others, C. Escude, *El fracaso del proyecto argentino: Educación e ideología* (Buenos Aires, 1990), esp. chap. 2; and H. Spalding, "Education in Argentina, 1890–1914."

6. *Monitor de Educación Común* 714 (June 1932).

7. Ministerio de Justicia e Educación, *Memoria del Ministerio de Justicia e Instrucción Pública: Correspondiente al año 1943* (Buenos Aires, 1944), 153ff.

8. Remember that Law 1420 had established that religious instruction should be provided by members of the clergy of different creeds on a voluntary basis *outside* regular classes.

9. Schoolteacher unions and organizations were traditionally liberal or left-wing. Back in 1914, the nationalist writer (later turned Peronist) Manuel Gálvez had parodied teachers in his novel *La Maestra Normal*, which provoked a strongly unfavorable reaction among schoolteachers. However, once Catholic religious instruction became mandatory, only a very few teachers refused to teach it. This might suggest that most of the members of this profession (much more predominantly female in 1943 than when Gálvez wrote his novel) were less ideologically committed than they were perceived to be.

10. In March 1947, an article in the official labor magazine *CGT* claimed that the workers opposed religious education because it was an antidemocratic measure that violated freedom of conscience. See Virginia Leonard, *Politicians, Pupils, and Priests: Argentine Education since 1943* (New York, 1989), 89.

11. The Laínez Law of 1905 had authorized the federal government to establish schools under its jurisdiction in those provinces that requested them.

12. V. Leonard, *Politicians*, 45.

13. Argentina, Consejo Nacional de Educación, *La educación común en la capital, provincias y territorios* (Buenos Aires, 1946), chap. 6.

14. See M. Plotkin, "Politics of Consensus in Peronist Argentina (1943–1955)" (Ph.D. diss., University of California, Berkeley, 1992), table 5.1, 184–85.

15. In an internal memo sent in May 1944 to the principal of School No. 19 from the Consejo Escolar for the fifth district, the secretary of the Consejo Escolar wrote: "One should definitely not tell the child about the beginning of this new class [religion]. The activity should start, the student will take the news home, talk it over with his parents, and they will be the ones who, if in disagreement, should bring their concern to school; but the authorities should only reply: The Consejo Escolar is located in Montes de Oca 455, where from 9 to 12 . . . a book has been opened to register all complaints." School No. 19, V Consejo Escolar, Archive, "Meeting Book." Teachers' meeting, May 30, 1944.

16. See, for example, the internal memo sent by the ministry to the school authorities dated March 29, 1951.

17. Ministerio de Justicia e Instrucción Pública, *Memoria del Ministerio de Justicia e Instrucción Pública: Correspondiente*.

18. The idea of requiring an oath from schoolteachers was not new. Back in 1920, Angel Gallardo, then president of the Consejo Nacional de Educación, had suggested the institution of an oath, which would have to be renewed annually. The reason Gallardo gave for the oath (which was apparently approved, but it is unclear if it was ever put into practice) was: "It is clear to all that the dissolvent preaching by newspapers and magazines and writings of advanced ideas are pervasive, and they could affect the basic fundamentals of the school or even of our nation if they take root in the children's souls." Argentina, Consejo Nacional de Educación, *La*

educación común en la capital federal, provincias y territorios nacionales (Buenos Aires, 1920).

19. Argentina, Ministerio de Educación de la Nación, *Labor desarrollada durante la primera presidencia del General Juan Perón* (Buenos Aires, 1952); Argentina, Ministerio de Educación, *La educación secundaria en la Argentina* (Buenos Aires, 1964).

20. "We will give each Argentine a future, declared the president to the directors of learning." *Democracia*, March 6, 1948.

21. Decree 1100, dated January 16, 1948, instituted "prelearning" (technical education) in the syllabi for the fifth and sixth grades of primary schools.

22. The conflict between the military authorities (and later Perón) and the universities was evident from the beginning. By March 1947, 1,073 university professors had been fired for ideological reasons. However, also from the beginning, groups of faculty formed that supported the policies of the new authorities (and later Perón), especially among the faculty of the medical school. These groups were led by Dr. Oscar Ivanissevich, Ramón Carrillo, and others. See Edward Johnson, "Education and Nationalism in Argentina, 1930–1966" (Ph.D. diss., University of California, Santa Barbara, 1973), 85.

23. Decree 26,941/47, April 9, 1947.

24. This text is taken from the introduction to the decree.

25. Although tuition fees were eliminated in 1949, public secondary education would only be free from 1952 onward.

26. Although the expansion of the technical education system was an important component of the social policy of Perón's government, the topic has not yet been studied in detail. One of the few studies is David Wiñar, "Poder político y educación: El peronismo y la Comisión Nacional de Aprendizaje y Orientación Profesional." Working Paper series, Centro de Investigaciones en Ciencias de la Educación, Instituto Torcuato Di Tella (Buenos Aires, 1970).

27. See the discussion in *DSCD* 1948, 3 (1984–1998).

28. On the projects of the conservative governments for establishing a system of technical education, see J. C. Tedesco, *Educación y sociedad en la Argentina (1880–1945)*.

29. *La Tribuna*, January 18, 1947.

30. *La Nación*, June 14, 1946.

31. Paulino Mussachio was a doctor whose previous official appointments had been under the military governments first established in 1943. These positions included secretary of welfare for the City of Buenos Aires, vice president of the National Commission on Culture, vice president of the Caja Nacional de Ahorro Postal. Another evidence of the secondary role that Perón's government assigned the Consejo Nacional de Educación was the fact that the administrators appointed by Perón were, in general, unknown figures. Until the coming of Peronism, the highest positions within the Consejo were reserved for members of the elite, polititians, or well-known scientists. It is interesting to note that during Perón's rule, the names of

almost none of the highly placed personnel within the educational system appeared in the annual editions of *Who's Who*.

32. The post of Secretary of Education was created by decree on February 24, 1948.

33. Law 13,548, 1949.

34. This topic will be discussed further in Chapter 8.

35. According to an official source published during the governance of Perón, the number of kindergartens increased from five in 1946 to 636 in 1951. See Argentina, Ministerio de Educación de la Nación, *Labor desarrollada durante la primera presidencia del General Juan Perón* (Buenos Aires, 1952).

36. A case in point is the celebration of Youth Week in 1948, which coincided with the anniversary of the Battle of Tucumán. An order issued by the ministry, dated September 7 of that year, established that "the authorities, the teachers, the students, the workers, and the employees, united by the same patriotic feeling, will participate in the celebrations." The program organized by the ministry was as follows: in Tucumán, "the people," led by authorities, would parade on the battleground. There, "representatives of the people" would light an "Argentine flame," while students, workers, and employees would listen to a speech that Perón would deliver in Buenos Aires, which would be broadcast by radio through loudspeakers. Simultaneously, in Buenos Aires, students, workers, and employees would participate in a "patriotic vigil" in the Plaza de Mayo, after which there would be an open-air Mass. To conclude, a teacher and an officer from the army would both deliver speeches.

37. From a speech delivered by Perón at the opening of the ordinary session of Congress, May 1, 1949.

38. Many of the tours organized by the ministry were held in the presidential residence, where Perón and Eva handed out toys to the children and often shared lunch and teatime with them. Although the use of the presidential residence as a place of tours for primary school students was certainly not new (President Justo had opened up parts of the residence for the same purpose), the possibility of getting physically close to the president or his wife was certainly a Peronist grace note.

39. Generally, this tension seems to be a feature of regimes usually characterized as "populist." See, among others, M. Conniff, "Introduction: Towards a Comparative Definition of Populism."

40. *La Nación*, June 24, 1950.

41. On many ocassions the Ministry polled teachers for their opinions on the functioning of extracurricular activities. In most responses, teachers stressed the lack of enthusiasm among parents and students, as well as the endemic problem of lack of funds. The latter was recognized by the ministry's secretary of didactics, Oscar Tolosa, who in a note dated July 12, 1948, suggested the possibility of charging those who wished to participate in the activities of the school clubs a small amount, since the state did not provide adequate funds.

42. See the text of the speech in *Boletín de Comunicaciones del Ministerio de Educación* 275 (April 24, 1953).
43. Decree 20,226, October 26, 1953.
44. *Boletín de Comunicaciones* 270 (February 1953), 351.
45. See Lila Caimari, *Perón y la Iglesia Católica: Religión, Estado y sociedad en la Argentina, 1943–1955* (Buenos Aires, 1995).
46. T. Halperín Donghi, *Historia de la Universidad de Buenos Aires* (Buenos Aires, 1962), 184.

Chapter 6, Pages 105–34

1. See editorial in *La Prensa*, September 21, 1946.
2. *La Nación*, April 2, 1950, 4.
3. On this point, see A. Ciria, *Política y cultura popular: La Argentina peronista (1946–1955)* (Buenos Aires, 1983).
4. The analysis of textbooks, whether issued under authoritarian regimes or not, has received attention in other countries, generating a very extensive literature, which cannot be fully enumerated here. See, among others, for Italy: Umberto Eco and Marisa Bonazzi, *I pampini bugiardi* (Rimini, 1972); T. Koon, *Believe, Obey, Fight: Political Socialization of Youth in Fascist Italy, 1922–1943* (Chapel Hill, NC, 1985), especially chap. 3. For texts on Franco's Spain, see C. Garcia Crespo, *Léxico e ideología en los libros de lectura de la escuela primaria (1940–75)* (Salamanca, 1983); Gregorio Camara Villar, *Nacional-Catolicismo y escuela: La socialización política del franquismo (1936–1951)* (Madrid, 1984). For the United States, see Michael Apple, *Teachers and Texts: A Political Economy of Class and Gender Relations in Education* (New York, 1986). On history texts in particular, see Volker Berghahn and Hanna Schissler, comps., *Perceptions of History: An Analysis of School Textbooks* (Oxford, 1987). For Latin America, see Giorgio Bini et al., *Los libros de texto en América Latina* (Mexico City, 1977); Ana Boggio, "La ideología en los textos escolares peruanos," in *Comunicación y Cultura* 2 (1973); Dante Moreira Leite, "Analise de contenido dos livros de leitura na escola primaria," in *Pesquisa e Planejamento* 4 (1962); Josefina Vazquez, *Nacionalismo y educación en México* (Mexico City, 1970). For Argentina, see Ana Nethol, "El libro de lectura en la escuela primaria en la Argentina," in *Comunicación y Cultura* 2 (1973); Catalina Wainerman and Rebeca Raijman, *La división sexual del trabajo en los libros de lectura de la escuela primaria argentina: Un caso de inmutabilidad secular* (Buenos Aires, 1984), and *El sexismo en los libros de lectura de la escuela primaria* (Buenos Aires, 1987); A. Ciria, *Política y cultura popular*.
5. U. Eco and M. Bonazzi, *I pampini bugiardi*.
6. This image was not realistic, since in Argentina, unlike the United States, almost all charity was centered in the Society of Beneficence. This body was almost completely financed by public funds. Perón's first government took over the society

and in practical terms replaced it with the Fundación Eva Perón. On the history and development of the Society of Beneficence, see Cynthia Little, "The Society of Beneficence in Buenos Aires, 1823–1900" (Ph.D. diss., Temple University, 1980). On the Fundación, see Chapters 7 and 8 of this volume.

7. Note to Deputy Nicanor Costa Méndez, published in *Monitor de Educación Común* 714 (June 1932).

8. *Privilegiados.*

9. See M. Conniff, "Introduction: Toward a Comparative Definition of Populism," in M. Conniff, ed., *Latin American Populism in Comparative Perspective* (Albuquerque, NM, 1983).

10. This, of course, is not the only possible interpretation of the poem. See T. Halperín Donghi, *José Hernández y sus mundos* (Buenos Aires, 1985), and Josefina Ludmer, *El género gauchesco: Un tratado sobre la patria* (Buenos Aires, 1988).

11. "Historical revisionism" is a historiographical trend that appeared in the 1930s and is linked to nationalist groups. This trend rejects the traditional liberal historiography completely and attempts to build an alternative one based on the revaluation of the Hispanic, *caudillista* tradition of the country. The heroes of the liberal pantheon are degraded to the category of "nation-sellers," while the *caudillos*— in particular, Juan Manuel de Rosas—are elevated to the category of national heroes. See T. Halperín Donghi, *El revisionismo histórico* (Buenos Aires, 1970).

12. See M. Plotkin, "La ideología de Perón: Rupturas y continuidades," in S. Amaral and M. Plotkin, comps., *Perón del exilio al poder* (Buenos Aires, 1993). For a perspective that places the origins of the relationship between Peronism and revisionism within the origins of Peronism, see D. Quattrocchi-Woisson, *Los males de la memoria* (Buenos Aires, 1995). See also Colin Winston, "Between Rosas and Sarmiento: Notes on Nationalism in Peronist Thought," in *The Americas* 39, no. 3 (1983).

13. C. Ibarguren, *La historia que he vivido* (Buenos Aires, 1954).

14. *Monitor de Educación Común* 726 and 727 (June–July 1933).

15. In the same way, the constitutional reform of 1949 came to be called "the *justicialista* Constitution." This Constitution came to be seen as an essential element of the Peronist imagery and is, naturally, conspicuously present in the texts.

16. Only three textbooks for primary school among the ones I was able to analyze mention Rosas in a neutral tone: *Manual Estrada para 4to grado*; *Patria justa* by Luisa de García; and *Alma de América* by León Benarós.

17. C. Winston, "Between Rosas and Sarmiento."

18. This tendency could be the result of certain components of Peronist ideology but also of a certain "bureaucratic memory," which existed in educational institutions.

19. Statements such as "All authority emanates from God" are repeated numerous times in the syllabi.

20. See Lila Caimari, *Perón y la Iglesia Católica: Religión, estado y sociedad en la Argentina, 1943–1955* (Buenos Aires, 1995).

21. See, among others, M. Navarro Gerassi, *Evita* (Buenos Aires, 1980); Julia Guivant, *La visible Eva Perón y el invisible rol político femenino en el peronismo: 1946–1952* (Notre Dame, IN, 1986); and the general analysis by C. Wainerman and R. Raijman on the representations of women's role in primary school textbooks in *La división sexual del trabajo en los libros de lectura de la escuela primaria argentina: Un caso de inmutabilidad secular* (Buenos Aires, 1984). See, in addition, the interesting oral history of the Partido Peronista Femenino by S. Bianchi and N. Sanchis, *El Partido Peronista Femenino* (Buenos Aires, 1988).

22. C. Wainerman and R. Raijman, *La división sexual del trabajo*.

23. M. Conniff, "Introduction."

Part IV and Chapter 7, Pages 135–64

1. Renzo De Felice, *Mussolini il Duce*, vol. 3, *Gli anni del consenso, 1929–1936* (Torino, 1974), chap. 2.

2. The Unión de Estudiantes Secundarios (UES) was a late attempt to organize youth. But its objectives were ambiguous and it was never able to attract mass participation.

3. T. Halperín Donghi, *Argentina: La democracia de masas* (Buenos Aires, 1986), 64.

4. The mythology around the FEP is so strong that it has even permeated otherwise fine pieces of scholarship such as Marysa Navarro Gerassi, *Evita* (Buenos Aires, 1981). To my knowledge, the best analysis of the FEP and of the social policies of Perón in general is the doctoral thesis of Peter Ross, "Policy Formation and Implementation of Social Welfare in Peronist Argentina, 1943–1955" (Ph.D. diss., University of New South Wales, Australia, 1988).

5. This idea is suggested but not elaborated on by T. Halperín Donghi, *Argentina: La democracia de masas*.

6. A large part of this section is based on data appearing in P. Ross, "Policy Formation."

7. According to Carlos Escudé, the health system in Buenos Aires at the turn of the twentieth century was extremely efficient for that era. During the first decade of the century, Buenos Aires compared favorably to cities such as New York, Philadelphia, and Montreal in terms of death rates and the number of hospital beds available per 1,000 inhabitants. See C. Escudé, "Health in Buenos Aires in the Second Half of the Nineteenth Century," in D. M. C. Platt, ed., *Social Welfare, 1850–1950: Australia, Argentina and Canada Compared* (London, 1989).

8. P. Ross, "Policy Formation," 75.

9. In 1888, for example, the SBC disputed with the Defensoría de Menores over the right to establish policies concerning abandoned children. As a result of

this conflict, in 1890 the state withheld the funds allocated to the SBC for the Casa de Expósitos. For a history of the SBC up to 1900, see C. Little, "The Society of Beneficence in Buenos Aires, 1923–1900" (Ph.D. diss., Temple University, 1980). See also Carlos Correa Luna, *Historia de la Sociedad de Beneficencia, 1852–1923* (Buenos Aires, 1925), and Sociedad de Beneficencia de la Capital, *Sociedad de Beneficencia de la Capital, 1823–1936* (Buenos Aires, 1936).

10. Sociedad de Beneficencia de la Capital, *Memoria correspondiente al año 1934* (Buenos Aires, 1935).

11. P. Ross, "Policy Formation," 237.

12. Vicepresidencia de la Nación, Consejo Nacional de Post-Guerra, *Ordenamiento económico y social* (Buenos Aires, 1945), 39.

13. P. Ross, "Policy Formation," 37, and J. Horowitz, *Argentine Unions, the State, and the Rise of Perón, 1930–1945* (Berkeley, 1990), 186.

14. P. Ross, "Policy Formation," 48.

15. CGT, *Anuario del Trabajo, 1948* (Buenos Aires, 1948), cited in P. Ross, "Policy Formation," 52.

16. J. D. Perón, "Discurso pronunciado por el General Perón al poner en posesión de su cargo al director del Instituto Nacional de Previsión Social, Dr. Roque V. Policicchio" (1950).

17. Presidencia de la Nación, Subsecretaria de Informaciones, *Segundo Plan Quinquenal* (Buenos Aires, n.d.), 47.

18. Gary Wynia, *Argentina in the Post-War Era: Politics and Economic Policy Making in a Divided Society* (Albuquerque, NM, 1978), 68–77.

19. See Objective III E 3: "Régimen de Asistencia Social," which reads: "National coordination of all organizations providing social aid at the national, provincial, and municipal level, and the consequent coordination with the social services of the professional associations and with the Fundación Eva Perón." Subsecretaria de Informaciones, *Segundo Plan Quinquenal*, 50.

20. On the relationship between Perón and the unions, see L. Doyon, "Organized Labour and Perón (1943–1955): A Study of the Conflictual Dynamics of the Peronist Movement in Power" (Ph.D. diss., University of Toronto, Canada, 1978).

21. During the government of Perón real wages rose at a faster rate than average income per capita:

Period	Index of real wage rates	Index of per capita GNP
1940–1944	100	99
1945–1949	142	118
1950–1954	159	110
1955–1959	166	117
1960–1964	164	124

Source: Carlos F. Díaz Alejandro, *Essays on the Economic History of the Argentine Republic* (New Haven, 1970), table 133, 538.

According to Peter Alhadeff, during the Peronist period, "economic policy was tailored to the redistribution of income." See P. Alhadeff, "Social Welfare and the Slums: Argentina in the 1930s," in D. C. M. Platt, ed., *Social Welfare, 1850–1950.* See also Pablo Gerchunoff, "Política Económica Peronista, 1945–1955," in G. Di Tella and R. Dornbusch, comps., *The Political Economy of Argentina, 1946–1983* (London, 1990).

22. See L. Doyon, "Organized Labour and Perón," table on p. 433.

23. The existence of such duality was suggested by Gino Germani in the mid-1950s, when he noted that out of the 1,800,000 industrial workers registered by the national census in 1947, there were 500,000 who had not been registered as such by the industrial census of 1946. Probably, as Germani pointed out, the difference can be explained by the existence of people who, although working within the industrial sector, did not work in organized firms but as artisans, and as such were not registered by the industrial census. See G. Germani, *Estructura social de la Argentina* (Buenos Aires, 1955), 169. Sergio Lischinsky has shown that during the Peronist period there was a significant proportion of workers who did not participate in the *cajas de jubilación* in "La afiliación al sistema previsional (1944–1955): Logros y dificultades en su expansión" (Buenos Aires, mimeograph, 1989).

24. See, for example, Mary Main (pseud. María Flores), *La mujer del látigo: Eva Perón* (Buenos Aires, 1955), 102.

25. Eva Perón, *La razón de mi vida* (Buenos Aires, 1951), 182.

26. Nicholas Fraser and M. Navarro Gerassi, *Eva Perón* (New York, 1981), 115.

27. See, for example, "Un acto de desagravio al General San Martín," in *Democracia*, September 1, 1946.

28. The Radical opposition also characterized the SBC as an oligarchic institution. In 1949, when discussing a subsidy to the FEP for the Campeonatos Evita, Radical Congressman Sobral noted of the SBC: "Hipólito Yrigoyen, when he became President of the Republic, donated his entire salary as president to the SBC, forgetting that in this same society there were ladies representing the regime he had just defeated." *DSCD* 1949 3:2062.

29. In spite of the fact that *Criterio* published a note in defense of the SBC, the Catholic Church had no official reaction. See "La Sociedad de Beneficencia," *Criterio*, August 1, 1946, 112.

30. The granting of the new salary scale to the employees of the SBC and other public employees was offered by the Ministry of Finance as an explanation for an increase in the national budget for 1947. See Ministerio de Hacienda de la Nación, *Boletín* 1, 37 (December 7, 1946). Thanks to Lila Caimari for calling this source to my attention.

31. Sociedad de Beneficencia de la Capital, *Un año de intervención* (Buenos Aires, 1947). See also "Hermosa realidad: Van a la escuela del Estado los niños de la Sociedad de Beneficencia," *Democracia*, April 22, 1948, 9.

32. The opposition members of Congress refused to show up to administer the oath to Perón on the day of his inauguration, transforming this formal official cer-

emony into a political statement against the government.

33. E. Perón, "Mensaje pronunciado el 27 de enero de 1947 dedicado a la mujer argentina por LRA Radio del Estado y la Red Argentina de Radiodifusión." E. Perón, *Discursos completos, 1946–1948*, vol. 1 (Buenos Aires, 1985), 32.

34. Eva's relationship with the unions is analyzed in detail by M. Navarro Gerassi in *Evita*.

35. Otelo Borroni and Roberto Vacca, *La vida de Eva Perón*, vol. 1, *Testimonios para su historia* (Buenos Aires, 1971), 136.

36. The gifts were to be distributed on the Fourth of June in celebration of the anniversary of the Revolution. *Democracia*, June 1, 1947. *Democracia* was instrumental in creating myths around Eva. As early as June 1947, we find notes such as the following: "A poor widow needs a sewing machine. She cries because she has nothing, not even a husband. Surely Eva will help heal her pain." There was also a tendency to associate Eva's name with elements of popular culture. The June 6, 1948, issue of *Democracia*, for example, featured on the front page a photo of Santa Claus carrying his traditional sack of gifts. The difference from the usual picture of Santa, however, was that, on one corner of the sack, one could make out the name "Eva."

37. *Democracia*, December 30, 1947.

38. Ibid., December 21, 1947.

39. Ibid., January 9, 1947.

40. Ibid., June 19, 1948.

41. See the by-laws in N. Fraser and M. Navarro Gerassi, *Eva Perón*, 117.

42. *DSCD* 2 (1951): 1327.

43. *Democracia*, January 11, 1949.

44. This law was a model of incoherence. It established that the FEP would be responsible for social tourism, previously the responsibility of the INR. The law transferred to the FEP all the resources of the INR, including a retention of 2 percent of bonus pay, 1 percent contributed by employers, and the money from the fines imposed on those who did not obey the law. Article 10 authorized the FEP to take charge of the administration and maintenance of any building or organization of social assistance owned or built by the state. Article 11 authorized state organizations to make donations in cash or other forms of payment to the institutions of social assistance owned by the FEP. However, Article 2 established that the FEP was a private institution, independent of the state, while the activities of the FEP "are of a public order and in the national interest." Finally, Article 14 donated to the FEP a building belonging to the University of Buenos Aires.

45. Law 14,042 of 1951 increased the tax to 6 percent.

46. "Fundación de Ayuda Social," *Primera Plana: Historia del Peronismo* 26 (December 27, 1966).

47. See, for example, Law 14,048.

48. M. Navarro Gerassi, *Evita*, 250.

49. N. Fraser and M. Navarro Gerassi, *Eva Perón*, 119.

50. Néstor Ferioli, *La Fundación Eva Perón* (Buenos Aires, 1990), 40.

51. The narration of this incident is based on information found in Vicepresidencia de la Nación, Comisión Nacional de Investigaciones, *Documentación, autores y cómplices de las irregularidades cometidas durante la segunda tiranía*, vol. 2 (Buenos Aires, 1958). Comisión 17: Cine, Teatro, Radio, 3–177.

52. The event may be followed in issues of *Democracia* during December 1950. See also *La Nación*, December 22, 1950.

53. Instituto Bernasconi, Archives, Libro copiador de notas; and Escuela 19, D.E. 5, Archives, Libro copiador de notas.

54. Fundación Eva Perón, *Memoria 1952* (Buenos Aires, n.d.), 65ff.

55. The government took over not only the SBC but also the Argentine Red Cross and other societies of social assistance in Buenos Aires and the interior. See *DSCD* 3 (1949): 2193.

56. Resolutions of June 17 and 26, 1949. Special permits for the collection of donations in the schools on special occasions, however, were granted to particular institutions such as the Asistencia Social al Cardíaco and, more significantly, to the Liga Patriótica Argentina.

57. Escuela 19, D.E. 5, Archives, Libro copiador de notas, 1953.

58. It is not clear whether the halfway houses were created by the FEP or the SBC. What is certain is that after the dissolution of the SBC, the homes were administered by the FEP.

59. *Democracia*, August 14, 1948.

60. Fundación Eva Perón, "Memoria 1954" (unpublished).

61. See S. McGee Deutsch, *Counterrevolution in Argentina, 1900–1932: The Argentine Patriotic League* (Lincoln, NE, 1986), 58.

62. See N. Stack, "Avoiding the Greater Evil: The Response of the Catholic Church to Juan Perón, 1943–1955" (Ph.D. diss., Rutgers University, 1976).

63. *Criterio* makes almost no mention of the FEP until the outbreak of open conflict between the Church and the state.

64. *Democracia*, December 10, 1948. As expected, the hospitals were named "Presidente Perón," "17 de Octubre," and "Coronel Perón." The hospital "17 de Octubre" was inaugurated after the death of Eva and was rebaptized "Evita."

65. According to Ross, only the polyclinic "Presidente Perón" in Avellaneda, with a capacity of six hundred beds, was finished by that time. See also *Revista de Arquitectura: Organo Oficial de la Sociedad Argentina de Arquitectos* 38 (1953): 370.

66. Fundación Eva Perón, *Memoria 1953* (Buenos Aires, n.d.). According to Ross, by the end of 1953, there were fifteen hospitals in the process of being built and eight not yet begun. Ross, "Policy Formation," table v.9.

67. Fundación Eva Perón, "Memoria 1954."

68. N. Ferioli, *La Fundación*, 70.

69. "I don't deny that my works help to consolidate the enormous political prestige of the General." E. Perón, *La razón de mi vida*, 233.

70. *Democracia*, June 30, 1949, 5.

71. Ibid., November 9, 1949.

72. Ibid., September 23, 1951, 2.

73. Ibid., July 15, 1949.

74. Fundación Eva Perón, *Memoria 1952*, 23.

75. Cited in N. Ferioli, *La Fundación*, 90–91.

76. *Democracia*, October 28, 1951, 2.

77. Fundación Eva Perón, *Memoria 1953*, 29.

78. In an interview given in 1972, Dr. Ramón Cereijo said that 1,000 had actually been built at a cost of $90 million. Instituto Torcuato Di Tella, *Proyecto de historia oral*.

79. Interview with Dr. Ramón Cereijo, Buenos Aires, August 25, 1989.

80. *Life* Magazine, April 11, 1949, cited in N. Fraser and M. Navarro Gerassi, *Eva Perón*, 122.

81. Teresa María Mazzatosta and Claudio Volpi, eds., *L'Italietta Fascista. Lettere al potere, 1936–1943* (Bologna, 1980), 11.

82. There is a famous picture, obviously fabricated, which has been reproduced many times in official publications, showing Eva in her limousine at night, while the illuminated clock in the tower of the Secretariat of Labor and Welfare shows the hour of 5:00 A.M.

83. See J. Taylor, *Eva Peron: The Myths of a Woman* (Chicago, 1979), 88 and 96.

84. This event, which culminated in a dramatic dialogue between Eva and the people gathered in the Avenida Nueve de Julio, was baptized by the official propaganda as the "Cabildo Abierto del Justicialismo." For details, see M. Navarro Gerassi, *Evita*, chap. 12, and Borroni and Vacca, *La vida de Eva Perón*, 260ff.

85. Cited in N. Fraser and M. Navarro Gerassi, *Eva Perón*, 127.

86. Instituto Torcuato Di Tella, *Proyecto de historia oral*. A similar story was told to Susana Bianchi and Norma Sanchís by one of their interviewees.

87. Cited in O. Borroni and R. Vacca, *La vida de Eva Perón*, 223.

88. Fundación de Ayuda Social María Eva Duarte de Perón, *Por la ruta de los cuentos mágicos* (Buenos Aires, n.d.).

89. Ibid.

90. Ibid.

91. Testimony of Angel Peralta, secretary general of the Federación de Obreros y Empleados Vitivinícolas y Afines, who had participated in the aid mission as a representative from the CGT. *Democracia*, September 29, 1949, 3.

92. Ibid.

93. Consejo Superior de la Medalla Peronista, "Entrega de la medalla peronista a la abnegación (1950)" (Buenos Aires, 1950).

94. See, for example, *Mundo Peronista* 64 (May 1954), 5.

95. On *Mundo Peronista*, see A. Ciria, *Política y cultura popular: La Argentina peronista (1946–1955)* (Buenos Aires, 1983).

96. *Mundo Peronista* 26 (August 1952).

97. *Mundo Peronista* 27.

98. The ministry finally ordered that at least one school per city and one classroom per school be given the name "Eva."

99. J. Taylor, *Eva Perón.*

100. See M. Coniff, ed., *Latin American Populism in Comparative Perspective* (Albuquerque, NM, 1982).

101. See, for example, the article "Ayuda social sí, limosna no," in *Democracia,* July 28, 1948.

102. On the development of the concepts of charity and philanthropy in Argentina, see Ricardo González, "Caridad y filantropía en la ciudad de Buenos Aires durante la segunda mitad del siglo XIX," in Diego Armus, comp., *Sectores populares y vida urbana* (Buenos Aires, 1984). For the concept of "social rights," see T. H. Marshall, "Citizenship and Social Class," in T. H. Marshall, ed., *Sociology at the Crossroads and Other Essays* (London, 1963).

Chapter 8, Pages 165–93

1. F. Luna, *Perón y su tiempo,* vol. 2, *La comunidad organizada, 1950–1952* (Buenos Aires, 1987), 211.

2. E. Perón, "Eva Perón habla a los gobernadores de provincias y territorios nacionales" (1950), HUPC.

3. In this section, I make extensive use of a series of interviews of women members of the PPF carried out by Susana Bianchi and Norma Sanchís, some of which were used in their *El Partido Peronista Femenino,* 2 vols. (Buenos Aires, 1986). I deeply thank Bianchi and Sanchís for giving me access to the original transcriptions of the interviews and for having granted me permission to use them in this work. The names of the interviewees, at their request, have been kept confidential.

4. S. McGee Deutsch, *Counterrevolution in Argentina, 1900–1932: The Argentine Patriotic League* (Lincoln, NE, 1986), 15.

5. P. Ross, "Policy Formation and Implementation of Social Welfare in Peronist Argentina, 1943–1955" (Ph.D. diss., University of New South Wales, Australia, 1988), 330.

6. Nancy Hollander, *La mujer: Esclava de la historia, o historia de esclava?* (Buenos Aires, 1974), 86.

7. Ibid., 280.

8. S. Bianchi and N. Sanchís, *El Partido Peronista Femenino* (Buenos Aires, 1986), 25.

9. Juan Bialet Masse, *Informe sobre el estado de las clases obreras en el interior de la república* (Buenos Aires, 1904), 181. Cited in N. Hollander, *La mujer,* 66.

10. C. Wainerman and M. Navarro Gerassi, *El trabajo de la mujer en la Argentina: Un análisis preliminar de las ideas dominantes en las primeras décadas del siglo*

XX (Buenos Aires, 1979). See also Donna Guy, *Sex and Danger in Buenos Aires: Prostitution, Family, and Nation in Argentina* (Lincoln, NE, 1991), 134–35.

11. *El Hogar* 19 (January 2, 1923): 694, cited in C. Wainerman and M. Navarro Gerassi, *El trabajo de la mujer*, 26.

12. C. Wainerman and M. Navarro Gerassi, *El trabajo de la mujer*.

13. Departamento Nacional de Higiene, *Guía Oficial* (Buenos Aires, 1913), cited in P. Ross, "Policy Formation," 325.

14. N. Hollander, *La mujer*, 87.

15. However, according to the Seminar on Feminism and Culture in Latin America, *Women, Culture, and Politics in Latin America* (Berkeley, 1990), Argentina was the Latin American country with the greatest number of women's periodicals published between 1800 and 1988: 73 in total. Mexico was second, with a total of 55 periodicals.

16. For an overview of early feminism in the southern cone (Argentina, Chile, and Uruguay), see Asunción Lavrin, *Women, Feminism, and Social Change in Argentina, Chile, and Uruguay, 1890–1940* (Lincoln, NE, 1995).

17. Manifran Carlson, *Feminismo! The Woman's Movement in Argentina from Its Beginnings to Eva Perón* (Chicago, 1987), chap. 4. See also S. McGee Deutsch, *Counterrevolution in Argentina*, 22. One of the objectives of the CNM was to provide a market for the sale of handcrafts made by women from upper-class families who had fallen into poverty, providing a way for them to avoid the dishonor of having their situation made public.

18. *Boletín del Museo Social Argentino* 1 (1912): 163.

19. On the Socialist Party, see R. Walter, *The Socialist Party of Argentina, 1890–1930* (Austin, TX, 1977).

20. M. Carlson, *Feminismo!* 162.

21. Ibid., 172.

22. On the issue of women and patriotism, see D. Guy, *Sex and Danger*.

23. S. McGee Deutsch, *Counterrevolution in Argentina*, 55.

24. Ibid., 87.

25. Ibid., 92. However, the truly militant women's group of the league never had more than 820 members (p. 94).

26. Cited in T. Halperín Donghi, *Argentina: La democracia de masas* (Buenos Aires, 1986), 33.

27. S. Bianchi and N. Sanchís, *El Partido Peronista Femenino*, 37–38.

28. M. Carlson, *Feminismo!* 186; and S. Bianchi and N. Sanchís, *El Partido Peronista Femenino*, 38.

29. Cited in O. Borroni and R. Vacca, *La vida de Eva Perón*, vol. 1, *Testimonios para su historia* (Buenos Aires, 1971), 133.

30. The contradictions concerning women in Eva's speech were analyzed by J. Guivant, *La visible Eva Perón y el invisible rol político femenino en el peronismo: 1946–1952* (Notre Dame, IN, 1986).

31. Cited in O. Borroni and R. Vacca, *Vida de Eva Perón*, 1:133.

32. In this sense, Argentina was following a worldwide tendency. France had granted women the vote in 1945, Chile in 1947. In Cuba, women had gained the right to vote in 1934.

33. In many places, above all in heavily Catholic countries, the Catholic Church supported the enfranchisement of women, reasoning that women could be more easily attracted to Catholic parties and act as a counterweight to leftist parties. One such instance is Spain before the Second Republic. In fact, during a constitutional convention there in 1931, the leftist parties and even some feminist groups who had fought for a long time for the enfranchisement of women provided only half-hearted support for this measure, perceiving that most women would vote for the conservatives of the right. See Marie-Aline Barrachina, "La section féminine de la phalange espagnole: L'exclusion du politique comme aboutissement d'un discours survalorisant," in Rita Thalmenn, comp., *Femmes et fascismes* (Paris, 1987), 122.

34. F. Malimacci, *El catolicismo integral en la Argentina (1930–1946)* (Buenos Aires, 1988), 75.

35. E. Perón, "Mensaje pronunciado el 27 de enero de 1947 dedicado a la mujer argentina por L.R.A. Radio del Estado y la Red Argentina de Radiodifusión," in E. Perón, *Discursos completos*, 1:42.

36. E. Perón, "Mensaje pronunciado el 12 de febrero de 1947 por L.R.A. Radio del Estado y la Red Argentina de Radiodifusión dedicado a la mujer argentina y su derecho de elegir y ser elegida," in ibid.

37. E. Perón, "Discurso pronunciado el 23 de setiembre de 1947 en Plaza de Mayo con motivo de la sanción de la ley que otorgó el derecho al voto a la mujer argentina," in ibid., 121.

38. E. Perón, "Discurso pronunciado el 26 de febrero de 1947 desde la Quinta Presidencial de Olivos por L.R.A. Radio del Estado y la Red Argentina de Radiodifusión," in ibid., 57.

39. E. Perón, *Discursos completos*, 1:58.

40. M. Navarro Gerassi, *Evita* (Buenos Aires, 1981), 107.

41. E. Perón, "Discurso pronunciado en el acto inaugural de la Primera Asamblea Nacional del Movimiento Peronista Femenino, realizado en el Teatro Nacional Cervantes de la Capital Federal el 26 de julio de 1949," in E. Perón, *Discursos completos*, 2:71.

42. E. Perón, *Discursos completos*, 2:72.

43. E. Perón, "La consigna inmortal," in *Mundo Peronista* 63 (1951).

44. M. Navarro Gerassi, *Evita*, 210.

45. As happened with Haydeé Longoni and Teresa Fiora, who were both expelled from the PPF.

46. "Discurso de Perón a las delegadas del PPF," *Democracia*, February 24, 1951.

47. *Mundo Peronista* 24 (1952).

48. Interview conducted by Susana Bianchi and Norma Sanchís, Buenos Aires.

49. The PPF was hierarchically organized. At the head was Eva, and under her were twenty-three "census delegates," each of whom supervised the subdelegates who were in charge of the UBs.

50. Interview conducted by Susana Bianchi and Norma Sanchís, Buenos Aires.

51. S. Bianchi and N. Sanchís, *El Partido Peronista Femenino*, 174.

52. Interview conducted by Susana Bianchi and Norma Sanchí, Buenos Aires.

53. Ibid.

54. Ibid.

55. Ibid.

56. E. Perón, "La consigna inmortal," in *Mundo Peronista* 63 (1952).

57. Lynn Stoner, *From the House to the Street: The Cuban Woman's Movement for Legal Reform, 1898–1940* (Durham, NC, 1991), 2.

58. For contemporary descriptions of the public attitudes of women from the beginning of the twentieth century to the 1930s, see Katherine Dreier, *Five Months in Argentina from a Woman's Point of View: 1918 to 1919* (New York, 1920); and Ezequiel Martinez Estrada, *Radiografía de la pampa* (Buenos Aires, 1942).

59. P. Ross, "Policy Formation," 341.

60. Secretaría de Estado de Trabajo, Oficina Nacional de la Mujer, *Evolución de la mujer en las profesiones liberales en Argentina, años 1900–1965* (Buenos Aires, 1970), 82–84, cited by P. Ross, "Policy Formation," 342.

61. *Mundo Peronista* 1 (May 1951).

62. In Chapter 5, we mentioned briefly the UES: the Unión de Estudiantes Secundarios (Union of Secondary School Students), created by Perón during his second presidency. These were clubs sponsored by the government for high-school students in which participation was semivoluntary. The female branch of the UES was housed in the presidential residence, and apparently Perón had sexual relations with at least one of the girls of the UES. I do not focus more closely on the UES here for two reasons: first, because there are no adequate sources; and second, because the UES was an institution closely linked with the educational system and, therefore, outside the scope of this chapter.

63. The titles of the stories published in this collection were "Adventures of Peronist Children," "Stories of the 17th of October," and other similar titles.

64. See, for example, "Peronchinlandia, el mundo de los peronchiquitos," in *Mundo Peronista* 4 (1951).

65. P. Ross, "Policy Formation," 280. However, it is interesting to note that in magazines such as *Mundo Infantil*, especially after Eva's death, the propaganda for the CE was presented in a way that suggested a certain lack of spontaneous enthusiasm for the competitions on the part of potential participants.

66. According to Congressman Visca, the congressional contributions covered only a tiny part of the costs of the organization of the CE. The major part of these costs was paid by the FEP. This does not appear to be totally correct, however. In

1949, for example, out of a total cost of $1,642,597, the subsidy given by Congress amounted to $950,000, or over 50 percent. See *DSCD* 2 (1950): 1108.

67. Leandro Gutíerrez and Luis Alberto Romero, *Sociedades barriales, bibliotecas populares y cultura de los sectores populares: Buenos Aires, 1920–1945* (Buenos Aires, 1989).

68. A note from the secretary of education dated June 26, 1948, stressed the "moral" character of the activities carried out in the clubs. It explicitly prohibited gambling, drinking, and the like, and recommended strong vigilance over the coed activities such as the choirs. Escuela 19, D.E. 5. Archive.

69. Note from Secretary of Didactics Oscar Tolosa, dated July 12, 1948. This note made clear that no budget provision had been made for the clubs, but that, nevertheless, it prohibited charging a fee for participation, in ibid.

70. The teachers of Public School 19 in the Fifth District, for example, said that people were not interested in the clubs, because, in Parque Patricios, the neighborhood in which the school was located, there were already other centers of social life, including a vacation school for children sponsored by the municipal government. Parents were only interested in the free movies shown at the club. Ibid., meeting on June 6, 1950.

71. Silvio Marzolini, for example, future star of the Boca Juniors, had played for Arzenal, champion of the CE in 1953, and had won a prize. Other clubs, such as the "Sacachispas" of Parque Patricios, would later become semiprofessional teams. Some clubs, which had offered soccer as one of several available sports, came to specialize in only soccer as a consequence of the CE.

72. The literature on the relationship between mass sports (especially soccer) and politics is enormous. To mention only two works that treat this theme, see Janet Lever, *Soccer Madness* (Chicago, 1983), and Duncan Shaw, *Fútbol y franquismo* (Madrid, 1987).

73. *Mundo infantil* 5 (1949).

74. Ibid., 17 (1949).

75. From Congressman Miel Asquía, *DSCD* 7 (1953): 1257.

76. *Mundo Infantil* 102 (1951).

77. Inserted in *DSCD* 2 (1950): 1148.

78. The words to the CE anthem: "We owe our club to Evita/ For this reason we sing our gratitude to her/ We comply with the ideals and the mission/ Of this New Argentina of Evita and Perón."

"We will go out to the field/ Anxious to win/ We will be sportsmen/With all our hearts/ To form a new/And great generation. If we win or lose/ We do not offend our rival. If we win or lose/ We do not lose our morale/ We will know how to defend with loyalty/ The soul of our *argentinidad*."

79. *Democracia*, March 7, 1950.

80. Out of the fifty neighborhood champions of Buenos Aires in the 1951 CE, eight bore names with patriotic significance (national heroes, Antártida Argentina,

etc.); one had a name associated with Peronism (Dr. Ramón Cereijo); seven included the name of their neighborhood (Almagro, Centenario [two], Patricios, Palermo [two], La Boca); four included the name of the institution that had created the club (Salvador, Hogar de Niños Gral. San Martín, Ciudad Infantil, and Escuela de Artesanos Almafuerte). The rest of the names were invented.

81. In the same year another Peronist magazine published by the Ministry of Education, *Argentina*, sold for $1.00.

82. I would like to express my gratitude to Lic. Clara Brafman who gave me access to her unpublished work on *Billiken* from the 1920s and 1930s. All the quotations from *Billiken* were kindly provided by her.

83. In 1919, Congress passed Law 10,903 creating the Patronato de la Infancia, making it easier for the state to take control of abandoned children, delinquents, and children of "immoral parents."

84. Letter from a nine-year-old girl published in *Billiken* 35 (1920).

85. *Billiken* (December 1927).

86. *Mundo Infantil* 4 (1949).

87. Ibid., 108 (1951).

88. Most of the Peronist publications, such as *Mundo Peronista*, mentioned only Perón and Eva. *Mundo Infantil* made an exception by mentioning Aloé.

89. *Mundo Infantil* 268 (1954).

90. Ibid.

91. Ibid., 110 (1951). Capital letters used in the original.

92. See, for example, *Mundo Infantil* 37 (June 1950), which, in the section "Su Majestad el Niño," tells the story of a child who had approached Perón during a boxing match to ask him for a bicycle. Of course, Perón promised it for the following day. In addition, Perón pulled out a $100 bill from his wallet and gave it to the astonished child. Similar stories abound in other contexts. During the celebration of May Day 1948, a child began to chant Perón's name. On hearing him, Perón had someone bring him to the official platform. Other children who observed this also asked to be brought close to Perón, and he agreed. At the end of the celebration, Perón and Eva distributed money among the children. *La Prensa*, May 2, 1948, 13.

93. *Mundo Infantil* 98 (1951).

94. Ibid., 100 (1951).

95. Similarly, children from anti-Peronist families secretly went to the post office during Christmas to get the presents sent there by the FEP. I have interviewed five people who told me similar stories.

96. Kristen Drotner, *English Children and Their Magazines, 1751–1945* (New Haven, 1988), 4.

97. On the "nondifferentiation" of women's tasks, see C. Wainerman and R. Raijman, *La división sexual del trabajo en los libros de lectura de la escuela primaria argentina: Un caso de inmutibilidad secular* (Buenos Aires, 1984).

Conclusion, Pages 195–202

1. T. Halperín Donghi, "El lugar del peronismo en la tradición política argentina," in S. Amaral and M. Plotkin, comps., *Perón, del exilio al poder* (Buenos Aires, 1993).

2. Ibid.

3. Interview with Joaquín Díaz de Vivar, Buenos Aires, July 23, 1989.

4. Interview with Manuel Molinari, Buenos Aires, July 30, 1989.

5. J. D. Perón, "Discurso pronunciado ante los rectores y directores de escuelas secundarias," July 14, 1947, reproduced in *Boletín del Ministerio de Justicia e Instrucción Pública* 89 (July 1947).

6. See, for example, Torcuato Luca De Tena, Luis Calvo, and Esteban Peicovich, *Yo, Juan Perón: Relato autobiográfico* (Buenos Aires, 1986), 28–29.

7. J. D. Perón, "Discurso de apertura del Congreso Nacional," May 1, 1954.

8. Jürgen Habermas, "The Public Sphere: An Encyclopedia Article," *New German Critique* 3 (Autumn 1974).

9. See, among others, Richard Hamilton, *Who Voted for Hitler* (Princeton, 1982); and Thomas Childers, *The Nazi Voter: The Social Foundations of Fascism in Germany, 1919–1933* (Chapel Hill, NC, 1983).

10. See J. Horowitz, "Industrialists and the Rise of Perón, 1943–1946: Some Implications for the Conceptualization of Populism," *The Americas* 47:2 (October 1990).

11. Carlos Waisman maintains that Peronism was a counterrevolutionary alternative and, thus, in this sense, resembled the European experiences. C. Waisman, *Reversal of Development in Argentina: Postwar Counterrevolutionary Policies and Their Structural Consequences* (Princeton, 1987).

12. During his exile in Madrid, Perón said, "We reversed things. That which was above we brought low, and that which was low we raised up." In Américo Barrios, *Con Perón en el exilio: Lo que nadie sabía* (Buenos Aires, 1964), 141.

13. Philippe Burrin, "Politique et société: Les structures de pouvoir dans l'Italie Fasciste et l'Allemagne Nazie," in *Annales, ESC* 3 (May–June 1988). Perón's attempts to correct this situation by searching for a counterweight to the power of the unions are analyzed in Part IV.

14. Adrian Littleton, *The Seizure of Power: Fascism in Italy, 1919–1929* (Princeton, 1987), chap. 1.

15. M. Plotkin, "La ideología de Perón: Rupturas y continuidades," in S. Amaral and M. Plotkin, comps., *Perón: Del exilio al poder.*

16. It is interesting to note that the term "resistance" had been used in 1945 by the opposition to Perón, in obvious reference to the French resistance during the Nazi occupation. For the later Peronist resistance, the reference is less clear.

17. See S. Sigal and E. Veron, *Perón o muerte: Los fundamentos discursivos del fenómeno peronista* (Buenos Aires, 1986).

SELECTED BIBLIOGRAPHY

The bibliography on Perón and Peronism is enormous. As early as 1956, less than one year after Perón's fall, the first review article on the literature about Peronism was published in the *Hispanic American Historical Review.* This review article was updated three years later. See Fritz Hoffmann, "Perón and After: A Review Article," *Hispanic American Historical Review* 36, no. 4 (November 1956); and *Hispanic American Historical Review* 39, no. 2 (May 1959). The best bibliography on Peronism that includes sources published in any language is Horvath Laszlo, *A Half Century of Peronism, 1943–1993: An International Bibliography* (Stanford: Hoover Institution, Stanford University, 1993). What follows is a selected list of bibliographical sources published in English and organized thematically.

Early Books on Peronism

Alexander, Robert. *The Perón Era.* New York: Columbia University Press, 1951.
Blanksten, George. *Perón's Argentina.* Chicago: University of Chicago Press, 1953.
Greenup, Ruth, and Leonard Greenup. *Revolution before Breakfast: Argentina, 1941–1946.* Chapel Hill: University of North Carolina Press, 1947.

General Works on Peronism

Brennan, James P., ed. *Peronism and Argentina.* Wilmington, DE: Scholarly Resources, 1998.
Crassweller, Robert. *Perón and the Enigmas of Argentina.* New York: Norton, 1987.

Turner, Frederick, and José Enrique Miguens, eds. *Perón and the Reshaping of Argentina*. Pittsburgh: University of Pittsburgh Press, 1983.
Waisman, Carlos. *Reversal of Development in Argentina: Postwar Counter-revolutionary Policies and Their Structural Consequences*. Princeton: Princeton University Press, 1987.

The Working Class and Peronism

Baily, Samuel. *Labor, Nationalism, and Politics in Argentina*. New Brunswick: Rutgers University Press, 1967.
Falcoff, Mark, and Ronald Dolkart, eds. *Prologue to Perón: Argentina in Depression and War*. Berkeley: University of California Press, 1975.
Horowitz, Joel. *Argentine Unions, the State, and the Rise of Perón, 1930–1945*. Berkeley: Institute for International Studies, 1990.
_____. "The Impact of Pre-1943 Labor Union Tradition on Peronism." *Journal of Latin American Studies* 15 (1983).
James, Daniel. *Resistance and Integration: Peronism and the Argentine Working Class, 1946–1976*. Cambridge: Cambridge University Press, 1988.
Munck, Ronaldo, and Ricardo Falcon. *Argentina: From Anarchism to Peronism: Workers, Unions and Politics, 1855–1985*. London: Zed Books, 1987.
Tamarin, David. *The Argentine Labor Movement, 1930–1945: A Study on the Origins of Peronism*. Albuquerque: University of New Mexico Press, 1985.

Industrialists and the Rise of Perón

Horowitz, Joel. "Industrialists and the Rise of Perón, 1943–1946: Some Implications for the Conceptualization of Populism." *The Americas* 47, no. 2 (October 1990).
Kenworthy, Eldon. "Did the New Industrialists Play a Significant Role in the Formation of Perón's Coalition, 1943–1946?" In Alberto Ciria, ed. *New Perspectives in Modern Argentina*. Bloomington: Indiana University Press, 1972.
Teichman, Judith. "Interest Conflict and Entrepreneurial Support for Perón." *Latin American Research Review* 16, no. 1 (1981).

The Peronist Party, Politics, and the State

Kirkpatrick, Jeane. *Leader and Vanguard in Mass Society: A Study of Peronist Argentina*. Cambridge, MA: MIT Press, 1971.
Little, Walter. "Electoral Aspects of Peronism, 1946–1954." *Journal of Inter-American Studies and World Affairs* 15, no. 3 (August 1973).
Potash, Robert. *The Army and Politics in Argentina*. Vol. 1: *From Yrigoyen to Perón*. Stanford: Stanford University Press, 1969.
Ranis, Peter. "Early Peronism and the Post-Liberal State." *Journal of Inter-American Studies and World Affairs* 21, no. 3 (August 1979).
Smith, Peter. "Party and State in Peronist Argentina, 1945–1955." *Hispanic American Historical Review* 53, no. 4 (November 1973).
Walter, Richard. *The Socialist Party of Argentina, 1890–1930*. Austin: University of Texas Press, 1977.

Peronist Ideology and Culture

Conniff, Michael. *Latin American Populism in Comparative Perspective*. Albuquerque: University of New Mexico Press, 1982.
Corradi, Juan. "Between Corporatism and Insurgency: The Sources of Ambivalence in Peronist Ideology." In Morris Blachman and Ronald Hellman, eds. *Terms of Conflict: Ideology in Latin American Politics*. Philadelphia: Institute for the Study of Human Issues, 1977.
James, Daniel. *Doña María's Story: Life History, Memory, and Political Identity*. Durham: Duke University Press, 2000.
King, John. *Sur: A Study of the Argentine Literary Journal and Its Role in the Development of a Culture, 1931–1930*. Cambridge: Cambridge University Press, 1986.
Laclau, Ernesto. *Politics and Ideology in Marxist Theory: Capitalism, Fascism, Populism*. London: Humanities Press, 1977.
Rein, Raanan. *The Franco-Perón Alliance: Relations between Spain and Argentina, 1946–1955*. Pittsburgh: University of Pittsburgh Press, 1993.
Stabb, Martin. "Argentine Letters and the Peronato: An Overview." *Journal of Inter-American Studies and World Affairs* 13, nos. 3-4 (July–October 1971).
Winton, Colin. "Between Rosas and Sarmiento: Notes on Nationalism in Peronist Thought." *The Americas* 39, no. 3 (1983).

Juan and Eva Perón

Dujovne Ortiz, Alicia. *Eva Perón*. New York: St. Martin's Press, 1996.

Frank, Gary. *Juan Perón vs. Spruille Braden*. Lanham, MD: University Press of America, 1980.

Fraser, Nicholas, and Marysa Navarro Gerassi. *Eva Perón*. New York: Norton, 1981.

Navarro Gerassi, Marysa. "Evita and the Crisis of 17 of October 1945: A Case Study of Peronist and Anti-Peronist Mythology." *Journal of Latin American Studies* 12 (1980).

Page, Joseph. *Perón: A Biography*. New York: Random House, 1983.

Perón, Eva. *Evita: Eva Duarte Perón Tells Her Own Story*. London: Proteus, 1978.

Taylor, Julio. *Eva Perón: The Myths of a Woman*. Chicago: University of Chicago Press, 1979.

Works of Fiction

Martínez, Tomás Eloy. *The Perón Novel*. New York: Vintage International, 1999.

_____. *Santa Evita*. New York: Vintage Books, 1997.

INDEX

of October coverage, 66, 72; violence against, 76

La Nueva República (magazine), 7

La Plata, Seventeenth of October demonstration in, 55

La Prensa (newspaper): Marcha de la Constitución y la Libertad coverage, 57; May Day coverage, 49; SBC takeover coverage, 145; Seventeenth of October coverage, 66, 76; textbook coverage, 107; violence against, 72

La Protesta (newspaper), 170

La Razón (newspaper), 66

La razón de mi vida (Eva Perón), 100, 108, 130

La Tribuna (newspaper), 95

La Vanguardia (newspaper), 57–58, 62, 66

La Víspera (magazine), 10

La Voz Nacional (magazine), 7

Labor Party (Partido Laborista), 59, 60, 62, 63

Laclau, Ernesto, 9, 12

Lanteri, Julieta, 169

Law 1420 (1884), 15, 85, 87

Law 11,672 (1943), 140

Law 13,100 (1947), 174

Law 13,478, 149

Law 13,941, 149

Law 13,992 (1950), 149

Law 14,028 (1951), 149

Law 14,044, 149

Law 14,126 (1952), 108

Law 14,297 (1953), 102

Law of Social Safety (1910), 4

Leadership: Bloch on, 161; charismatic, 30–31, 43, 56, 75, 136, 160–63; Perón on, 21–22

Legitimacy. *See* Political legitimacy

Leisure time, 136, 182, 186

Liberal consensus, 3–18, 26–29; basis of, 3; breakup of, 1, 7–8, 12–13, 16–18; conservative opposition to, 6–7; "double delegitimization" and, 6, 29; education and, 85; elites and, 3–4, 6, 7–8; imperialism and, 8, 9, 29; nationalist opposition to, 6–7; perceived threat to, 4–6; at Perón's beginning, 195; political parties and, 4

Liberalism, 1, 26–29, 84, 126–27

Liberating Revolution, 39, 106, 150, 200–202

Libraries, growth in number of, 182

Lieux de mémoire, 44, 70

Liga Argentina de Empleados Públicos (Argentine League of Civil Servants), 148

Liga Patriótica Argentina, 7, 170

Llambías, Joaquín, 89

Llorente, Ignacio, 163–64

Lonardi, Eduardo, 200

Longoni, Haydeé, 171

López, Estanislao, 125

López, Vicente Fidel, 125

López Serrot (Radical deputy), 148–49

López y Planes, Vicente, 125

Losada de Genta, Lila, 89

Loyalty Day (Día de la Lealtad), 43, 63

Lugones, Leopoldo, 5, 7, 18

Maetzu, María de, 16

Mallea, Eduardo, 16

"Manifiesto de la Liga Republicana" (1933), 7

Manzi, Homero, 33

March of the Constitution and Freedom (Marcha de la Constitución y la Libertad, 1945), 27–28, 57, 58

Marechal, Leopoldo, 9, 33

"Martín Fierro" (Hernández), 120

Martín Fierro (journal), 8, 122

Martínez, Tomás Eloy, 201

Martínez Estrada, Ezequiel, 17, 31–32

Martínez Zuviría, Gustavo, 33, 35, 86

Massone Pharmaceuticals, 150

May Day, 41–51, 59–62, 69–82; 1946 celebration, 59–62; 1947 celebration, 70–71; 1948 celebration, 73–75; 1949 celebration, 77; Anarchists and, 46, 47, 69–70, 74, 75, 80, 81; Catholic Church and, 48, 74; CGT and, 48–49, 60, 74, 79; Communists and, 48; "double contamination" of celebrations, 48; Eva Perón and, 59, 73–74; flags in celebrations, 48–49, 61, 77; Peronization of celebrations, 39, 43–45, 49–51, 60–62, 68–71, 73–75, 77–78, 81–82; Perón's speeches on, 50–51, 56, 60, 70, 74–75, 79; press coverage of celebrations, 46–47, 70–71, 77; prohibition against newspaper publication on, 46–49, 68; Queens of Labor and, 73–74, 79; rituals, 73–74, 79; Socialists and, 41–

Latin American Silhouettes
Studies in History and Culture

William H. Beezley and
Judith Ewell
Editors

Volumes Published

Brian Loveman and Thomas M. Davies, Jr.,
eds., *The Politics of Antipolitics: The
Military in Latin America*, 3d ed.,
revised and updated (1996).
Cloth ISBN 0-8420-2609-6
Paper ISBN 0-8420-2611-8

Dianne Walta Hart, *Undocumented in L.A.:
An Immigrant's Story* (1997).
Cloth ISBN 0-8420-2648-7
Paper ISBN 0-8420-2649-5

William H. Beezley and Judith Ewell, eds.,
*The Human Tradition in Modern Latin
America* (1997). Cloth ISBN 0-8420-
2612-6   Paper ISBN 0-8420-2613-4

Donald F. Stevens, ed., *Based on a
True Story: Latin American History
at the Movies* (1997).
Cloth ISBN 0-8420-2582-0
Paper ISBN 0-8420-2781-5

Jaime E. Rodríguez O., ed., *The Origins of
Mexican National Politics, 1808–1847*
(1997). Paper ISBN 0-8420-2723-8

Che Guevara, *Guerrilla Warfare*, with revised
and updated introduction and case studies
by Brian Loveman and Thomas M.
Davies, Jr., 3d ed. (1997). Cloth ISBN 0-
8420-2677-0   Paper ISBN 0-8420-2678-9

Adrian A. Bantjes, *As If Jesus Walked on
Earth: Cardenismo, Sonora, and the
Mexican Revolution* (1998; rev. ed.,
2000). Cloth ISBN 0-8420-2653-3
Paper ISBN 0-8420-2751-3

A. Kim Clark, *The Redemptive Work: Railway
and Nation in Ecuador, 1895–1930*
(1998). Cloth ISBN 0-8420-2674-6
Paper ISBN 0-8420-5013-2

Louis A. Pérez, Jr., ed., *Impressions of Cuba
in the Nineteenth Century: The Travel
Diary of Joseph J. Dimock* (1998).
Cloth ISBN 0-8420-2657-6
Paper ISBN 0-8420-2658-4

June E. Hahner, ed., *Women through Women's
Eyes: Latin American Women in*
Nineteenth-Century Travel Accounts
(1998). Cloth ISBN 0-8420-2633-9
Paper ISBN 0-8420-2634-7

James P. Brennan, ed., *Peronism and Argentina*
(1998). ISBN 0-8420-2706-8

John Mason Hart, ed., *Border Crossings:
Mexican and Mexican-American Workers*
(1998). Cloth ISBN 0-8420-2716-5
Paper ISBN 0-8420-2717-3

Brian Loveman, *For la Patria: Politics and
the Armed Forces in Latin America*
(1999). Cloth ISBN 0-8420-2772-6 Paper
ISBN 0-8420-2773-4

Guy P. C. Thomson, with David G. LaFrance,
*Patriotism, Politics, and Popular
Liberalism in Nineteenth-Century
Mexico: Juan Francisco Lucas and the
Puebla Sierra* (1999).
ISBN 0-8420-2683-5

Robert Woodmansee Herr, in collaboration
with Richard Herr, *An American Family
in the Mexican Revolution* (1999).
ISBN 0-8420-2724-6

Juan Pedro Viqueira Albán, trans. Sonya
Lipsett-Rivera and Sergio Rivera Ayala,
*Propriety and Permissiveness in
Bourbon Mexico* (1999).
Cloth ISBN 0-8420-2466-2
Paper ISBN 0-8420-2467-0

Stephen R. Niblo, *Mexico in the 1940s:
Modernity, Politics, and Corruption* (1999).
Cloth ISBN 0-8420-2794-7
Paper (2001) ISBN 0-8420-2795-5

David E. Lorey, *The U.S.-Mexican Border
in the Twentieth Century* (1999).
Cloth ISBN 0-8420-2755-6
Paper ISBN 0-8420-2756-4

Joanne Hershfield and David R. Maciel, eds.,
*Mexico's Cinema: A Century of Films and
Filmmakers* (2000). Cloth ISBN 0-8420-
2681-9 Paper ISBN 0-8420-2682-7

Peter V. N. Henderson, *In the Absence of Don
Porfirio: Francisco León de la Barra*

and the Mexican Revolution (2000).
ISBN 0-8420-2774-2

Mark T. Gilderhus, The Second Century: U.S.-
Latin American Relations since 1889
(2000). Cloth ISBN 0-8420-2413-1
Paper ISBN 0-8420-2414-X

Catherine Moses, Real Life in Castro's Cuba
(2000). Cloth ISBN 0-8420-2836-6
Paper ISBN 0-8420-2837-4

K. Lynn Stoner, ed./comp., with Luis
Hipólito Serrano Pérez, Cuban and
Cuban-American Women: An
Annotated Bibliography (2000).
ISBN 0-8420-2643-6

Thomas D. Schoonover, The French in
Central America: Culture and
Commerce, 1820–1930 (2000).
ISBN 0-8420-2792-0

Enrique C. Ochoa, Feeding Mexico: The
Political Uses of Food since 1910
(2000). ISBN 0-8420-2812-9

Thomas W. Walker and Ariel C. Armony,
eds., Repression, Resistance, and
Democratic Transition in Central
America (2000). Cloth ISBN 0-8420-
2766-1   Paper ISBN 0-8420-2768-8

William H. Beezley and David E. Lorey,
eds., ¡Viva México! ¡Viva la
Independencia! Celebrations of
September 16 (2001).
Cloth ISBN 0-8420-2914-1
Paper ISBN 0-8420-2915-X

Jeffrey M. Pilcher, Cantinflas and the Chaos
of Mexican Modernity (2001).
Cloth ISBN 0-8420-2769-6
Paper ISBN 0-8420-2771-8

Victor M. Uribe-Uran, ed., State and Society
in Spanish America during the Age of
Revolution (2001). Cloth ISBN 0-8420-
2873-0   Paper ISBN 0-8420-2874-9

Andrew Grant Wood, Revolution in the
Street: Women, Workers, and Urban
Protest in Veracruz, 1870–1927 (2001).
ISBN 0-8420-2879-X

Charles Bergquist, Ricardo Peñaranda, and
Gonzalo Sánchez G., eds., Violence in
Colombia, 1990–2000: Waging War and
Negotiating Peace (2001).
Cloth ISBN 0-8420-2869-2
Paper ISBN 0-8420-2870-6

William Schell, Jr., Integral Outsiders: The
American Colony in Mexico City, 1876–
1911 (2001). ISBN 0-8420-2838-2

John Lynch, Argentine Caudillo: Juan
Manuel de Rosas (2001).
Cloth ISBN 0-8420-2897-8
Paper ISBN 0-8420-2898-6

Samuel Basch, M.D., ed. and trans. Fred D.
Ullman, Recollections of Mexico: The
Last Ten Months of Maximilian's Empire
(2001). ISBN 0-8420-2962-1

David Sowell, The Tale of Healer
Miguel Perdomo Neira: Medicine,
Ideologies, and Power in the
Nineteenth-Century Andes (2001).
Cloth ISBN 0-8420-2826-9
Paper ISBN 0-8420-2827-7

June E. Hahner, ed., A Parisian in Brazil:
The Travel Account of a Frenchwoman
in Nineteenth-Century Rio de Janeiro
(2001). Cloth ISBN 0-8420-2854-4
Paper ISBN 0-8420-2855-2

Richard A. Warren, Vagrants and Citizens:
Politics and the Masses in Mexico City
from Colony to Republic (2001).
ISBN 0-8420-2964-8

Roderick J. Barman, Princess Isabel of
Brazil: Gender and Power in the
Nineteenth Century (2002).
Cloth ISBN 0-8420-2845-5
Paper ISBN 0-8420-2846-3

Stuart F. Voss, Latin America in the
Middle Period, 1750–1929 (2002).
Cloth ISBN 0-8420-5024-8
Paper ISBN 0-8420-5025-6

Lester D. Langley, The Banana Wars:
United States Intervention in the
Caribbean, 1898–1934, with new
introduction (2002). Cloth ISBN 0-8420-
5046-9   Paper ISBN 0-8420-5047-7

Mariano Ben Plotkin, Mañana es San Perón:
A Cultural History of Perón's Argentina
(2003). Cloth ISBN 0-8420-5028-0
Paper ISBN 0-8420-5029-9

Allen Gerlach, Indians, Oil, and Politics:
A Recent History of Ecuador (2003).
Cloth ISBN 0-8420-5107-4
Paper ISBN 0-8420-5108-2

Karen Racine, Francisco de Miranda: A
Transatlantic Life in the Age of
Revolution (2003). Cloth ISBN 0-8420-
2909-5   Paper ISBN 0-8420-2910-9